Buildings and projects by

Troughton McAslan Architects

トロートン・マッカーズラン・アーキテクツ：時代を超えた英国建築

CONTENTS

PROCESS :Architecture

Front Cover: Apple Computers' Facility
Back Cover: 3 St. Peter's Street

表紙:アップルコンピューター社
裏表紙:セント・ピーターズ・ストリート3番地

PRO
:Arch

論文

No.105

Publisher: Murotani Bunji

Editor-in-Charge: John McAslan

Writers: Thomas Fisher, Rowan Moore, Kenneth Powell

Editorial Staff: Miwako Ito, Yumiko Fujimaki

Editorial Assistants: Kazuto Mizuse, Chie Ishikawa. Kyoko Shibazaki, Tomoko Tatsukawa, Tomoko Amemiya

Translator: Rei Kuroki

Cover Design: Takahisa Kamijyo (Kamijyo Studio)

Published by Process Architecture Co., Ltd., Tokyo, Japan

Printed by TOPPAN PRINTING Co., (S)Pte., Ltd. Isozaki Printing Co., Ltd., Tokyo, Japan

Executive and Editorial Office
1-47-2-418 Sasazuka Shibuya-ku Tokyo, Japan
Phone(03)3468-0131, 0132 Fax(03)3468-0133

ISBN 4-89331-105-0

第105号
発行日:1992年9月1日
発行人:室谷文治
責任編集者:ジョン・マッカーズラン
執筆:トーマス・フィッシャー、ローワン・ムーア、ケネス・パウエル
編集部:伊藤美和子、藤巻由美子
編集アシスタント:
水瀬和人、石川智恵、芝崎恭子、龍川朋子、雨宮智子
翻訳:黒木 玲
表紙デザイン:上條喬久(上條スタジオ)
制作・写植:㈱協和クリエイト、㈲ユニット、大西写植
製版:TOPPAN PRINTING Co., (S)Pte., Ltd.
印刷:磯崎印刷㈱
発行所:株式会社 プロセスアーキテクチュア
〒151 東京都渋谷区笹塚1-47-2-418
電話 03-3468-0131 FAX 03-3468-0133
振替 東京6-57446
取次店:トーハン、日販、大阪屋、栗田出版販売、誠光堂

Editor's Note

My first recollections of wanting to be an architect date from childhood. I remember an interest in art and drawing which manifested itself in meticulously copying everything from JMW Turner's watercolours to reproducing minature versions of album covers and banknotes - early enthusiasms which eventually blossomed into a passion for architecture.

I took up a place to read architecture at the University of Edinburgh in 1972- although I knew little about architecture at this point beyond an interest in traditional Scottish buildings - the medieval tower houses, brochs and castles - and a lively regard for the work of the pioneering Scotish architect Charles Rennie Mackintosh and the great Catalan modernist Antonio Gaudi. My university career was unspectacular, and my commitment to and passion for architecture did not develop fully until a four-year period spent intermittently working and travelling in the United States during university vacations between 1975 and 1979.

I worked first in Baltimore with RTKL Associates. I remember being enchanted by that city with its elegant brownstones, tough cast iron buildings and animated waterfront. I travelled extensively in the north eastern states to see the work of Louis Kahn, Frank Lloyd Wright and H H Richardson, to the cities of Washington, Philadelphia, New Haven and New York, and to meet people who were genuinely passionate about architecture. I ended up in Boston, where I worked with Cambridge Seven Associates, introducing me to the type of practice I hoped eventually to run - groups of design teams operating in an open studio environment.

By late 1979 I felt it was time to make another move. I had been introduced to Richard Rogers in the US and returned to Britain to work in his studio at the end of that year. London seemed the right place to be at that time, with Rogers, Foster, Stirling, ABK, Grimshaw, Dixon and others all producing exciting work. During my three years in the Rogers' office, I helped design, detail and supervise on site Rogers' Patscentre Laboratory in Cambridge, as well as gaining the experience of working in an international office during a dynamic period. It was here too that I met my partner, Jamie Troughton who was a key member of the Lloyds' design team. Jamie left to form the practice in 1982, and I joined him six months later.

Architecturally, our ideas were already developing from an interest in the international modernism I had seen in the US through the work of Louis Kahn, Frank Lloyd Wright, Eero Saarinen, Mies van der Rohe and others, combined with a continued love of history: Richardson, Holabird and Roche, Sullivan and the Chicago School; to an understanding from Rogers' office of the potential in the use of high technology in architecture. Rogers' high-tech introduced us to a new set of influences (represented in our early projects at Design House and Shepherd's Bush). But we are developing a much tougher architecture than high-tech and my background makes me ever-conscious of tradition, honesty, restraint, climate, materials, economy, practicability and solidity; which combines itself well with Jamie Troughton's continued interest in the opportunities which engineering offers to our architecture.

Slowly our work has evolved through its high-tech period (1984-86) and tentative experiments with modernism (1986-88) to a more direct modernist vocabulary. Among our latest projects, the large office commissions at Bolsover Street, Hardwick Street, Rosebery Avenue and Canary Wharf are straightforward, robust office buildings; the Kobe Institute exhibits a timeless, modernist vocabulary; and the Canning Town Underground Station is a tough engineering influenced project. Our work is evidence of a rigorous and rational approach, in which the appearance of the building emerges from careful consideration of the brief, programme, client's requirements, users' needs, and constraints of site and budget.

Jamie and I would like to keep our office medium sized, with an international portfolio of projects; we are not interested in developing a large, commercial practice. Our offices is open and non-hierarchical, with Jamie taking responsibility for management and overall strategies and myself for design. A one-to-one relationship with the client and an intimate working team are important to us - our most rewarding and successful work has been that in which the building design is developed in collaboration with the end-user. The emphasis in our recent work on transport, educational buildings and the refurbishment and sensitive reinterpretation of modernist masterpieces such as Mendelsohn's De La Warr Pavilion is one which we hope to continue. **John McAslan**

編集言

私が初めて建築家になりたいと考えたのは，ごく幼い子供の頃である．アートや描くということへの関心はまず，J.M.W.ターナーの水彩画をそっくりコピーし，レコード・アルバムのカバージャケットや紙幣を細かく模写するという形で現われた．こうした子供の頃の熱中が，次第に建築への情熱に発展していった．

1972年にエジンバラ大学で建築を学ぶことになったが，この時点では，私は建築について，伝統的なスコットランドの建物への関心以外に，ほとんどなにも知らなかった．中世の砦や城郭建築，紀元前の円形の石造建築であるブロッホ，そして特にスコットランドのパイオニア的建築家チャールズ・レニー・マッキントッシュやカタロニアのモダニストであるアントニオ・ガウディの作品への傾倒ぐらいである．私の大学での経歴はさほど取り立てていうべきことはなく，私が実際に建築に携わり，情熱を発揮し始めたのは，1975年から1979年にかけて大学の休暇を利用しながら，アメリカ国内を働きながらいろいろなところを旅してまわった，4年という歳月を経てからであった．

まず，最初に働いたのは，ボルチモアのRTKLだった．エレガントな褐色砂岩と強靱な鋳鉄による建物，生き生きとしたウォーターフロントというボルチモアの街並みに魅了された．アメリカの北東部を中心にルイス・カーン，F.L.ライト，H.H.リチャードソンなどの作品を精力的に見てまわり，ワシントン，フィラデルフィア，ニューヘブン，ニューヨークといった都市を訪れ，本当に情熱を持って建築に携わっている人々に数多く出会った．その後，ボストンに辿り着き，ケンブリッジ・セブン・アソシエイツで働くことになった．ここでの経験によって私は，これから取り組んでいくべき仕事のやり方を習得した．つまり「スタジオというオープンな雰囲気の環境で機能していくデザイン集団」が，その答えである．

1979年も終わる頃，私は行動を起こすべきであると感じた．ある時，アメリカでほんの短い時間，リチャード・ロジャースに会う機会があり，その結果，年末には英国に戻り，彼の下で仕事をすることになった．ロジャース，フォスター，スターリング，ABK，グリムショー，ディキソン，その他のすばらしい作品をつくり出している建築家たちに囲まれたロンドンは，当時の私が仕事をするにふさわしい場所だった．ロジャース事務所の3年間に，ケンブリッジのパットセンターの計画から実施設計，工事監理にいたるまでを担当した．同時に，これは建築界の激動の時期に国際事務所で仕事をするという経験を得たことになる．そこで私の現在のパートナーであるジャミー・トロートンに出会ったのである．彼はロイズビルのデザインのキーパーソンであったが，私より一足先に1982年にロジャース事務所を辞めて独立し，その半年後に私は彼に合流した．

建築的な私たちの考えは，建築におけるハイテクの活用を充分に認識した上で，アメリカでのカーン，ライト，エーロ・サーリネン，ミースといった建築家の作品に見たインターナショナル・モダニズムへの関心に，リチャードソン，ホラバード&ローチ，サリバン，シカゴ派の建築家たちの作品を好むという，歴史的な建築への情熱をミックスしたところに収斂していった．ロジャース事務所のハイテクという特徴は，トロートン・マッカーズランの初期の作品，たとえばデザイン・ハウスやシェパード・ブッシュといった作品に顕著にその影響が現われている．しかし，私たちはその方向をハイテクを超えた，より強靱な建築に向かわせ，スコットランド人気質という背景が，伝統，誠実，抑制，気候，マテリアル，経済，実際性，安定といったものを常に私たちに意識させる．これは，ジャミー・トロートンが常に建築へのエンジニアリングの寄与に深い関心を寄せ続けたことと相まって，その方向に推進していったともいえる．

1984年から1986年というハイテクの時期，そして1986年から1988年にかけてのモダニズムの試練の時期を徐々に脱して，さらに率直なモダニストのボキャブラリーへと変換していった．最近作では，ボルソバー・ストリート，ハードウィック・ストリートそしてローズベリー・アベニュー，キャナリーワーフなどの大規模なオフィス建築は，直截な表現のたくましいオフィスビルであり，一方，セント・キャサリン神戸校の場合は，時間を超越した，モダニスト的な表現，カニングタウン地下鉄駅では，力強い技術に裏打ちされた建築となっている．私たちの作品は，設計条件，プログラム，クライアントの要望，使用者のニーズ，敷地や予算条件の熟考から建物の全貌が決定するという，正確かつ合理的な設計手法の結果である．

ジャミーも私も事務所は中規模のままに維持しつつ，国際的なあらゆる仕事をしていきたいと考えている．大規模であるけれども実務的でしかない事務所という組織には全く関心がない．オフィスはオープンで階級制度もない．ジャミーはマネージメントと全体の運営戦略に，そして私はデザイン全般を統括している．クライアントとも所員とも一対一の関係がなによりも重要である．建物のデザインが，そこを使う人たちと一緒に計画できたときにはじめて，最も価値のある成功例が生まれる．教育施設や交通施設，モダニストの最高傑作であるメンデルゾーンのデ・ラ・ワーパビリオンの改修といったような分野の仕事の比重が最近特に重くなっているが，これは私たちが望む方向でもある． **ジョン・マッカーズラン**

ARTICLES

論文

The Empiricism of Troughton McAslan

by Thomas Fisher

トロートン・マッカーズランの経験主義　トーマス・フィッシャー

One of the great gifts England has given the world is empiricism. Established in the late 17th and early 18th Centuries by John Locke, George Berkeley, and David Hume, empiricism is a frame of mind that values real experience of abstract argument, particular facts over universal truths, pragmatic solutions over ideological statements, and the experimental methods of science and technology over the deductive reasoning of logic and mathematics. Although 300 years old, empiricism remains widely influential, but just as widely misunderstood, especially when seen as synonymous with Modernism. A closer look at the work of Troughton McAslan - a model of architecture empiricism - allows us to unravel some of this confusion and begin to clarify what we mean when we speak of Modern Architecture.

Empiricism has been most commonly applied to buildings that use technology as a means of expression, such as the "High Tech" architecture of Richard Rogers or Norman Foster. That label is misleading, though, when you compare say, Rogers' work to that of Troughton McAslan. Jamie Troughton and John McAslan both worked in Richard Rogers' office before starting their own practice in 1983 and, like Rogers, they produce buildings in which technology plays an expressive role. But Rogers differs in seeking, through technology, a maximum flexibility of plan and changeability of parts, resulting in buildings that, with their external structures and exposed mechanical systems, look similar from one project to the next. His work is, if anything, the opposite of empirical: an idealistic statement about the ability of modern technology to achieve absolute freedom.

Troughton McAslan's architecture offers no such absolute; it is not idealistic, but pragmatic. Their Acton Vocational Training Centre, for example, has a hybrid structure in response to the varied requirements of the program. It achieves a high degree of flexibility for the training areas under a vaulted steel-truss roof, but the classrooms and offices, which require less variability, occupy a more fixed concrete and masonry structure. Troughton McAslan's empiricism also gives greater weight to the experiential aspects of architecture than to the technology behind it. At their railway station at Redhill, they have exposed the perforated beams and steel cable bracing of the circular roof, but they also have painted out those structural elements, as if to reinforce the empiricist view of technology as a means rather than as an end in itself.

Other Troughton McAslan work reveals a similar empiricist view of history. Consider their office building at Canary Wharf. It occupies a middle ground between two extreme positions regarding the place of history in design. At one extreme are some of the other buildings at Canary Wharf, which drape themselves in the period costume of Edwardian England or Fascist Europe. These buildings look to history to give them the meaning they otherwise lack, however ambiguous that meaning might be. At the other extreme is the building such as the Mies-designed tower and plaza recently proposed for the centre of London, which would have ripped a hole in the city's historic fabric. Such architecture adheres to the Hegelian belief that progress will one day bring us to the end of history, to an absolute freedom from constraint.

Empiricists such as Troughton McAslan generally have too much respect for particular facts and evolutionary ideas to either mimic the past or wish it away. Their Canary Wharf building, with its elegantly minimal

英国が世界に与えた恩恵の１つに経験論がある．17世紀末から18世紀初めにかけて，ジョン・ロック，ジョージ・バークリー，デイビッド・ヒュームらによって確立された哲学で，すべての観念は感覚的な実際の経験から生ずるというものである．個々の事実は普遍的な真実に勝り，実用的な解答は観念に勝り，科学やテクノロジーの経験的な手法は論理や数学の演繹論に勝るというものである．すでに300年を経た現在でも，経験論は大きな影響力をもっているが，特にモダニズムと同義語と見られるという点で，多分に誤解されている．建築における経験主義の典型といえる，トロートン・マッカーズランの作品をくわしく眺めることは，この混同を解きほぐし，近代建築について語るときにそれがなにを意味するかを，明確にすることになる．

経験主義は，リチャード・ロジャースやノーマン・フォスターのハイテク建築に見られるように，表現の手段としてテクノロジーを使うことで，建築にごく一般的に適用されている．しかし，この分類法はトロートン・マッカーズランの作品をロジャースのそれと比較して考察するときに大変まぎらわしい．ジャミー・トロートンとジョン・マッカーズランは２人とも，1983年に自分たちのオフィスを設立する以前，ロジャースの事務所で働いていた．そして当時はロジャースと一緒に，テクノロジーが表現に大きな役割を果たすという方法で設計していた．しかし，ロジャースはテクノロジーを通してプランのフレキシビリティやパーツの可変性を最大に追求し，その結果，構造も設備システムも外側にはっきり現われるという，どのプロジェクトもよく似た特徴をもつ建物となった．すなわちロジャースの作品は経験主義とは反対のものである．近代のテクノロジーが絶対的な自由を達成するための観念論的な声明なのである．

トロートン・マッカーズランの建築には決してそのような絶対論は存在しない．観念的でなく，実用的である．たとえば，彼らのアクトン職業訓練センターは，求められたさまざまなプログラムに対してハイブリッドな構造で応えている．すなわち，スチールトラスのヴォールト屋根の下の訓練スペースで高度なフレキシビリティをつくり出す一方で，それほど変化を必要としない教室やオフィスには，コンクリートや組積造の頑丈な構造を採用している．トロートン・マッカーズランの経験主義は，建築を支える技術より，建築の経験的な側面に重点を置いている．レッドヒル駅舎計画では，穴開きの梁や丸屋根のスチールケーブルの筋違を露出して使うと同時に，これらの構造要素を，ペンキで塗りつぶしてしまってもいる．つまり，テクノロジーの経験論的な意味合いを，それ自身が目的でなく方法であるということで経験主義を強く表明している．

トロートン・マッカーズランの他の作品は，歴史に対して同様な経験論者的な見方を示している．キャナリーワーフのオフィスビルを見ると，デザイン的に歴史を表現した２つの極端な建物の間に位置して建っている．その極端な例の１つは，キャナリーワーフのその他のビルにいくつか見られるものであるが，エドワード朝風の英国あるいはファシストのヨーロッパの時代の意匠を身にまとっている．それがなければ意味を欠くために，意味づけのためにこれらの建物は歴史を参考にしている．しかし，そのためにかえってその意味が不明瞭になってしまっている建物である．もう１つの極端な例の建物は，近年ロンドンの街中に提案されているミース風の超高層ビルやその広場によく似たもので，市の歴史的な街並みに穴を開けるような存在である．それらの建物は，進歩がいつの日かわれわれを歴史の結末，制約からの絶

curtain wall, avoids the historicism of some of its neighbours, but the structure also rejects the idealism of Mies in its acceptance of constraint, such as holding the street walls and obeying the height limits of the neighbourhood. Likewise, in their two studio buildings in the St Peters Street area, Troughton McAslan have carefully grafted Modernist elements - asymmetrical facades and mass-produced components such as steel windows and glass block walls - onto existing industrial structures. And in their Merton Road office and warehouse, the firm has produced a Modernist building that nevertheless remains grounded in the particulars of its location, maintaining the height, rhythm, and scale of the adjacent structures. There is an inductive quality to such work; the requirements of each project differ and so too does the form of each building.

This raises another issue: the widespread confusion of empiricism and rationalism. To understand that distinction, compare Troughton McAslan's work to that of a rationalist architect such as Mario Botta. Botta's buildings, with their strong geometry, clear symmetry, centred compositions, and heroic scale, reveal the rationalist tendency to impose a mathematical order onto life; his is a deductive, a priori architecture, in which formal order dominates functional diversity.

Troughton McAslan seek order in their work, but of a very different kind. In projects such as their St Catherine's College in Kobe, Japan, they achieve unity, not through the imposition of symmetry, centrality or geometry, but through the use of repetitive modules in plan and of proportional systems in elevation. Like most of Troughton McAslan's work, this building avoids the self-referential, closed order of rationalism and offers, instead, an open-ended system that allows for change and growth. the empiricist seeks to uncover and reinforce the order of life, not to impose an abstract order upon it.

I have not meant to suggest here that empiricism completely defines the production of Troughton McAslan. Nor have I intended to place empiricism beyond reproach. What I hope is evident from this discussion, however, is the lack of precision and understanding that surrounds the current debate about Modern architecture. That debate usually portrays Modern architecture as monolithic, when in fact is has always embraced many conflicting viewpoints, including longstanding disputes among empiricists, idealists, and rationalists. To speak of Modern architecture, without reverence to these various ideas, is to say nothing. And to claim that Modern architecture is dead, without presenting coherent arguments against the complex and varied philosophies embedded within it, is sheer folly. If nothing else, Troughton McAslan show that at least the empirical aspect of Modern architecture are still very much alive and capable of generating work of considerable power.

Thomas Fisher is executive editor of 'Progressive Architecture'.

対的解放に導くというヘーゲル哲学を支持している.

トロートン・マッカーズランのような経験主義者は,過去を模倣するにしても追放するにしても，事実や革新的な思想を非常に尊敬する.彼らのキャナリーワーフ・ビルは,優雅でミニマルなカーテンウォールによって，周辺の建物のもつ歴史主義を退け，通りに面しては壁を立て，近隣の高さ制限に従うことで制約を受容しつつ，同時に構造的にはミースの観念主義を排している．その上，セント・ピータース通りの2つのスタジオ作品では，非対称のファサード，スチール窓やガラスブロックといった大量生産部品の採用によって,トロートン・マッカーズランは注意深くモダニスト的な要素と現存する工業的な構造を合体させている．マートンロードのオフィス・倉庫では，特殊な敷地にもかかわらず，隣接する建物の高さ，リズム，スケールを維持しつつ，モダニスト的な建物をつくり出している．これらの作品には，プロジェクトによって求められる要望が異なれば，建物の形態も異なるという，帰納的な特質がある.

これはまた，経験主義と合理主義の混乱という別な問題も引き起こした．しかし，トロートン・マッカーズランの作品を合理主義であるマリオ・ボッタなどの建築家のそれと比較してみると,その差が明確にわかる．ボッタの建物は，強い幾何学的な形態，シンメトリー，中心性のある構成，スケールの誇張などによって，人々の生活に数学的な様式を課するという合理主義特有の傾向を表している．ボッタの建築は，フォーマルな様式が機能的な多様性より優れているという，演繹的な選ばれた建築である.

トロートン・マッカーズランは彼らの作品に様式を追求するが，それも他とは違った種類の様式である.日本の神戸に建つセント・キャサリン・カレッジの場合などは，シンメトリーや中心性，幾何学的といったものを課することなしに，平面の反復するモデュールの使用，エレベーションの均衡などによって一体性をつくり出している.トロートン・マッカーズランのほとんどの作品と同様，このカレッジも自己参照的な要素をなくし，合理主義的様式を打ち切り，その代わりに使用する人と共に変化，成長していけるような，強い制限のない建物としてつくられている．経験主義者は日常生活の中の様式を追求し，強化するが，そこに観念的な様式の強制はしない.

私は,経験主義だけでトロートン・マッカーズランの作品を定義するつもりは毛頭ない．まして経験主義が非の打ち所のないものだというつもりもない．ただ明らかなことは，近代建築を取り巻く昨今の議論に正確さと理解が欠けているという点である．近代建築は，実際は矛盾するさまざまな考え方をもち，経験主義者，観念論者，合理主義者すべてを含めてずっと議論され続けているにもかかわらず，往々にしてこれらの議論は近代建築を単一なものとしてとらえている．さまざまな考えを尊重することなしに近代建築を語ることは無意味である.同様に，そこに含まれる複層した多様な哲学に対する一貫した論争もなしに，近代建築は死んでしまったと規定することは全く馬鹿げている．いずれにしても，少なくとも近代建築の経験主義的な考え方がいまでも生き続けており，かなりの重要さでプロジェクトを統合する力となっていることをトロートン・マッカーズランの作品は示している.

Transcending Modernism

by Kenneth Powell

モダニズムを超えて　ケネス・パウエル

Background

The 1980s saw a revolution in British architecture, with the Modern Movement, finally labelled Post Modernism, steadily advancing. Responding initially to a popular thirst for history and decoration, for context and congruity, Post Modernism has been gradually revealed as an architecture of surface, show and excess - an empty husk which blossoms only when allied with the rarest of architectural qualities: wit.

The Modernist values of discipline, logic, reason, structural integrity, and a concern for functional expression, have, as a consequence, been increasingly re-examined. Was Modernism "just another style"? Its social ambitions, for example, once derided, now seem more worthy of respect.

But is there now, as some have suggested, a school of Neo-Modernists? There has certainly been a degree of revival, though not an uncritical one. The revivalists, in this instance, as in the great revivals of the past, have learned from their precursors - and from their mistakes. The virtues of colour, ornament and "sense of place", and a concern for the user/consumer, cannot again easily be set aside. Neo-Modernism is, of course, no more than a convenience label, but it reflects a real movement away from the feverish obsession of the Post Modernist era with superficial decoration and towards a new seriousness and rationality. Many years ago, Berthold Lubetkin defined the true objectives of modern architecture as "genuine change, development and transformation". The formula holds good today.

Origins

Jamie Troughton (born 1951) and John McAslan (born 1954) founded their practice in 1983. To be exact, McAslan joined Troughton, who had set up on his own a year before. The two had met in the office of Richard Rogers, which they both joined in 1979. (Troughton had previously spent three years with Foster Associates, McAslan two years in the US working for Cambridge Seven Associates). Lloyd's, of course, dominated the Rogers office at the time - Troughton became a team leader on the project. It was a place to get practical experience young - McAslan was in charge of the Cambridge Patscentre project at the age of 25. The Rogers influence is - understandably - very evident in the partnership's earliest independent work. But Troughton McAslan quickly developed through the preoccupation with technology which they had embraced at the Rogers office, seeking to temper the idea of architecture as "pure machine" with a leavening of history.

Early Days

Refurbishing buildings is a perennial activity - built fabric usually outlives the uses it serves. But the energy crisis of the 1970s gave a great impetus to the cause of re-use. Inevitably, Troughton McAslan's first substantial project was rehabilitation.

Design House at Camden Town, completed in 1984, was in origin a mundane, but substantially built, 1950s car showroom occupying a promi-

背景

英国の建築界は1980年代に近代建築運動から，ついにポスト・モダニズムに到達するという大変革を見た．歴史や装飾への，またコンテクストや適合への社会の渇望を反映して，ポスト・モダニズムは表層的でショー的な，そして過度のものとして建築に徐々に現われてきた．それはしかし，理知という質をもたない，中身のない空虚な徒花としてである．

結果として，規律，論理，道理，構造的無欠性，機能的表現というモダニストの特質がこれを機会に問い直された．モダニズムは単なる１つのスタイルだったのだろうか．かつては省みられなかった，この社会的な問いが尊重され始めた．

しかし，一部で指摘されるように，そこには現在ネオ・モダニストという一派が存在するのだろうか．大きな流れではないが，たしかにある種のリバイバルは存在している．現代のリバイバリストもまた，過去の偉大なリバイバルのように，先駆者や過去の過ちから多くを学ぶ．色彩や装飾，場の観念の価値，使用者／消費者の関心などを再び安易に退けることはできない．もちろん，ネオ・モダニズムは都合のよいラベルではあり得ない．しかし，すばらしい装飾性をもったポスト・モダニスト時代の熱狂から導き出された，新たな真剣さや合理性への方向という運動を反映している．かつて，バーソルド・リベトキンは近代建築の真の目的は「純粋な変化，発展，変容」であると定義した．この公式は現在も通用する．

発端

トロートン・マッカーズランは1983年に彼らの活動を開始している．正確にいえば１年前に独自に活動を開始していたトロートンにマッカーズランが合流したのである．２人は1979年に共にリチャード・ロジャースの事務所で働いていた．それ以前にトロートンは３年ほどフォスター・アソシエイツに，マッカーズランはアメリカのケンブリッジ・セブンに２年ほど在籍していた．当時のロジャースの代表作であるロイズ本社ビルをトロートンはチームリーダーとして担当している．マッカーズランは25歳の若さでケンブリッジのパットセンター計画の責任者になって，実地の経験を積んだ．彼らの初期の仕事から，ロジャースの影響が大きいことは明白である．しかし，トロートン・マッカーズランは，建築を歴史に影響される「純粋な機械」とする考え方を追求しながら，ロジャースの事務所で体得した技術先取の思想を独自に発展させていった．

初期

ビルの改修はいつの時代も存在する．建物は長く使われ続けるものである．1970年代のエネルギー危機が再利用に拍車をかけた．必然的にトロートン・マッカーズランの初期の重要な仕事がこうした改修計画であった．

1984年に完成したカムデンタウンのデザインハウスは，もともとリージェントパークに近い，目立つ場所に1950年代に建てられた，ごく普通のかっちりとした自動車のショールームであった．建物の外観は外壁が張り替えられ，ハイテク以上にフォーマルな品位のあるものになり，インテリアもまた，ロジャース流の突出したやり方でクライアントのスタジオらしく根本からつくり直された．実に大胆でスタイリッシュなスタートであった．マッカーズランはこの作品をシーザー・ペリのパシフィック・デザインセンターの影響が大きいと述懐している．ロジャースの影響からの脱却は，彼らの次の作品であるスタジオビル

nent corner site near Regent's Park. The exterior of the building was transformed by recladding, giving it a formal dignity which already looks beyond High Tech. The interior was also radically recast for the studio user client, with the extruded services of the Rogers school clearly on display. It was a bold and stylish start. (McAslan cites Cesar Pelli's Pacific Design Centre as a definite influence.) The working-out of the Rogers influence continued at their next studio building - the conversion of a 3,000 square metres warehouse - for a design group in Shepherd's Bush (1984-85). This is a good example of High Tech tempered by common sense.

Troughton McAslan's retreat from High Tech was signalled by a growing interest in the romantic Modernism of the 1930s. McAslan, the practice's principal designer, looked back not so much to early Corb or Mies but to the more romantic Modernists like Erich Mendelsohn and his De La Warr Pavilion at Bexhill-on-Sea and Frank Lloyd Wright, whose Johnson Wax building has become a perennial Troughton McAslan influence. Both the partners venerate Pierre Chareau's Maison de Verre - indeed, it was Rogers who introduced them to this extraordinary building.

One of the firm's most problematic and, in the event, most tortuous jobs - the apartment block by the River Thames at Rotherhithe (1986-90) - illustrates the stream of inspiration. The site was a gap between recently completed housing in a decent, if ordinary, version of the now-familiar "Docklands vernacular" look. The London Docklands Development Corporation was inclined to demand more of the same, but support from SAVE and the Royal Fine Art Commission helped to sway the planners, as did critical endorsement from the *Architects' Journal*.

Alexander Thomson: Villa, Glasgow, Scotland
グラスゴーのビラ(アレキサンダー・トムソン設計)

Francisco Berenguer: Chapel, near Barcelona, Spain
バルセロナ近郊の教会(フランシスコ・ベレンゲル設計)

に引き継がれた．それは，1984年から85年にかけてシェパード・ブッシュのデザイン・グループのために3,000㎡の倉庫を改修したものである．これは常識的な範囲でハイテクを駆使した好例である．

トロートン・マッカーズランのハイテクからの乖離は，1930年代のロマンティックなモダニズムへの関心の高まりによって引き起こされた．マッカーズランは初期のコルビュジェやミースにはあまり関心をもたず，ロマンティック・モダニストであるエリッヒ・メンデルゾーンや彼のベックスヒル・オン・シーにあるデ・ラ・ワー・パビリオン，そしてライトの，特にジョンソンワックスビルに大きな影響を受けた．また，2人ともピエール・シャローのメゾン・ド・ヴェールを崇拝していた．実は，このすばらしい作品を彼らに教えたのはロジャースであった．

彼らの最も問題作であり，最も曲がりくねった作品となった，ロザーヒースのテムズ川沿いのアパートメント(1986－90年)は，インスピレーションの傾向を明確に表わしている．敷地は，最近完成したばかりの，いわゆるドックランド・バナキュラー風の立派なハウジングの間に位置している．ロンドン・ドックランド開発公社はまわりの建物と同じデザインを要求していた．しかし，SAVE(英国遺産の保護団体)や王立ファインアート委員会の支持が，公社のプランナーの意見を覆させたのである．それと同時に「アーキテクツ・ジャーナル」誌はこれを大いに評価した．

Maturing

The Rotherhithe scheme seems to be part of the period of 1986-87 when Troughton McAslan were redefining their position. Their entry for the Indira Gandhi Arts Centre competition (1986) shows a firm intention to learn from the existing architecture of New Delhi, both native Indian and European. Though unsuccessful, the project was well reviewed and provided excellent practice for the office in the demanding business of master-planning. The more recent scheme for the British High Commission building in Nairobi (1989) is equally contextual, putting practical considerations first while referring to a tradition of European building in Africa.

Having come to terms with history and relaxed the ties which led from the Rogers office, Troughton McAslan were well placed to enter a period of relatively frenetic activity. Between 1988 and 1989 four significant buildings were completed and the office grew to a total complement of over twenty.

This was a period when Troughton McAslan began to grapple with the problems of building in towns. What architect these days does not lay claim to being an Urbanist? But how can the architect faced with a minor contribution to a quite ordinary street express his commitment? Troughton McAslan faced the challenge at Alexander House (1988-89) on the drearier fringes of Wandsworth with the commission for a warehouse and office building. Polychromatic banded brick was their response to the variegated Victorian streetscape. Now brick is not an obviously "modern" material, though there is no clear reason why it should not be. At Alexander House, brick - tough, exact engineering brick - was simply right for the site. In giving the building a Commendation, the Civic Trust noted that it attempted "no shallow connections with adjacent architecture...yet it does respond well to both position and place".

London is largely a Victorian city, but the Georgian image of the capital remains more fashionable. Kensington and Chelsea Council has an inordinate love of recycled stock brick, which accords well with carriage lamps, potted bay trees and the other paraphernalia of gentrification. Troughton McAslan fell foul of this prejudice at Pond Place (1987-88), a rather nondescript mews close to South Kensington underground station.

The local authority and some local residents wanted a recycled stock facade to the little studio block planned for an infill site there. The architects proposed bands of blue and red brick recalling the 19th century tradition, though the design has a distinct flavour of Italian Rationalism. The matter eventually went to a planning appeal. Almost inevitably, given the present timorous state of British taste, the council won. ("A victory for cocktail party politics," says Troughton.) The facade has had to be rendered over. How fortunate that such a rigid aesthetic code did not prevail a century ago, when the Victorians enriched South Kensington with churches and public buildings in a bewildering variety of materials!

円熟期

ロザーヒース計画は，トロートン・マッカーズランが彼らの立場を再定義する時期(1986-87)の重要な部分を担っていた．1986年のインディラ・ガンジー・アートセンターのコンペ応募案は，ニューデリーに存在する，インド本来の建築とヨーロッパ的なものの両方から学びとろうとする意図が明白に表われている．入選しなかったが，このプロジェクトはよく考えられており，彼らのオフィスにとってマスタープランの必要性を認識した優れた実績となった．ごく最近(1989年)のナイロビの英国高等弁務官事務所計画もまた同じコンテクストで，まず最初にアフリカにおけるヨーロッパ建築の伝統を参照して設計されている．

実績を積み，ロジャース事務所から受け継いだものから脱し，トロートン・マッカーズランはいまその活動の全盛期に突入している．1988年から1989年にかけて，４つの重要な作品が完成し，事務所員も20人以上に成長した．

トロートン・マッカーズランは，都市の中における建物の問題に取り組み始めた．いまや建築家はアーバニストたることを止めてしまった．しかし，それではどうして建築家として都市に寄与することができるだろう．トロートン・マッカーズランは，アレキサンダーハウス(1988−89年)でこれに挑戦した．荒涼としたワンズワースの端に建つ倉庫とオフィスビル計画である．多色レンガを帯状に使った外観が，さまざまな建物が混在する街並みへの解答であった．いまや，レンガはモダンな材料ではない．しかしこれを使ってはいけないという理由はない．アレキサンダーハウスでは，堅い工業レンガが敷地にふさわしい材料であった．この建物はシビック・トラストから「周辺の建物となんら関係なく建っているにも係わらず，その場所や位置に充分に適応している」との賞賛を得た．

ロンドンは大きくはビクトリア朝風の都市である．しかし，首都としてのジョージ王朝風のイメージもファッショナブルな形で残っている．ケンジントンやチェルシーの議会はリサイクルの保存レンガに異常なほどの情熱をもっている．それは，馬車のランプや植木鉢の月桂樹など上流社会を表わす装置類とよく調和するのである．トロートン・マッカーズランはサウスケンジントンの地下鉄駅近くのごく普通の馬屋であったポンドプレイス(1987−88年)で，この偏見と真っ向から対立した．

挟まれた狭隘な敷地に建つ小さなスタジオ建築に対して，地元の自治体や住民の一部は，リサイクルのレンガの外観を求めた．設計者は，19世紀の伝統的な，そしてイタリアの合理主義の香りの強いデザインである青と赤のレンガの縞模様を提案した．問題は結果として計画のアピールに行き着き，現在の英国の時宜的な嗜好から，ほとんど必然的に市当局側が勝った．「カクテルパーティ的な政治の勝利」だとトロートンは評している．ファサードは描き直された．さまざまな材料によるビクトリア風の建築が教会や公共建築に採用されてサウスケンジントンを豊かにしていた１世紀前には，幸いなことに，こんな厳格な美的制約は普及してはいなかった．

飛躍

ストックレーパークに1987年から89年にかけて建てられたアップルコンピュータ本社ビルは，土地のランドマーク的存在の5,000㎡の大きな建物である．「時期的にむずかしい仕事だった」とマッカーズランは述懐する．しかし，結果として14か月で完成した建物は，どちらかというとスタイリッシュな建物に囲まれているが，決して遜色のない見事な出来ばえである．

High Ambition

The Apple Computers headquarters block at Stockley Park, built in 1987-89, was a largish building (5,000 square metres) which was a landmark in the evolution of the practice. Apple was "difficult at times" confides McAslan, but the resulting building (completed in fourteen months) has an exuberance which makes it stand out even amidst some stylish neighbours.

But wasn't Stockley Park a difficult location for such urban-minded Modernists? Where are the streets? Troughton McAslan's response was to create an internal "street" through the building. It's a device to which they have returned subsequently, (One obvious precedent is Henning Larsen's Trondheim University). The Apple building certainly seems to have satisfied the clients, who came back with a commission for a further block.

Owen Williams: Daily Express Building, London, England
デイリー・エクスプレスビル(オーエン・ウィリアムズ設計)

Pierre Chareau: Maison de Verre, Paris, France
パリのメゾン・ド・ヴェール(ピエール・シャロー設計)

ストックレーパークは，都市の建築を目指すモダニストにとってはむずかしい敷地である．通りはどこにあるかはっきりしていない．トロートン・マッカーズランの解決法は，建物の中に内部通路を設置することであった．ヘニング・ラーセンのトロンハイム大学という先例が1つあるが，彼ら独自の考案といえる．アップル本社ビルは確実にクライアントを満足させることができ，引き続き隣接地での設計を依頼された．

アップル社の最初の仕事で，マッカーズランはある雑誌に発表するに際して「ここで私たちは過去の様式を模倣するのでなく，また他の文化を引用するのでもない，独自のスタイルを追求した」といっている．さらに大規模な仕事が入ってくるという予測が，この追求を強化した．マッカーズランの関心は，19世紀末のフリースタイルの建築家たち，ガウディや他のカタロニア地方のモダニストであるベレンゲルやドメネク・イ・モンタナ，そしてマッキントッシュの陰になって目立たないながら，偉大なグラスゴーの建築家たち，サーモン，ギレスピー，バーネット，トムソンといった建築家たちに集中していた．彼はまたジャン・プルーベやオーエン・ウィリアムズといった建築技術者にも傾倒していた．グレン・マーカットを目下は最も尊敬している．

ドックランドのキャナリーワーフの建物の設計を依頼された1988年に，トロートン・マッカーズランのスタイル追求は表面化した．彼らはドックランドプロジェクトに起用された最初の英国建築家であり，さらに，40,000m²という規模は彼らのこれまでの仕事の最大規模のものである．ディベロッパーであるオリンピア&ヨーク社としては，キャナリーワーフが，外国からの輸入品であるアメリカン・コマーシャルスタイルの大量のディスプレイにとどまらないイメージを持っていた．彼らがトロートン・マッカーズランに求めていたものは「形態と組織の明快さがある，モダンでかつ流行に左右されない永久的な設計」であった．

At the time of the first Apple commission, McAslan was quoted in a magazine article to this effect: "We are trying to find a style which isn't imitating the past yet is not from another culture." The prospect of more large-scale jobs seems to have intensified their search. McAslan's enthusiasm is most deeply fired by those architects who pioneered a new Free Style at the end of the 19th century - Gaudi and the other Catalan Modernists like Berenguer and Domenech i Montaner, and the great Glasgow architects who still tend to languish, to a degree, in Mackintosh's shadow: Salmon, Gillespie, Burnet and Thomson amongst them. He is equally enthusiastic about architect engineers like Jean Prouve and Owen Williams. Glenn Murcutt is a much admired contemporary.

The search for a style came to the fore when, in 1988, Troughton McAslan were asked to design a building at Canary Wharf in Docklands. They were the first British practice to be commissioned there and this was - at 40,000 square metres - by far their biggest job to date. It was also a clear indication that the developers, Olympia & York, were not content to have Canary Wharf dismissed as an alien import, a massive display of the US commercial style. Olympia & York asked Troughton McAslan for a design "modern but timeless and enduring, with a clarity of form and organisation".

Troughton McAslan's interpretation of the brief was to design a "wrapped skin" building in the tradition of their beloved Johnson Wax tower and of Owen Williams' series of buildings for the "Daily Express".

Erich Mendelsohn: De La Warr Pavilion, Bexhill-on-Sea, England
デ・ラ・ワー・パビリオン(エリッヒ・メンデルゾーン設計)

トロートン・マッカーズランはまず，彼らの崇拝するライトのジョンソン・ワックス風の，そしてオーエン・ウィリアムズの「デイリー・エクスプレス」のための一連の建物に見られる「包まれた外観」の建物を提案した．

マッカーズランは，この建物を隣接して建つシーザー・ペリの超高層と比較して，「ウイスキー瓶の横に建つピーナッツ」と謙遜をこめて称している．しかしまさにその通りで，建物は効果的で聡明な対立する存在となっている．

評価

歴史への参照は他の最近作に顕著である．1988年から1990年に設計されたレッドヒル駅舎は，チャールズ・ホールデンに，特に彼のサウスゲート・ピカデリーライン駅に敬意を表した作品である．ホールデンは健全で模範的であり，彼の近代性は伝統に根ざしている．したがって，ここでトロートン・マッカーズランはホールデンのデザインと直接対話しようとした．あるいは，プラットホーム上にかかる既存の鋳鉄のキャノピーを保存したのは，単なる常識的なことなのだろうか．

1989年のコンペに入選した，アクトンの新しいロンドンの地下に展開する職業訓練所は，歴史や文脈の尊重が，その時代の模倣を意味するという考えへの反発を表明したものである．そのデザインは鉄道の線路に面した郊外道路に沿らず，そこに覆い被さるように建っている．内部が見事である．ここでもまた，内部に道路が貫通している．線路に向かってさまざまなワークショップが扇型にとりつき，小さな中庭を点在させ，通りに面して教室や事務室が配置されている．通りに面した低層棟は，レンゾ・ピアノのIRCAMに呼応してパネル化されたレンガ貼り，ワークショップの外壁はメタルである．

McAslan, in a self-disparaging moment, suggested that the building would relate to the Cesar Pelli tower "like a peanut alongside a whisky bottle". This is hardly just. The building will provide an effectively luminous counterpoint.

Values

Historical references run through other recent projects. The Redhill Station (1988-90) pays a degree of homage to Charles Holden and to his Southgate Piccadilly Line station in particular. Holden is a sound enough model: modernity rooted in tradition. And the scheme shows a concern for conversation - or is it just plain common sense to retain the existing cast-iron canopies over the platform?

The successful competition entry for a new London Underground training centre at Acton (1989) is a riposte to the idea that a respect for history and context implies period pastiche. The design is not subservient to the suburban streets which border the tracks, yet it declines to overshadow them. The glories are within. Here is the building as internal street again. The various workshops fan out towards the tracks, leaving small-scale courtyards, housing classrooms and offices on the street side. The low blocks to the street will be brick-clad, the brick set in panels echoing Piano's IRCAM, the workshops will be metal clad.

Troughton McAslan are, first of all, sound, practical builders - an ideal which transcends all the "isms" on the architectural scene. But they have ideals too. They are searching for an architecture which is more than surface and style. I look forward immensely to their work in the 90s, which now includes projects abroad with a building completed in Japan - the Kobe Institute, for St Catherine's College in Oxford - as well as the completion during 1991 and 1992 of four major London office schemes at Canary Wharf, Hardwick Street, Rosebery Avenue and Bolsover Street. And looking further ahead, they will extend their portfolio of transport projects with the completion of two Jubilee Line Extensions Stations at Canning Town and Stratford by 1996. Their buildings have an admirable toughness and "bite". Above all, Troughton McAslan have a tremendous enthusiasm for what they are doing. Their work deserves to be celebrated.

Kenneth Powell is architecture correspondent of the 'Daily Telegraph'.

Glenn Murcutt: Farmhouse, Jamberoo, Australia
オーストラリアの農家(グレン・マーカット設計)

Louis Kahn: Richards Medical Laboratory, Philadelphia, USA
リチャーズ医学研究所(ルイス・カーン設計)

トロートン・マッカーズランはまず第一に正統派で実用的であり，あらゆる建築の何々主義といったものを超越した考えに立っている．しかし，彼らもまた理想をもっている．それは表層やスタイル以上のものを追求することである．私は彼らの90年代の仕事に大いに期待している．オックスフォード大学セント・キャサリン・カレッジ神戸校などの海外での仕事や，1991年から1992年にかけて完成を見るキャナリーワーフ，ハードウィック・ストリート，ローズベリー・アベニュー，ボルソバー・ストリートの4つのロンドンのオフィスビル計画などが楽しみである．さらに，交通施設でも活躍が期待される．1996年までにはカニングタウンやストラットフォードのジュビリー線の鉄道駅増築計画が完成するはずである．しかし，柔弱になっては困る．彼らの作品はいつの時代も尊敬すべきタフさと刺激性をもっている．なかでも，トロートン・マッカーズランは自分たちのやっていることに膨大な情熱をかけている．彼らの作品は充分賞賛に値する．

Expression and Restraint

by Rowan Moore

表現と抑制　ローワン・ムーア

Troughton McAslan are leading protagonists of a generation of young architects that came to prominence in the mid-1980s. In their early days they were the subject of occasional favourable reviews in the architectural press: ten years later they have become established names, both nationally and internationally.

Like many of their contemporaries, they are well educated in architectural theory and history, particularly of the 20th century, and are young enough to view both the Modern Movement and the Post Modern reaction with a detachment uncoloured by polemic. As a result they are able to learn from both, although they have an obvious distaste for the excesses of Post Modernism, and their background in the offices of Rogers and Foster clearly indicates which way their preferences lie.

The resulting architecture is most readily described as an imaginative and honest expression of doing the job appropriately and well, of finding solutions that are not just efficient but also elegant, and which inform and create spaces. Like High Tech architecture, Troughton McAslan's work is technologically ambitious, but it is always rooted in the practicalities of a brief or site. Thus different circumstances have given rise to buildings as varied as Apple Computers' headquarters, and Alexander House offices, the Riverside apartments and most recently St Catherine's College Kobe. Their architecture reflects the fact that, in recent years, dogmatism and ideology have become the property of the more extreme traditionalists, leaving innovative architects to express themselves in their work.

Troughton McAslan's open minded approach allows them to employ a range of techniques, from fast track to traditional construction, and to choose when to express structure or services, and when to suppress or modify them in the interests of the hierarchy of a street, or the demands of context. They know how to make purely stylistic gestures without compromising the integrity of a project. Unlike earlier generations, they are able to see Modernism as partly a matter of style, which is how the influence of the more romantic Modernists like Owen Williams and Mendelsohn finds its way into Troughton McAslan's work. Their other major influences, from both the present and the past, are those architects and engineers who have combined technological inventiveness with a pragmatic flexibility in its application, such as Perret, Chareau and Kahn.

With the pressures of fast growth during the 1980s boom, current architecture for those building in London became more a matter of action than of thought. In this context Troughton McAslan have made the most out of restricted briefs, and they have avoided the bland reasonableness and descent into pure problem solving that are the most obvious hazards of this type of work. The high output of their ten years has also given them the opportunity to develop their work through experience. At present it is a matter of refinement and making simple, of learning how to achieve more with less, which is making their architecture both more rational and more expressive. With projects like St Catherine's Kobe, Hardwick Street, St Peter's Street and Colebrooke Place they are demonstrating the values of a growing restraint.

Experience has enabled their work to acquire a greater consistency, which can be attributed to a clearer division of responsibilities in the office, with Troughton becoming the business strategist and McAslan very much the designer. They are now in a position to build on their experience, and to demonstrate that they are more than highly efficient pragmatists.

In the last decade the reaction to sterility too often meant meretriciousness: Troughton McAslan have shown that a building can be rich and varied without excessive theatrics, and that simplicity and intellectual toughness need not exclude imagination and invention.

Rowan Moore is an architect and freelance architectural critic.

●　●　●

トロートン・マッカーズランは，1980年代中ごろから頭角を現わし始めた，若き建築家世代の主唱者的立場にある．駆け出しのころは建築業界誌等で時折，好意的な批評を受ける程度であったが，5年後には英国内外に広く名が知れわたるようになった．

他の同世代建築家たちのほとんどがそうであるように，彼らは20世紀の作品を中心に理論や歴史に精通しており，また，モダニズム建築とその後に来るポスト・モダニズムの反動，この２つの潮流を学派内部の論争に巻き込まれることなく，一歩離れた場所から冷静に見守ることのできた若い世代に属している．そのため，偏見に染まることなく，両方の潮流から学び取ることができたわけだが，彼らが過度なポスト・モダニズムを好まないことは明らかで，また，ロジャースやフォスターの設計事務所に在籍していたバックグランドを思い出してみれば，彼らの指向する方向性が読み取れる．

彼らの設計した建築物は，まさに，「的確でよい仕事」という表現がぴったりくるような，正直で創造性あふれるもので，問題を解決する手法も，ただ有能であるばかりでなく，気品をも漂わせており，それが空間を生み出す根本となっている．ハイテク建築物と同じく，トロートン・マッカーズランの作品は技術的には非常に野心的なものであるが，常に現場状況に合わせた実際性に根ざしている．このため，アップル・コンピューター本社ビルやアレキサンダー・ハウス・オフィス，リバーサイド・アパートメントなど，その場の付随状況の違いが，実に多様な作品を生み出す要素となっている．ドグマティズムやイデオロギーというものは極端な伝統主義者の領域となってしまい，革新的な建築家にとって，作品とは思うままに自己を表現できる場であるという事実を彼らの最近の建築物は端的に反映している．

トロートン・マッカーズランの偏見のない自由なアプローチは，ファースト・トラック方式から伝統的な建築方法まで，様々なテクニックを駆使させており，また，時には構造やサービスを思う存分に表現し，時には通り全体のヒエラルキーや建築物に要求される内容に合わせて表現すべき対象を変更，抑制する，その自由な選択を可能にさせている．彼らは，プロジェクト全体の統合性を損なうことなく，純粋にスタイリスティックなジェスチャーを示すやり方をよく認識している．以前の世代とは異なり，彼らはモダニズムをある部分では様式の１つに過ぎないと捉えることが可能で，そこにはオーエン・ウィリアムスやメンデルゾーンのようなもっとロマンティックなモダニズム推進者の影響を見ることができる．この２人のほかにも，トロートン・マッカーズランが影響を受けている過去，そして同世代の人々には，ペレやシャロー，カーンなど，適用の場において，技術的な発明力を実際的な自在性と結びつけている建築家や技術者がいる．

1980年代の建築ブームは，急速な成長と短期間での建設というプレッシャーを増大させ，現在ロンドンでみられる新しいビルを設計した建築家たちは，じっくり構想を練るというより，まず行動するタイプが多いようである．このような状況のなかで，トロートン・マッカーズランは限られた準備段階を最大限に利用することによって，退屈な理性主義や現代建築の持つ明らかに危険な側面である問題解決至上主義に陥ることを避けている．建築家としてのキャリア初期に多くの仕事をこなした彼らは，実際の経験を通して作品を発展させていく好機に恵まれた．現在は，いかに洗練させ，「単純化する」かという点，つまり，いかに少ないもので多くを生み出すかを学ぶ時期にさしかかり，それによって彼らの作品はより合理的で，より表現力豊かなものになってきている．セント・ピーターズ・ストリートやコルブルック・プレイスのようなプロジェクトにおいて，彼らは以前以上に，抑制という概念の価値を明瞭化している．豊かな経験が彼らの仕事に強力な一貫性を与えていることは疑いようがなく，それはトロートンが戦略立案者，マッカーズランが設計者，というように，オフィスにおける２人の責任分担が次第に明確になってきていることにも起因しているのかも知れない．そして今，彼らは積み重ねてきた経験を駆使できる立場にあり，自分たちが有能な実際主義者以上の存在であることを明らかにしつつある．

過去10年間，無味乾燥な作風の反動とは，どぎついまでの華麗さを意味した．そのなかで，トロートン・マッカーズランは過度に大袈裟にならずとも，豊かで多様な様式を作り出すことが可能であり，創意工夫が理性的な堅実性と両立しうることを見事に証明している．

BUILDINGS AND PROJECTS

主な作品と計画案

STUDIOS

During the 1980s, Britain's economic boom created a demand for new offices - while traditional industry slumped. On the one hand, the boom produced a spate of new custom-built office blocks - particularly in the City of London and London Docklands (see the Canary Wharf development)- in the aftermath of the "Big Bang" of 1986. The market in this case was international. But at the same time small businesses prospered, especially those associated with construction (including architects themselves), design, advertising and public relations. Industrial decline had left a reservoir of empty space - in the form of soundly built and often architecturally distinguished buildings- which could be converted to studios for small firms. The Conservative government's relaxation of planning regulations made it easier to build developments which mixed office and light industrial uses. The "B1" space, as it became known because of a clause in the new legislation, was one of the distinctive building types of the 1980s in Britain.

Troughton McAslan had begun in practice with the studio development at Design House, Camden Town - an economical refurbishment of a nondescript car showroom. The studios at Shepherd's Bush were in the same vein - both schemes reflect the influence of Richard Rogers. The St Peter's Street project in Islington was altogether a more considered scheme, expressive of an increasingly cool and considered approach by the firm to design. In its modest way, it looks back to traditional Japanese buildings and to the Maison de Verre, that perennial favourite of the architects of the Rogers/ Foster academy.

Close to St Peter's Street - and for the same client - is Colebrooke Place, where Troughton McAslan have completed the conversion of a basic shed into studios. If anything, the approach is even more simple and refined, with decisive and distinctive "interventions". Two further phases are underway at Colebrooke Place. Developments of this kind have a positive role, reusing abandoned buildings and giving new life to areas of the inner city as well as being nurseries for young firms. Though they were borne out of the 1980s boom, they look set to continue to flourish during the 1990s. Though none of the buildings which provided the raw materials for these Troughton McAslan's projects was especially distinguished, the practice has - typically - treated them with respect and imagination, fastening on their best features to provide the basis of the "interventions".

There is no scope in this kind of work for flamboyance, excess or extravagance - the emphasis is on effective, economical space. Perhaps working in this field has strengthened Troughton McAslan's practical bent, their distaste for the superfluous and the baroque. It has been an important element in the maturing of the practice's style. ***—Kenneth Powell***

3 St Peter's Street, Studio Interior
セント・ピーターズ・ストリート3番地，スタジオ内部

Photo by Peter Cook

スタジオ建築

1980年代の英国では，伝統的な産業の低迷の一方で経済復興ブームが新たなオフィススペースの需要を生み出した．1986年のビッグバンの余波の中で，ロンドン中心部やキャナリーワーフ(62頁参照)で特に，新しいオフィスブロックが続出した．マーケットは国際的であった．しかし，同時にまた小さなビジネス，特に建設(建築家の仕事も含めて)，デザイン，広告関係などの分野の仕事も繁栄し始めた．工業の衰退は多くの空きスペースのストックを生み出した．それらはしっかりと建てられ，建築的にすぐれたものも多いため，小さな会社のスタジオに容易に転換できる．保守党政府の計画関連法規制の緩和によって，オフィスと工業的な用途の混在した開発が容易となった．地下１階に関する新しい法律の条項によって，1980年代の英国の顕著なビルディングタイプが現出したのである．

トロートン・マッカーズランはカムデンタウンのデザインハウスの仕事が処女作である．ごく一般的な自動車のショールームのローコストな改修計画である．シェパード・ブッシュのスタジオも同じ延長線上にある．この両作品はリチャード・ロジャースの影響を受けている．アイリントンのセント・ピーターズ・ストリート計画は，それらを合わせてもう一歩進めたもので，マッカーズランの慎重なデザイン手法で，クールに表現されている．そこには，日本の伝統的な建物の特質，そしてロジャース／フォスター学派の建築家が非常に好きなメゾン・ド・ヴェールの影響が強く見られる．

セント・ピーターズ・ストリート近くにあり，同じクライアントのコルブルックプレイスで，トロートン・マッカーズランは倉庫をスタジオに改修した．そこでの手法は，決定的かつ明確な「介在」による，シンプルで洗練されたものである．コルブルックプレイス計画は引き続き第２期，第３期が建設中である．この種の開発は，見捨てられた建物の再利用，都心に新たな生命を吹き込み，若い組織を育成するという大事な役割を担っている．1980年代のブームによって生まれたとはいえ，その傾向は1990年代の現在にも引き継がれている．これらのどの作品もトロートン・マッカーズランにとってそれほど華々しいものではないが，それらを大事に設計した実績が，「介在」という彼らの最大の特質を形成する基盤となった．

この種の仕事に華々しさや過度，贅沢はなにも存在しない．強調はなんの意味ももたない，経済的なスペースである．多分，この種の仕事がトロートン・マッカーズランにもたらしたものは，実用的なものが好きでバロック的な華々しさは嫌いだということの確認であろう．これは設計を続け，成熟していく上で重要な要素である．

Design House
London, England, 1984

デザインハウス

All photos by Peter Cook

▲Mezzanine, with first floor studio　1階スタジオを見下ろせる中2階
◀Exterior view at night　夜の外観

Troughton McAslan's first commission, attracting widespread attention when it was completed in 1984, was the conversion of a garage showroom into design studios in London's Camden Town. The design developed techniques and approaches learned at Richard Rogers' office (where Jamie Troughton and John McAslan once worked) and applied them to the low cost refurbishment of the showroom into offices for a design company. It also embodies the pragmatic approach that has run through much of Troughton McAslan's work since.

As in the practice's later conversions, the structure and profile of the existing building have been put to maximum use. With a minimum of interference the old spaces have been adapted to answer the needs of a new and wholly different use. The double height showroom has been made into open plan office space overlooked by a gallery to the rear, underneath which are cellular offices looking back into the old showroom through a glazed wall. Through the extensive use of glazing the work carried out in the building is on display both to the outside world and within the company.

The latent qualities of the original building, and its pleasing quirkiness, have been preserved, but transformed out of recognition by clearer organisation and sharper detailing. Where the old

デザインハウスはロンドンのカムデンタウンにあった自動車のショールームからの改修である．これはトロートン・マッカーズランの処女作であり，1984年に完成したときは多くの注目を集めた．デザインは，トロートンとマッカーズランの両者がかつて働いていたリチャード・ロジャース事務所で学んだ技術や方法論を発展させて，自動車のショールームをデザインオフィスにローコストで改修することに応用したものである．それ以後のトロートン・マッカーズランの実用主義的方法論をここですでに体現していた．

最終的に，既存の建物の構造や仕上げはできるだけ多くそのまま利用されている．最小限の介在によって，古いスペースは新しい全く別な用途のニーズに適応させた．２層吹抜けのショールーム部分は建物後部のギャラリーから見下ろすことのできるオープンプランのオフィススペースとなった．ギャラリーの下にはガラス壁に仕切られた個室のオフィスがショールームに向かって並んでいる．建物にガラスを多く用いることで，内部の仕事の様子が外部にディスプレイできると同時に内部でも相互に見渡せる．

もとの建物のもっていた目に見えない特質や，その快適な気まぐれ性はうまく残しつつ，明快な

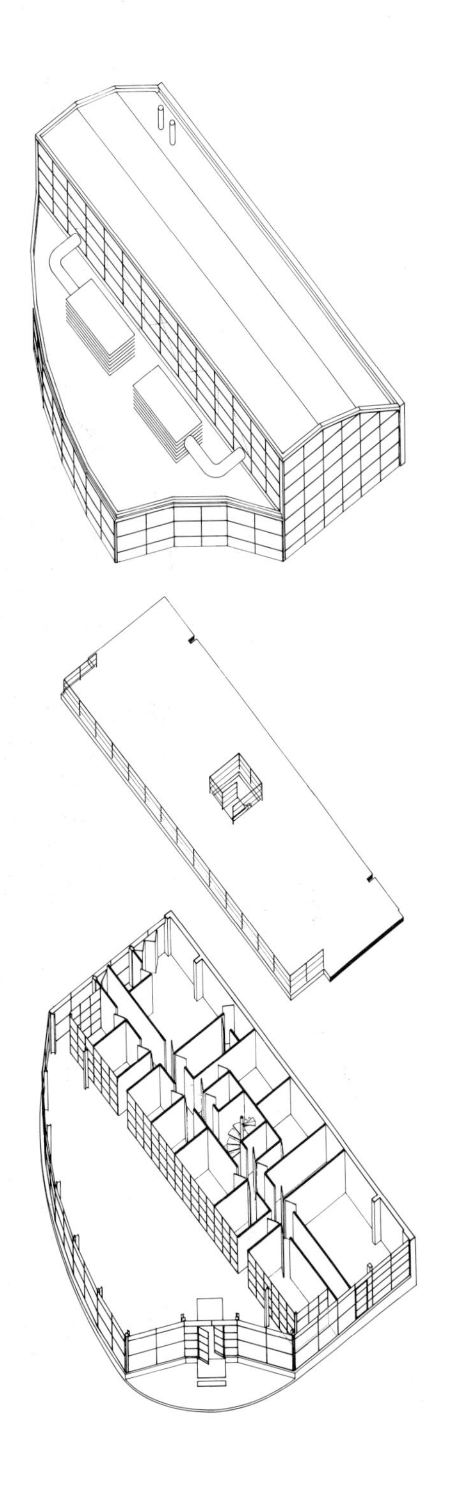

Cut-away axonometric

Exterior view of the entrance at night 夜の入口外観

building was dominated by a clumsy fascia sign, Design House now derives a new integrity from the consistency of its finishes: blue aluminium panels and glazing bars, white walls and minimal balustrades. What was once little more than a shed is revealed to be a surprising and original structure.

組織とより鮮明なディテールによって明らかな変換をなし遂げている．ぎこちないダッシュボードのサインが特徴となっていた古い建物から，デザインハウスは一新し，青いアルミのパネルや輝く建具，白い壁，最小限の手すりといった，その仕上げの整合性からくる新しい清廉な建物に生まれ変わった．かつては小さな小屋にすぎなかったものが，驚くべき個性的な建物に変身した．

Exterior prior to conversion 改築前の外観，通り側壁面のカーブを活かして改築された

Photo by Peter Cook

Shepherd's Bush
London, England, 1985

シェパード・ブッシュ

This West London three-storey, concrete framed warehouse was converted into the headquarters of a leading design company. The architects' task was twofold: solving the functional problem of organising space and services flexibly and efficiently, and finding an imagery appropriate to both the existing structure and its new use.

Troughton McAslan's first move was to reorganise the interior of the building about a new triple height volume, toplit by an existing roof light. It is about this volume, overlooked by both cellular and open plan offices, that primary circulation takes place. Ancillary accommodation, and further cellular office space, is housed at either end, leaving a clear open plan area between.

The building's character derives from both the large scale interventions and the treatment of individual elements and furniture. This varies from High Tech at its most robust and sculptural - the air conditioning ducts that mark the culmination of the central space - to the refinement of the reception "box", which is demountable to allow for expansion and change within the company. The purpose-made desks and lighting fall between these extremes: they are elegant constructions, but emphasise the way they are assembled with pronounced joints and changes of material.

With a combination of architecture, interior design and furniture design, a continuity is established between the industrial quality of the original building and the more urbane life it now leads.

The commission for the Shepherd's Bush offices gave Troughton McAslan the chance to manufacture an uplighter design they had already developed, which has since undergone further refinements and been used in a number of their projects.

The design is based on the expression of individual elements. As in their buildings, Troughton McAslan are interested in articulating the way an object is put together. The result is a slightly anthropomorphic uplighter in which reflector, base, frame and transformer are clearly expressed, and each element has its own personality which is derived from both its physical and functional properties.

Although they are primarily architects, Troughton McAslan, like their Free Style predecessors, see no absolute barrier between the design of buildings and of objects.

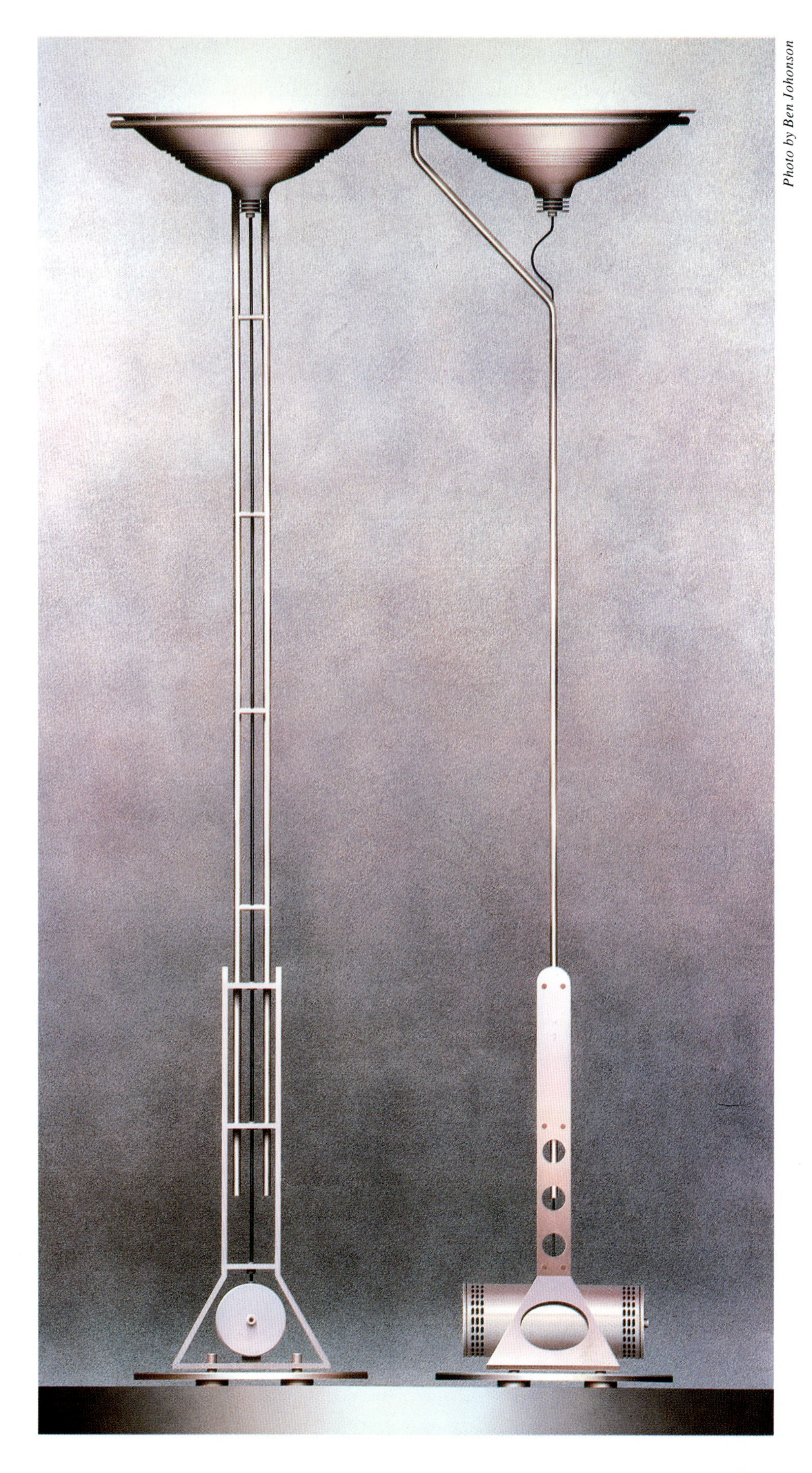

Photo by Ben Johonson

▶Painting of the uplighter, 'Scene in Another Light'
上を照らす照明の絵,「もう1つの光の中のシーン」
Opposite page: Atrium space *(photo by Richard Bryant)*
右ページ：アトリウムの空間

Photo by Richard Bryant

Atrium space at night　夜のアトリウムの空間

Interior during conversion　改築中の内部

ロンドン西郊の３階建てのコンクリートの倉庫が著名なデザイン会社の本社に改修された．ここでの建築家の仕事は２つの要素から構成される．１つは業務内容に合ったフレキシブルでかつ効率よいスペースとサービスを確保するという機能的な問題，もう１つは既存の建物と新しい用途をいかにうまくイメージとして結びつけるかという点である．

トロートン・マッカーズランの計画は，既存の屋根窓を活用してトップライトからの光があふれる３層吹抜けの新たな空間をつくってインテリアを再編成することであった．この吹抜け空間はオープンプランのオフィスからも個室からも見渡せ，かつ主な動線となる．補助的な室や追加の個室オフィスは建物の両端に配置し，中央はオープンプランのエリアが専有する．

大規模な介在，それぞれ個別の要素や家具什器の両方から建物の性格づけが導き出された．中央スペースの真中に陣取る空調ダクトのたくましい，彫刻的な形態が表わすハイテクから，業務内容に合わせて拡張したり，変更が容易にできるよう，取り外し可能な応接室の純粋な箱にいたるまで，さまざまである．両サイドには特注のデスクや照明器具が並ぶ．それらは優雅に空間を構成しているが，明快なジョイントと材質の変化を強調して組み合わせられている．

建築，インテリア・デザイン，家具デザインの結合によって，工業的な特質と新しい，より都市的な特質が連続性をもち得ている．

シェパード・ブッシュの仕事はトロートン・マッカーズランに，彼らがそれまで経験し，数多くのプロジェクトで使っていたデザイン手法をさらに発展させる好機となった．

個別の要素をそれぞれに表現することがデザインの基調である．トロートン・マッカーズランは，それぞれのものがつなぎ合わさるときのアーティキュレーションに関心が深い．結果として，彼らのデザインは，少しばかり人体的な形態の中に，ガラス，基部，フレーム，変換といったことを明確に表現し，各要素は物理的，機能的の両方から導き出された特質をもって存在している．

トロートン・マッカーズランは建築家であるが，かつてのフリースタイルの先駆者たちと同様，建物をデザインすることとオブジェのデザインの間に絶対的な障壁は設けていない．

Photo by Richard Bryant

Conference Room area in the centre of the atrium　アトリウム中央に位置する会議室

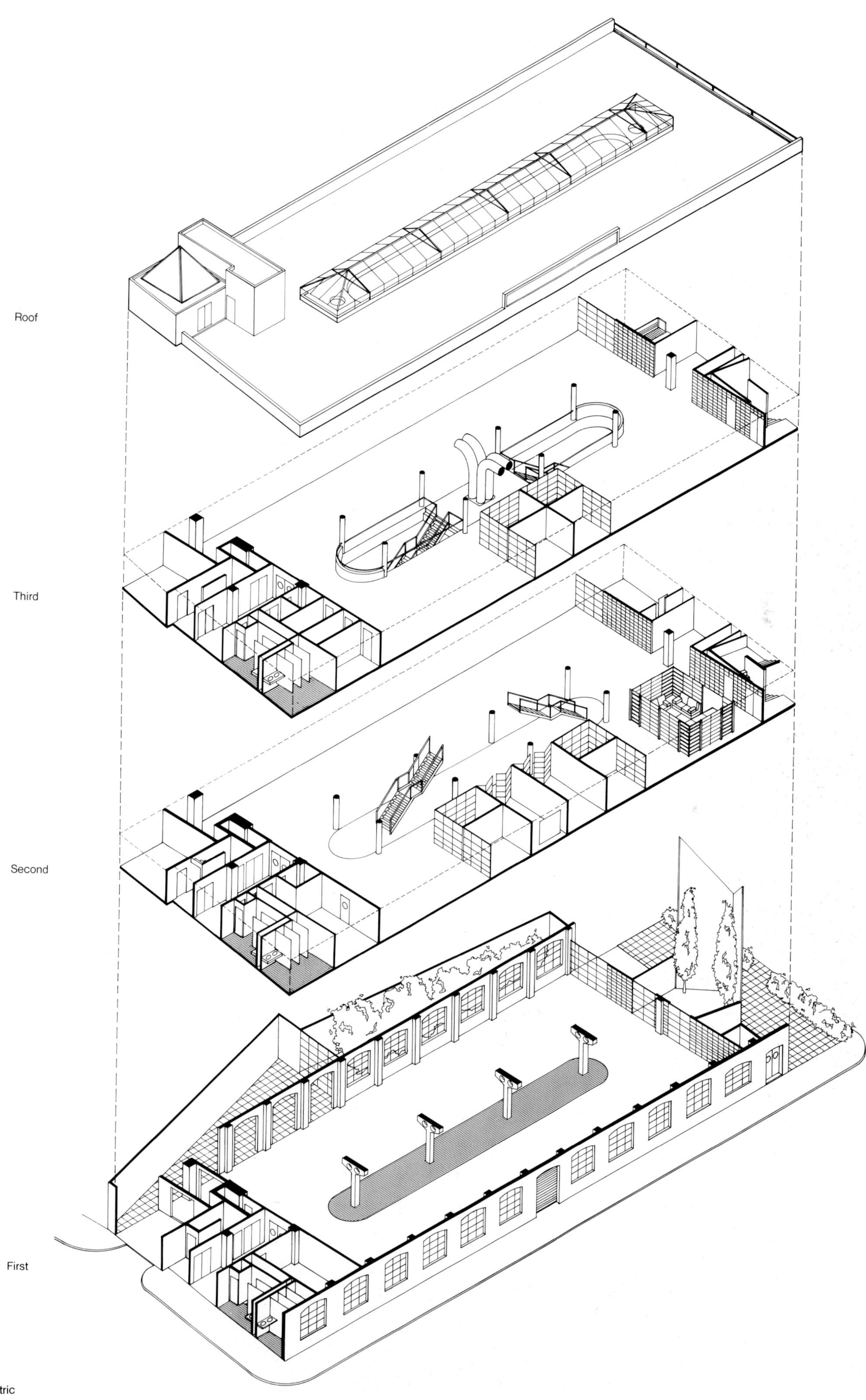

Cut-away axonometric

3 St. Peter's Street

London, England, 1988

セント・ピーターズ・ストリート 3 番地

Alongside major new-build commissions such as Canary Wharf and Apple Computers, Troughton McAslan have maintained their interest in the low cost refurbishments with which their practice started, refining their expertise as they go. 3 St Peter's Street, a small project on an exceptionally tight budget, shows how such expertise can produce quality in the most stringent circumstances. Set in a sea of the crumbling brickwork of which so much of London is made, it introduces an unexpected intimacy and refinement. The brief was to convert a redundant and decayed workshop into studios for an advertising agency at low cost.

To get the most out of this, Troughton McAslan employed a multiple strategy: contractual, constructional and aesthetic. The project was broken into individual, separately negotiated packages, while the existing fabric was retained wherever possible. The building's original light industrial quality was allowed to remain, which meant that electric cabling and structure could be exposed without compromising the whole, which was lifted out of the ordinary by a few well chosen moves. The design of the building rests on the balance between the rough and irregular existing building, and the refinement of the interventions, the two being unified by similar materials and a shared simplicity and directness.

The new work centres round a double height entrance space that echoes the court outside and allows light into the depths of the interior, and about new elements of quality that run through the building. The entrance space contains an elegant staircase, and is mediated with the courtyard outside by a modification of the old workshop facade.

This facade consists of a window, a door, a beam and a downpipe that neatly express the organisation of the interior while simply stating the elementary qualities of a building: structure, enclosure, the admission of light. Its vocabulary is derived from its light industrial setting, reinterpreted to create order, to lift the scale of the tiny courtyard, and to make a well balanced composition of lightness and weight, vertical and horizontal.

Photo by Peter Cook

Studio Interior　スタジオ内部

キャナリーワーフやアップル・コンピューターなどの全く新たな建物の設計をする一方で，トロートン・マッカーズランは，ローコストな既存の建物の改修という，彼らの当初からの仕事を続けることで，専門的な知識と経験をより一層磨いている．この計画も，非常に予算の厳しい，小さなプロジェクトであり，これまでの経験が非常にきつい条件の中で有効に活かされた例である．ロンドンの大抵の街がそうであるように，崩れかけたレンガの建物が密集する街の中に，予期せぬ親密感のある高品位な建物を生み出した．使われないで荒廃していた作業場が広告会社のスタジオにローコストで改造された．

この計画でトロートン・マッカーズランは，契約的，構成的，美的という複数の戦略を立てた．既存の構成要素はできる限り残され，それぞれ個別の要素に分解された．建物本来の軽工業的な特質を残し，妥協することなしに，電気配線や構造体は露出させ，いくつかの大きなものが取り除かれた．建物は全体として，ラフで不規則な形の既存の要素と，改修による介在の純粋な形態の間で微妙なバランスを保ちながら，その両者を相似の材料や共通のシンプルさと直截さによって一体化している．

スタジオは外の庭に呼応し，内部に光を導入する建物内部を走り抜ける新たな要素としての，2層吹抜けのエントランス空間を設け，そこを中心に執務空間が配置されている．ここにはエレガントな階段があり，もとの作業場のファサードを改修した外観が，中庭に面して建っている．

このファサードには窓，ドア，梁，縦樋があり，建物の基本的な構成，すなわち構造や部屋割り，光の入り方などを見せると同時に，内部の組織を的確に表わしてもいる．ボキャブラリーは，軽工業的な背景から引き出しながら，それを再解釈して新たな秩序をつくり出し，小さな中庭のスケールを拡大し，軽快さと重厚さ，垂直と水平が巧妙にバランスされた構成としている．

◀Exterior of the studio looking towards the main entrance from the courtyard　中庭から中央入口の方向に見たスタジオの外観
Photo by Peter Cook

First floor plan　1階平面図

Cutaway axonometric of the steel staircase construction

1. 33mm diameter mild steel CHS handrail and uprights
2. Stainless steel intermediate wires
3. Polished stainless turn buckle
4. 30mm deep mild steel tray with ribbed rubber inlay
5. 12mm mild steel bracket supports bolted to mezzanine frame
6. 33mm diameter mild steel CHS framed stringer
7. 12mm mild steel bracket supports bolted to floor slab

▶View into the studio entrance area from the courtyard
中庭から見たスタジオ入口部分の眺め
Photo by Peter Cook

Staircase detail　特徴的な線でデザインされた緊張感のある階段細部

◀Exterior detail of entrance at night
夜の入口外部詳細
All photos by Peter Cook

1 St. Peter's Street
London, England, 1991

セント・ピーターズ・ストリート１番地

This project consists of the conversion of a small existing brick building and insertion of a three storey glazed link fronting the street. This link is then connected on each level to the previous conversion at 3 St Peters Street.

この計画は，小さなレンガ造の既存の建物の改造と，３層のガラス張りの通りに面した接続スペースの挿入である．接続スペースによってこの建物は，先のセント・ピーターズ・ストリート３番地と各階で接続する．

▲Link view　リンクの眺め
◀Exterior view　外観

Photos by Peter Cook

1-3 Colebrooke Place

London, England, 1990

コルブルックプレイス1-3番地

This is a further example in the line of completed studio developments which started with Design House and continued at St Peter's Street, each involving the upgrading of industrial space into studio offices. Where Design House is the most overtly High Tech of the three, and 3 St Peter's Street has a primitive robustness, 1 - 3 Colebrooke Place is noticeably calmer and more abstracted.

Like its near neighbour, 3 St Peter's Street, it demonstrates how a mundane existing structure (a post-war shed) can be economically transformed beyond recognition with rational architectural and structural interventions. The strategy is to use the existing fabric to the full, and heighten it with carefully chosen, well placed elements and new finishes of quality.

Internally the space is divided by a central row of columns supporting a mezzanine floor. This provides additional usable area and connects the building to a retained block at the rear, housing cellular offices and ancillary accommodation. The mezzanine runs down one side of the building, creating a double height toplit space on the other. On entering the bulding one comes into this airy and generous space, overlooked by the mezzanine, the entrance being defined by a curved, freestanding canvas screen with the enclosed staircase to one side.

The white exterior is a simple reflection of the interior, its structure and organisation summarised by the T-shaped post and lintel on the entrance facade. The entrance itself is picked out by a clear glass door set into a wall of acid etched glass. As at 3 St Peter's Street, the materials develop from the light industrial aesthetic of the original structure to a hitherto alien level of finish and refinement; from painted brickwork, profiled steel decking and exposed structure, to oil treated oak floors and etched glass.

この作品はデザインハウスに始まり，セント・ピーターズ・ストリートにつながる一連の，工業的な空間をスタジオに改修するという仕事の１つである．いままでの３つのスタジオの実例の中で，デザインハウスは最もハイテク的なものであり，セント・ピーターズ・ストリート３番地は力強い表現であった．コルブルック・プレイス１－３番地は目立って穏やかな観念的な作品である．

すぐ近くにあるセント・ピーターズ・ストリート３番地と同様に，戦後に建てられた倉庫という世俗的な既存の建物を，いかに経済的に，合理的かつ建築的，構造的介在によってもとの面影もないほど見事に変身させ得るかを示している．方法は，既存の構造をできるだけ活用し，それを注意深く選り分け，要素をうまく配置し，新たな仕上げを施して質的に高めることである．

Exterior in context　既存のフォルムを残しながらすっきりとまとめられた外観

Exterior before conversion　改築前の外部

Photo by Peter Cook

First floor studio with mezzanine　1階スタジオから中2階を見る

Interior detail

All photos by Peter Cook

内部空間は，中央に並ぶ中2階を支えている柱列で大きく2分されている．これは空間の使い分けを可能にし，さらに敷地後ろにある付属屋に配置された個室オフィスや補助的な部屋につながる．中2階が建物の長手に沿って片側にあり，屋根頂部のトップライトからの光が2層分のスペースを照らしている．建物に入ると，中2階からも見下ろせる広々とした明るい室内に導かれる．エントランスはカーブを描く自立するキャンバス張りのスクリーンで区画され，片方には円形の壁に内包された階段がある．

外観はインテリアを反映して真っ白で，建物の構造や構成は，妻側エントランスのファサードの柱とリンテルからなるT字型に要約されている．エントランスは，エッチングガラスの壁にはめこまれた透明ガラスのドアで際立たせている．3セント・ピーターズ・ストリートでもそうであったように，軽工業的な既存建物の美学から今日の全く異なる仕上げや装飾にいたるまで，塗装したレンガや中2階のスチールデッキなどの露出した構造から油引きしたオーク材の床やエッチングガラスにいたるまで，さまざまな材質が使われている．

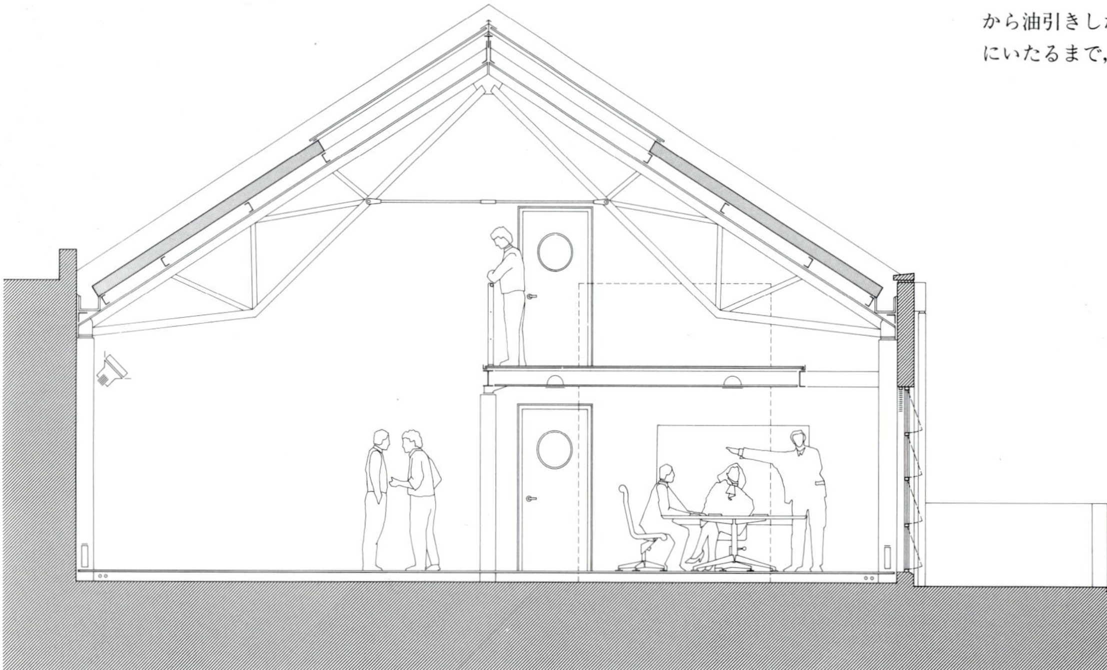

Cross-section through the building

View into the studio　スタジオ内部

OFFICES

British architecture during the years since the foundation of Troughton McAslan has been overwhelmingly commercial in character, so that even the acknowledged masters like Rogers, Foster, and Stirling have been driven increasingly into the commercial field. Retailing has remained in Britain the preserve of specialist firms - and little of value has been produced in consequence beyond the tiny specialist projects by the likes of Jiricna,Chipperfield and Coates. In the field of office building, however, some distinguished projects have been commissioned with a small number of developers - and Stanhope is a case in point - achieving a reputation for enlightened patronage. The private sector, to this extent, has done something to compensate for the near-collapse of public patronage.

Of course, property companies are constrained by the obligation to turn in profits for their shareholders - they are unlikely to inovate beyond a point where they cease to produce a readily marketable product. Only very slowly is the office block being recast. Nonetheless, the range of Troughton McAslan's commercial projects hint at the breadth of definition that lies behind the term "office block". The essential division lies, of course, between speculative schemes (such as their building at Canary Wharf) and those commissioned by the future users and designed to accord with their needs (such as the Apple Headquarters at Stockley Park).

Troughton McAslan's office schemes also vary in scale from the little block in Pond Place, Kensington, which relates closely to the various "studio" developments carried out by the firm, to building FC3 at Canary Wharf (at 40,000 square metres the largest commission the practice has completed to date).

Canary Wharf is a notable achievement for Troughton McAslan. Apart from one proposed block by the Italian Aldo Rossi, everything else in this vast Docklands scheme has been designed by American practices like SOM, Kohn Pedersen Fox, and Cesar Pelli. Though overwhelmingly a Post Modernist exercise, Canary Wharf was always intended to be stylistically diverse (though the overall plan is essentially Beaux'Arts in character). Troughton McAslan's building shows the influence of the Romantic Modernism of Frank Lloyd Wright (and of the Johnson Wax building in particular). Though the completed block has a more solid and substantial character than early models suggested, it retains a lightness of touch and refinement of detail which sets it far above the typical commercial work of the '80s. The interior is, inevitably, mostly standard office space, yet the architects have succeeded in giving the ground floor (which links to a dockside promenade) something of the character of an internal street. The building is one of a small number of buildings which provide an excuse for a tour of recent Docklands architecture.

The competition winning landmark office building proposed for a critical site at the very gateway to Docklands may soon add to this select band. Involving the retention of a listed building, the scheme generated by McAslan with Aidan Potter is a typical design, not extravagant or showy, and declines to make too much fuss about something which should be simple. The building rejects, of course, the facile Post Modernist pretence that an office building can or should take on the look of a town hall or palace. It is simply appropriate to the task in hand.

At Rosebery Avenue and Hardwick Street, in the Clerkenwell area of London, the task was to fit into a dense urban mesh and to create one new building alongside a refurbished block. Stylish refurbishment is the theme too at Bolsover Street. At Alexander House on a drab street in south London, discretion was not the aim. The area needed an infusion of life. The polychromatic facade, influenced (to an degree unusual for this practice) perhaps by the Rationalism of Rossi and others, provides this.

Troughton McAslan's urban office schemes underline their commitment to civic values and to history. It was ironic therefore that the Pond Place building, a considered response to a Victorian back street , had to be "toned down" at the direction of the local planning authority. At Stockley Park, near Heathrow Airport, there is no history and the "context" had to be created.

But the list of architects working there reads like a roll-call of modern architecture in Britain - Rogers, Foster, Ritchie, Arup Associates - and Troughton McAslan. Their Phase I block for Apple Computers has a tremendous exuberance which enables it to make its mark amongst its variegated neighbours - though it is essentially a modest and straightforward building with few "frills." It is amongst their most distinctive jobs to date.

In short, Troughton McAslan have managed to create a group of office buildings in a wide variety of locations which are notable for their undemonstrative pragmatism and quiet originality. Against the odds - for none of the projects was expensive - these buildings are at the core of the practice's achievement. ***—Kenneth Powell***

Canary Wharf and Building FC3 (centre) during construction
建設中のキャナリーワーフとFC3ビル

オフィス建築

トロートン・マッカーズランが事務所を設立して以来，英国では商業・業務建築が圧倒的に優勢であった．したがって，有名な建築家であるロジャースやフォスターやスターリングでさえも次第に商業・業務建築の世界に引きずり込まれていった．小売店舗は英国では独特の専門の設計者の領域として維持され，その結果，ジリクナやチッパーフィールド，ナイジェル・コーツといった一部のスペシャル以外にはそこにはほとんど価値が見出されなかった．しかし，オフィスビルの世界では，いくつかの特徴のあるすぐれたプロジェクトが，わずかばかりのディベロッパーによって進められた．ディベロッパーの1つスタンホープはその好例であり，パトロネージを啓発したという評判をとった．その意味で，ほとんど崩壊に近い公的なパトロネージを補うために，プライベートなセクターがいくらかある役割を果たしたのである．

むろん，営利会社は株主に利益を還元するという債務によって規制されているため，まだ市場価値のある製品の生産を中止させるまで革新的にはなれない．しかし，非常にゆっくりではあるがオフィスブロックはつくり直されてきつつある．にもかかわらず，トロートン・マッカーズランの商業施設計画の領域は，オフィスブロックの言葉の裏に隠れた意味の広がりを暗示している．もちろんキャナリーワーフのような投機的な計画と，発注者が使用者であるためそのニーズに合わせてデザインできるというストックレーパークのアップルコンピューター本社ビルのような計画の間には基本的に大きな違いが存在している．

トロートン・マッカーズランのオフィス計画は，彼らのこれまでの主要な仕事であったスタジオ作品に似た，ケンジントンのポンドプレイスのような小さな規模のものから，40,000㎡というこれまでに完成した仕事の中では最大規模であるFC 3キャナリーワーフ計画にいたるまでさまざまである．

キャナリーワーフはトロートン・マッカーズランの代表作である．イタリアの建築家アルド・ロッシ設計の建物からわずか1ブロック離れた敷地に建つ予定である．このアルド・ロッシとトロートン・マッカーズラン以外の，広大なドックランド地区のその他の建物はすべて，たとえばSOMやKPFやシーザー・ペリといったアメリカの建築家によって設計されている．キャナリーワーフの全体計画は基本的にボザール的な特徴をもつが，個々の建物は圧倒的にポスト・モダニストの作品が多く，スタイリッシュな多様性を誇示している．そんな中でトロートン・マッカーズランの建物は，フランク・ロイド・ライトのロマンティック・モダニズム，特にジョンソン・ワックスビルの影響を受けている．完成した建物は計画当初の模型より一層かっちりと完結したものになっているが，80年代の商業施設のもっていた個性以上の軽快さ，洗練されたディテールを実現させている．インテリアは必然的に標準的なオフィススペースであるが，1階ではドック側のプロムナードにつながる内部の通りを生み出している．昨今のドックランド建築見学ツアーの数少ない対象建物の1つになっている．

コンペで当選した新しい計画であるドックランド・オフィスビルは，ドックランドの入口という重要な敷地に建つランドマーク的な建物である．保存修復して再利用する建物を含むこの計画を，マッカーズランはアイデン・ポッターと協働で，ティピカルで華美でなく，シンプルであるべきものを飾り立てすぎることなく設計している．もちろんオフィスビルが市庁舎か宮殿に見えるというような，安易なポストモダニスト風は排除している．要するに適切な設計である．

ロンドンのクラーケンウエル地区にあるローズベリー・アベニュー／ハードウィック・ストリートの作品は，市街地の密集地域にうまくフィットさせ，改修された街並みに沿って新しい建物を建てることであった．ボルソバー・ストリートの計画もまたスタイリッシュな改修がテーマであった．サウス・ロンドンのうす汚れた通りに建つアレキサンダー・ハウスでは，思慮深さは求められなかった．この地区は生命の息吹を必要としていたため，ロッシや他の合理主義からの影響を多少受けて，この種の計画としては異例の，多色のファサードが出現した．

トロートン・マッカーズランの都市におけるオフィスビル計画は，市民にとっての価値や歴史に重点が置かれている．したがって，敷地後ろの通りのビクトリア風に呼応してデザインしたポンドプレイスビルが，市の計画局の指示で設計変更させられたことは皮肉なことであった．ヒースロー空港近くのストックレーパークでは，あまり歴史のない地区であったため，「コンテクスト」は新たに創出された．

しかし，ここで仕事をする建築家は，まるで英国の近代建築を一堂に集めたような顔触れである．ロジャース，フォスター，イアン・リッチー，アラップ・アソシエイツ，そしてトロートン・マッカーズランである．トロートン・マッカーズランのアップル・コンピューター社の第1期部分は，基本的には装飾の少ない控え目で直截な建物であるが，さまざまな建物が混在する周辺環境の中で，充分に目立たせることが可能な豊かな表現となっている．そして，トロートン・マッカーズランのこれまでの作品の中でも最もすばらしいものである．

概して，トロートン・マッカーズランは，さまざまな場所に，一群のオフィスビルを設計してきた．それらは，彼らの目立たない控え目な実用主義と穏やかな独創性で高く評価されている．予想に反して，どのプロジェクトも質素なものであるにもかかわらず，それらの建物は彼らの業績の中心的な存在である．

Photo by Robin Barton

Pond Place
London, England, 1988

ポンドプレイス

Exterior view in context　通り側外観

▶Entrance detail　入口部分

Photos by Peter Cook

18

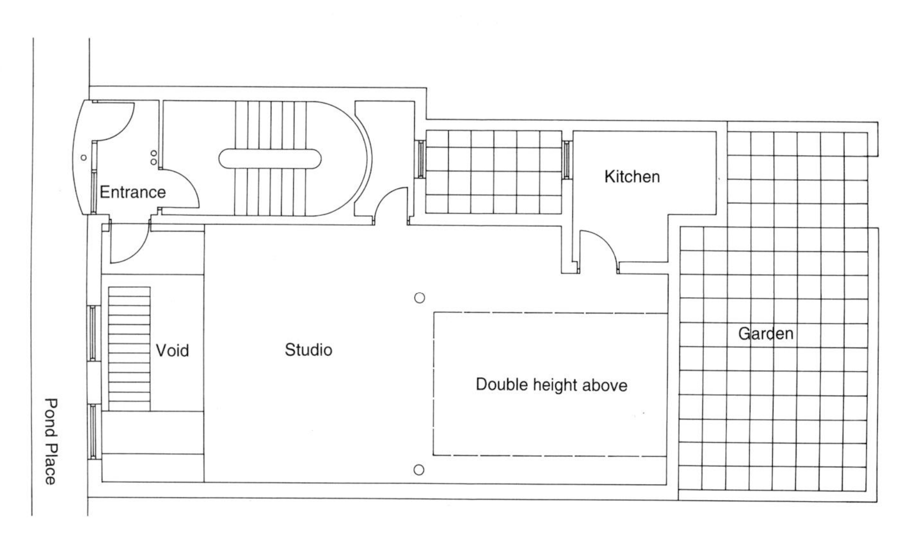

First floor plan

This urban office building consists of a small four floored infill scheme with concrete frame and brick elevations located within a conservation area.

The plan generates a series of single and double volume office spaces and has an organisational form which is interpreted from the traditional buildings which Pond Place adjoins.

Despite support from amenity groups and the Royal Fine Art Commission, Troughton McAslan were obliged to alter the principal street elevation from a polychromatic brick facade, to a more traditional rendered appearance due to objections raised by the local planning authority.

保存地区の街並みの中に，コンクリートのフレームにレンガによるファサードの４層の小規模なオフィスビルをはめ込んだ計画である．

プランは１層あるいは２層吹き抜けのオフィスが連なる形で，全体として周辺の伝統的な建物から引き出した有機的形態になるようにまとめている．

市民団体や王立ファインアート委員会の支持があったにもかかわらず，トロートン・マッカーズランは，市の計画局の反対によって，通り側の当初の多色レンガのファサード案を伝統的なおとなしいものに変更を余儀なくされた．

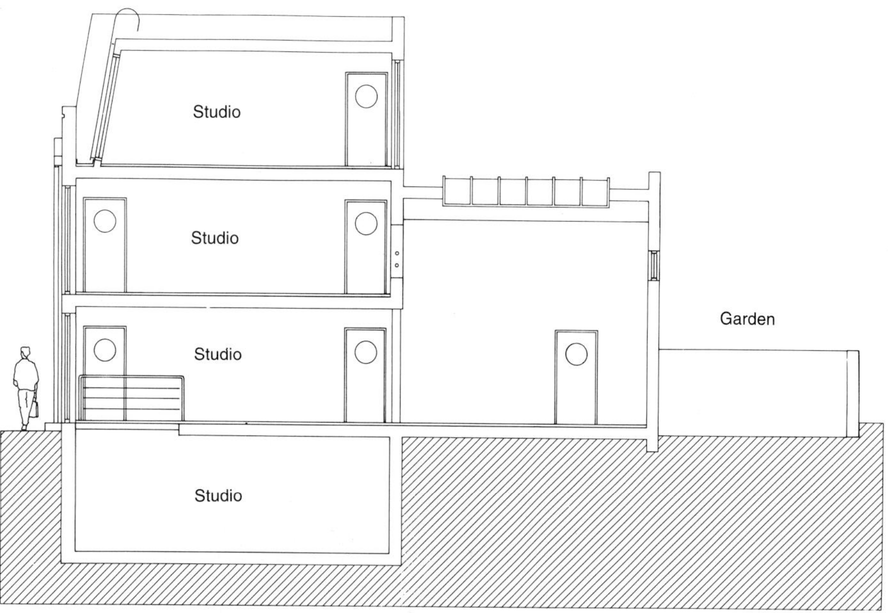

Building section

Building during construction　建設中風景

Axonometric

Street context

First floor office studio　I 階事務所内部

Alexander House
London, England, 1989

アレキサンダーハウス

The office building in context　アレキサンダーハウス外観
Photo by Richard Bryant

Set in a typically mixed and varied London street, Alexander House challenges the common belief that contextualism is synonymous with imitation. In contrast with the largely residential setting, the project consists of offices with a warehouse and distribution building behind, and expresses itself accordingly with its bold forms, its strip windows at top and bottom and its hard edged materials. But it also takes care to reinforce the enclosure of the street, to echo its rhythms and scale, and to recess the upper storey to reduce the new building's apparent bulk. It maintains continuity with its surroundings while asserting its difference and individuality.

It achieves this through its unprejudiced choice of influences, and its mixture of traditional and modern techniques, reminiscent of the rational expressionist architects whom Troughton McAslan admire. Although it is a predominantly brick building, the brickwork is at times supported in long horizontal bands achievable only with reinforced concrete. On the flat elevation the brickwork is treated as a thin, light cladding material broken up by expansion joints; however, in the adjacent curved stair tower the brick appears solid and load bearing.

If Alexander House plays games with the expectations of traditional construction, it does the same with the purities of Modernism. It is almost an exercise in structural honesty - bare concrete columns boldly expressed and distinguished from strip windows and infill - but the effect is offset by the frankly decorative stripes, which bind the disparate elements of the elevation together.

Meanwhile, standing clear of this complex game, is the elegant entrance stair and ramp, a piece of design which is entirely of its own time.

The project demonstrates how much Troughton McAslan have developed from their High Tech origins and their willingness to learn from different periods and individuals. In this they are typical of their generation: the dogmatism of earlier decades has been left behind and elements and techniques from the past and present can be manipulated with tolerant freedom. At Alexander House Troughton McAslan have, within a limited budget, used this freedom to create a well planned, well lit and purposeful building.

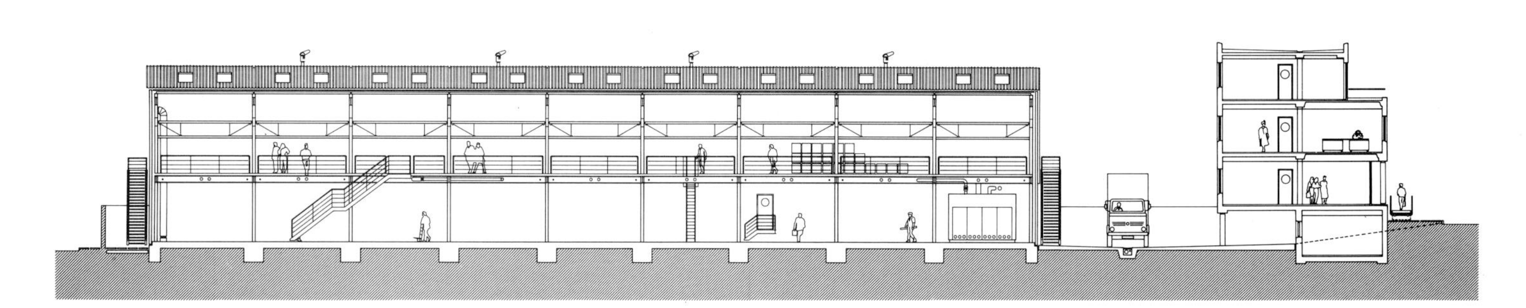

Section

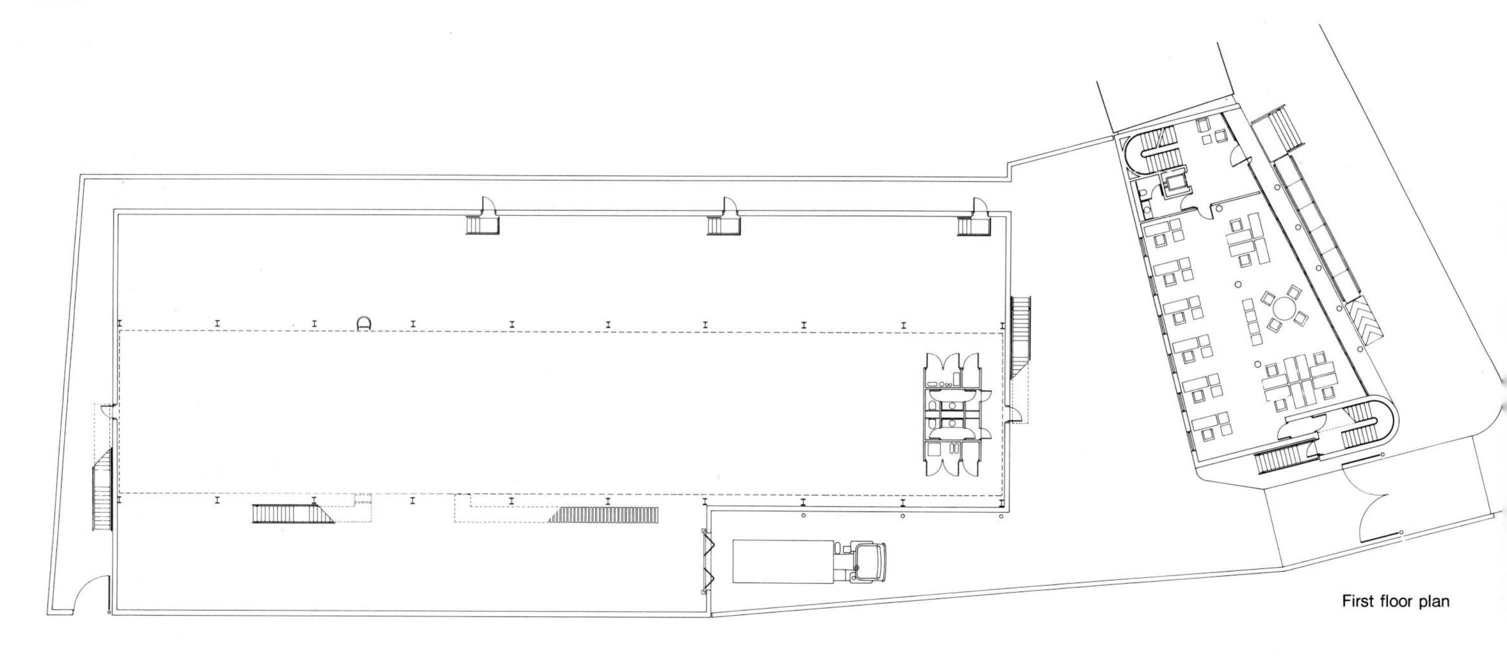

First floor plan

ロンドン特有のさまざまな建物が混在する通りに位置し，街並みのコンテクストの形成は模倣と同義語であるというこれまでの常識に挑戦した計画である．住居施設がほとんどという周辺環境とは対照的に，敷地後ろに倉庫と配送センターがあるオフィスビルであるため，形態や最上階と地上階の帯状の開口部，幾何学的な素材を使って，大胆にその特質を表現している．同時に通りの環境を取り入れて強化し，周辺のリズムやスケールに呼応させ，新しい建物のボリュームをあまり大きく目立たせないために上階を少し引っ込ませている．違いと個性を主張しながら，周辺環境との連続性を維持している．

伝統とモダンの影響を公平に受け，ほどよくミックスしながら，トロートン・マッカーズランの尊敬する合理的な表現主義の建築家を思い起こさせるような作品に仕上げている．明らかにレンガの建物であるが，レンガの横縞模様は鉄筋コンクリートの支持で可能になっている．平面的な壁の部分では，レンガはエキスパンション・ジョイント以外はすべて薄く，軽快な外装材の表情をもつが，建物端部の階段室棟のカーブしたレンガ壁は重厚な構造壁の表情をもっている．

アレキサンダーハウスが伝統的な建築の期待を裏切るものであるなら，モダニズムの純粋主義をもだましていることになる．打放しコンクリートの柱，横長の窓やレンガ壁といった構造に忠実で大胆な表現は，ある意味では装飾的な縞模様によって，全く異質なエレベーションの要素を結合させるということで相乗効果を発揮している．

しかし，ここでの試みが最も端的に現われているのは，現代のデザインにふさわしいエレガントなエントランスの階段と斜路である．

このプロジェクトは，トロートン・マッカーズランが彼らの初期のハイテク指向の強い作品から発展し，さまざまな時期，個性から学びとろうとする意思が明確に表現された．これは彼らの世代に典型的な特性である．それは，少し前の独断主義を脱却し，過去や現在の要素や技術は全く自由に巧みに操られている．この作品でトロートン・マッカーズランは，限られた予算の中で，自由な表現を駆使して，よく計画された光いっぱいの目的にふさわしいビルをつくり出した．

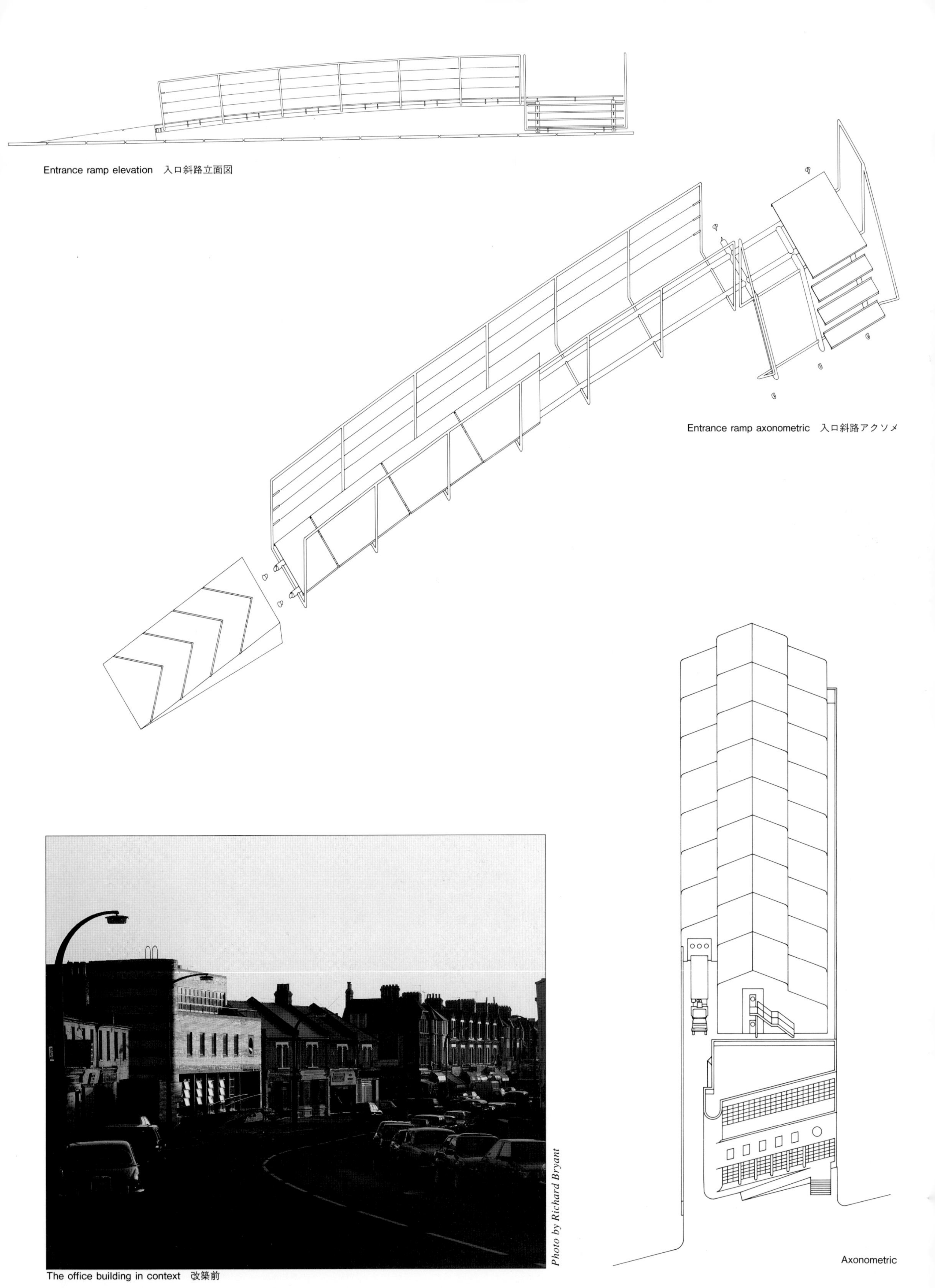

Entrance ramp elevation　入口斜路立面図

Entrance ramp axonometric　入口斜路アクソメ

Axonometric

Photo by Richard Bryant

The office building in context　改築前

Photo by Richard Bryant

Detail of the office building　線で構成された斜路とファサード

Photo by Richard Davies

Interior of warehouse　倉庫内部

▶Entrance detail at night　入口斜路を通して内部を見る
Photo by Richard Bryant

ALEXANDER HOUSE
155

Apple Computers' Facility, Stockley Park

Heathrow, England, 1989/1991

アップルコンピューター社

At Stockley Park Troughton McAslan applied their inventive, open minded use of technology to a building type and a constructional approach that constitutes one of the greatest challenges to contemporary architects.

The brief was for a new facility for Apple Computers with Stanhope Properties as developer, 5,000 square metres in area and to be completed in fourteen months using fast track management contract techniques.

Within this period construction was divided into separate phases of "shell and core" and "fit out". The site, a business park close to Heathrow airport designed to attract high quality companies with its good design, transport connections and landscaped setting, is built on formerly derelict land.

On such projects the architect is under pressure of time, and the subdivision of construction into separate packages can mean that he finds himself doing little more than designing an acceptable wrapping for a building largely determined by external pressures. In a new, as yet incomplete setting, the contextual approach developed by Troughton McAslan for urban sites is hardly applicable. The challenge to the architect is to produce positive architecture from a brief that provides few hints.

Troughton McAslan's response was to create a simple pavilion that holds its own in its open, park-like setting, but which encloses and defines spaces adjoining the building. The open plan, two-storey interior is focussed about an internal street and gallery, while, with the completion of Phase II, an entrance court will be created centred on the expressive entrance tower to Phase I.

The construction of the building reflects Troughton McAslan's experience with Rogers and Foster, but reinterpreted in the relaxed, pragmatic manner they have developed since establishing their own practice. It grows out of the imaginative response to simple problems such as the admission of daylight, the exclusion of direct sunlight and the provision of escape stairs. These have generated the translucent glass walls and tensile shades that characterise the elevations, and make them into simple expressions of structure and enclosure.

This is not to say that Apple is simply a functional exercise. The same problems could easily be solved more prosaically and with less flamboyance. What it exemplifies is rather that balance of display and practicality that characterises the most convincing High Tech architecture, and which Troughton McAslan understand well.

View of Phase I looking north across the lawn
芝生を通して眺めたI期棟北側
Photo by Alastair Hunter

第1期　1989年

この計画でトロートン・マッカーズランは，創意に富んだビルディングタイプ追求の技術，現代建築への最大の挑戦の1つといえる構成主義的アプローチを堂々と駆使している．

5,000㎡の敷地にスタンホープ地所をディベロッパーとして建設されたアップルコンピューター社の新施設で，CM技術を活かして14か月という短期間で完成している．

工期は大きく「外殻とコア」と「装置類」の2つに分けられた．敷地は，それまでは荒廃して放置されていた，ヒースロー空港に近いビジネスパーク内にあり，ここはグッドデザイン，交通の便のよさ，ランドスケーピングなどで企業にふさわしい高度な質を表現している．

このような計画では，設計者は往々にして時間の制約という条件の下で，工期を圧迫する要因になる建設過程の細分化を増やさないように，ただ外側のパッケージに包まれただけのデザインをすることが多い．新しい未完成な環境の中では，トロートン・マッカーズランがこれまで都市の中で手がけてきたコンテクスチュアルな方法論は通用しない．敷地からなんのヒントも得られないような状況の下で，個性的な建築を生み出すことが建築家の役割である．

トロートン・マッカーズランの解答は，開放的で公園のような環境の中にシンプルなパビリオンをつくり，その環境に包まれながら明確に施設の空間を認識できるような建物とすることであった．オープンプランの2層のインテリアは，内部の通りとギャラリーを焦点として配置されている．また第2期工事が完成すると，第1期のエントランスタワーを中心とするエリアにエントランスコートが誕生する．

建設方法はトロートン・マッカーズランのロジャースやフォスター時代の経験を反映しているが，しかし，それをそのままの形でなく，事務所設立以来発展させてきた，もう少しリラックスし，実用的な再解釈を施した上で採用している．すなわち，昼光の導入，直射日光の排除，避難階段の設置などの単純な問題に対して，イメージ豊かな対応という形に発展させている．これらは，透明ガラス壁，個性的な外観を構成する張力テントのシェード，構造と外皮による単純明快な表現に現われている．

建物が機能的であるのはいうまでもない．そうした問題は当然のこととして，派手な表現なしに容易に解決されている．大抵のハイテク建築を特徴づけているディスプレイと実用性のバランス以上に，トロートン・マッカーズランが十分にこうした施設を理解していることは明らかである．

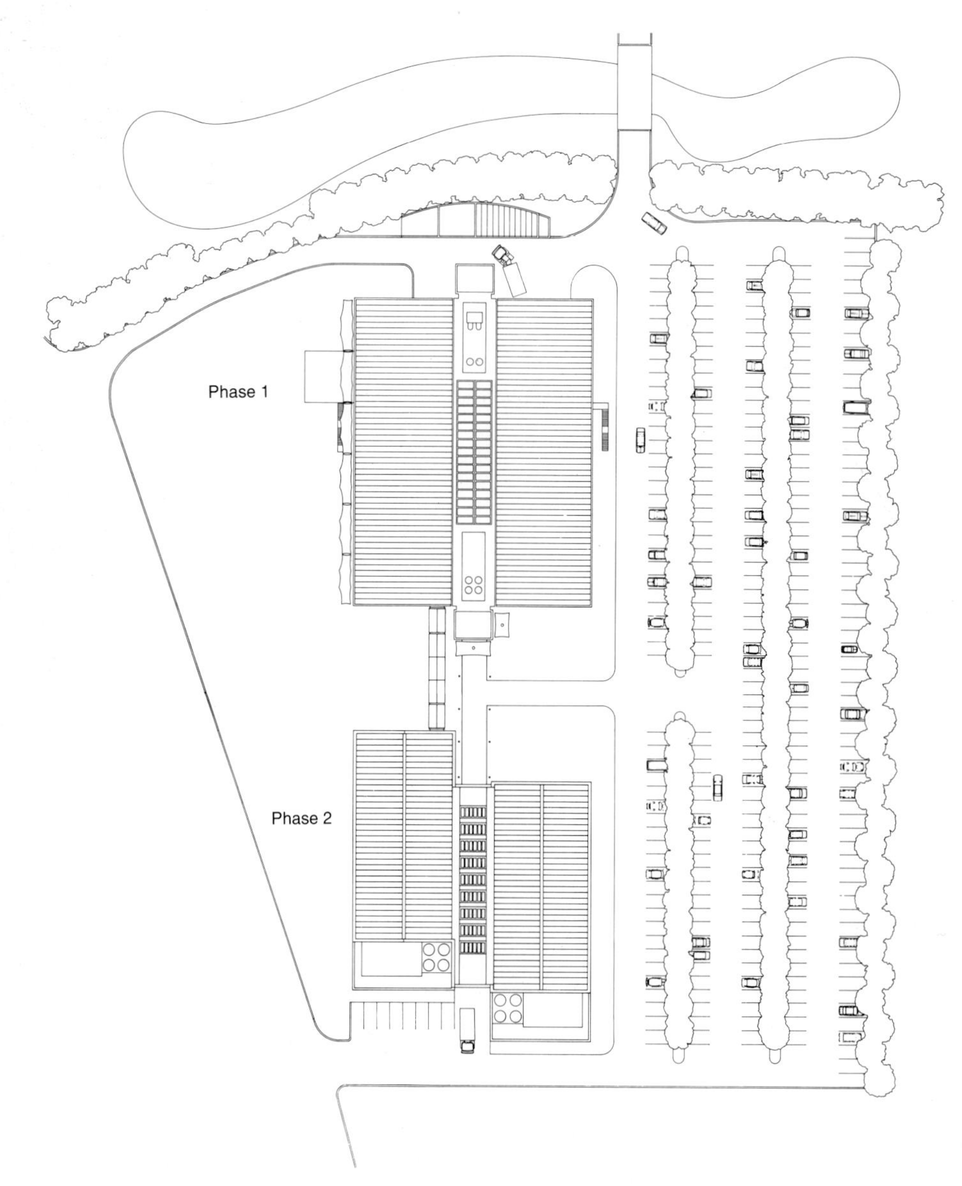

Site plan of Phase I and Phase II　敷地平面図．上部が1期棟，下部2期棟

By staggering its two sections Phase II completes the entrance courtyard to the project as a whole, but it also continues the organisational and structural themes of Phase I. The central, toplit circulation spine follows the same axis as the equivalent space in Phase I, and the detailing and treatment of the elevations have a consistency throughout the scheme, Like the first phase, Phase II is clad in translucent insulating panels above and below a central strip of windows. The area of clear glazing is on the ground floor to reflect the different nature of the spaces at that level.

Given its position to the rear of the site, Phase II is more discreetly and simply detailed, allowing Phase I to represent the company to the outside world, and to act as the more dominant and conspicuous of the two.

第2期　1991年

2期に分かれていたこのプロジェクトも，2つの建物の間にエントランスコートが完成して全体が完結した．第2期も第1期の構成，構造が継承されている．中央のトップライトから光が入る内部ストリートはの通りは第1期のそれと同じ延長にあり，外部のディテールや仕上げも第1期と共通である．窓ガラスの上下に半透明の断熱パネルを挿入しているのも1期，2期ともに共通である．1階の透明ガラス部分は，さまざまな自然の様子を映し出している．

敷地の奥側に位置する第2期は，外界に向けては第1期の建物が同社を代表し，より目立つように，1期より一層控え目でシンプルなディテールでまとめられている．

Detail of Phase I south elevation
Photo by Peter Cook
I 期棟南側側面

Interior volume of Phase I　I 期棟内部

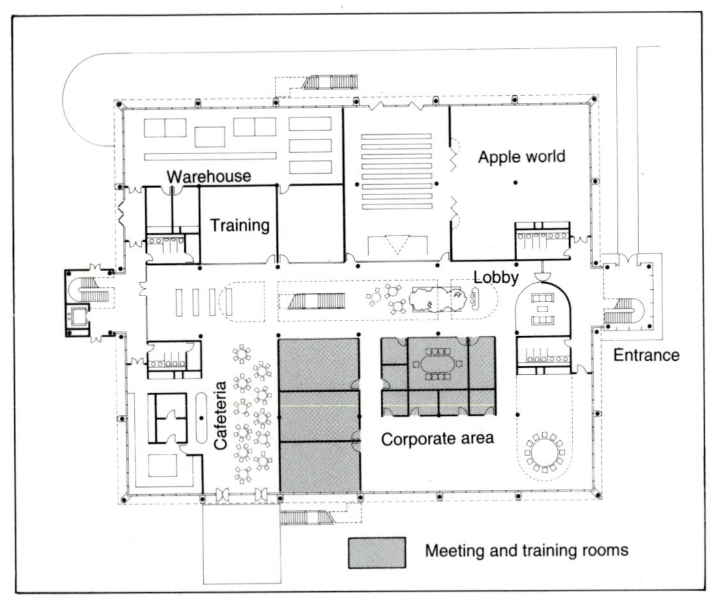

Phase I first floor plan　I 期棟 I 階平面図

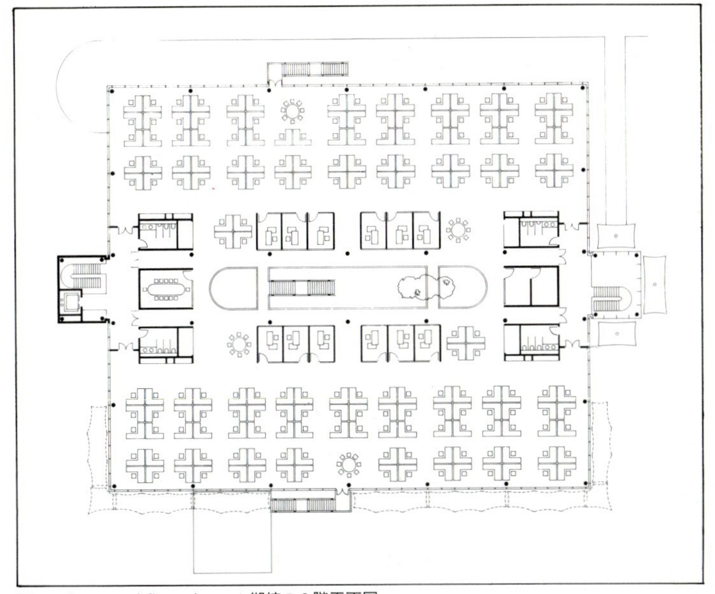
Phase I second floor plan　I 期棟の 2 階平面図

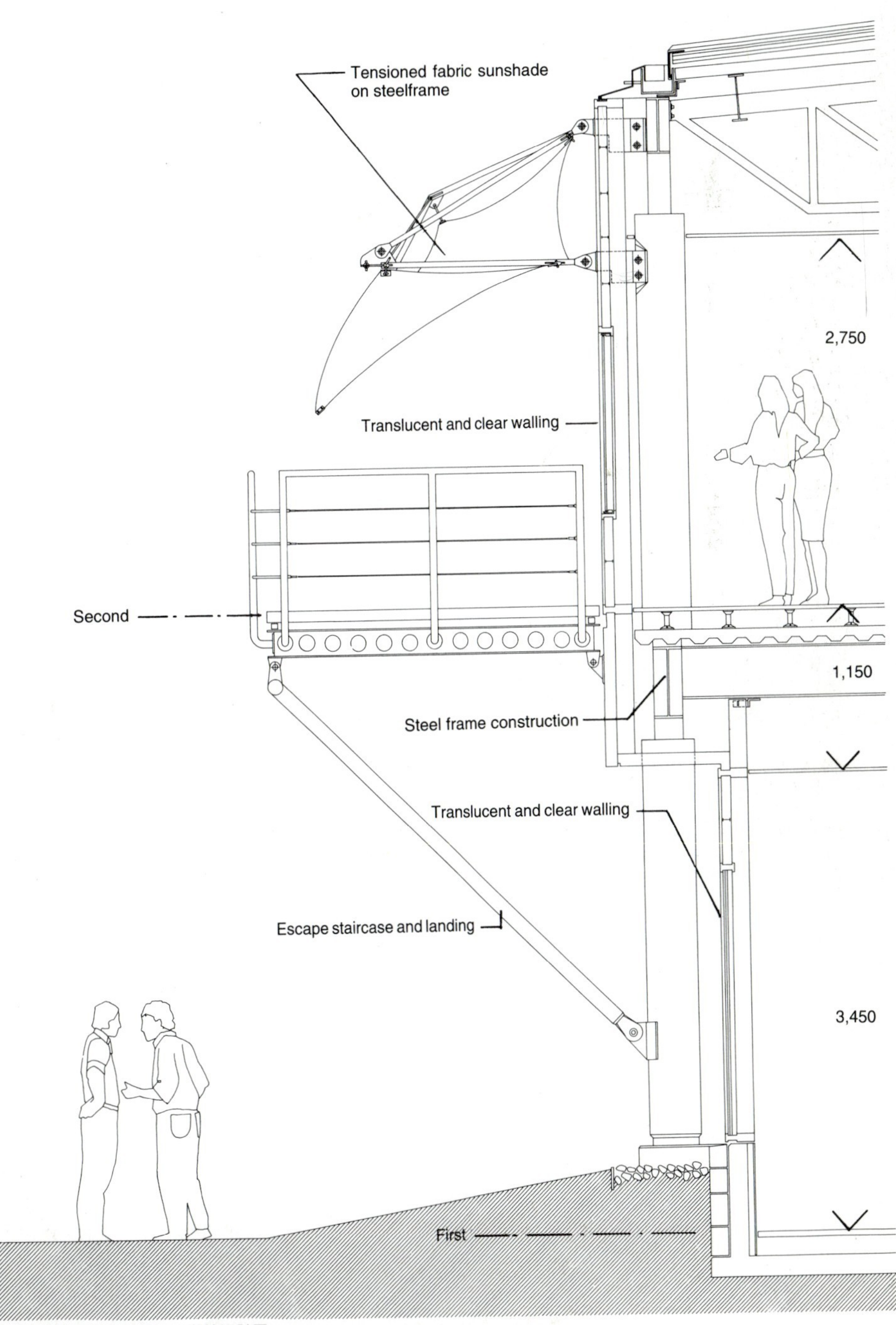

Edge detail of Phase I　I 期棟矩計図

Detail of Phase II elevation　2 期棟の窓まわり

Next page : Detail of Phase I south elevation
次ページ：I 期棟南側側面
All photos by Peter Cook

Huntsworth Mews
London, England, 1990

ハンツワース・ミューズ

6-16 Huntsworth Mews was designed to provide 500 square metres of office accommodation on a long narrow site behind Marylebone Station. The building was conceived in scale and proportion to relate to the surrounding low rise mews buildings. Although the gridded three storey front elevation exaggerates the true size of the building (as it is only 6m deep), it reflects precisely the columns and floor slabs of the concrete structure behind.

The building is organised into a central core comprising of reception, lift and top-lit stairs with two wings of office space to either side. This internal organisation is expressed on the front elevation with the office wings having a fully glazed elevation and the central core being denoted by a rendered wall with an entrance recess at street level.

ハンツワース・ミューズ6-16番地はメリルボーン駅裏の細長い敷地に建つ500のオフィスビルである．周辺の低層の建物にプロポーションやスケールを合わせて設計された．格子状の３層分の正面外観は，実際以上に建物のサイズを強調し(奥行わずか６m)，その背面にある柱と床スラブによるコンクリート構造を正確に表現している．

建物は，受付スペースやエレベーター，トップライトのある階段室などからなるコアを中央に，その左右にオフィススペースという平面である．この内部配置は外観にもそのまま現われ，オフィススペースは大きな開口部によって，中央コア部分は１階で玄関の引っ込みをもつ壁面で表現されている．

View of the building in context　建物外観

Bolsover Street
London, England, 1991

ボルソバー・ストリート

Set in a typical West End street Chadwickham House is an office development of 2,700 square metre contained within an existing turn of the century grade II listed building and a new-build extension to the rear. The design response to the site was to retain the external stone and brick character of the existing building as much as possible whilst strongly contrasting the new extension with it. To emphasise this contrast the new structure is clad in white glazed concrete blocks, glass blocks and a white powder coated curtain walling system.

Internally the contrast between the new accommodation and the refurbished accommodation has been minimised. This has been achieved by stripping out the service core within the existing building and then stabilising the whole structure with a concrete frame thus forming large open spaces (36m × 10m). These spaces are slightly unexpected as they feel more like modern office accommodation rather than the more cellular type space one would expect to find in a building of this nature. The problem of low floor to ceiling heights within the existing building was overcome by designing an uplighter which cantilevers off downstand beams to provide an even reflected light throughout. Thus suspended ceilings have been avoided.

The circulation pattern within the development echos that of the original building - (ie. central main entrance leading directly to the principal staircase with escape stairs situated at either end of the building). The main staircase and lifts are housed within the new core on axis with the entrance door. The staircase is a sculptural concrete element cantilevering from floor to floor rising the full height of the six storey volume in which it is housed. It is flanked to one side by a dramatic 18m tall glass block wall enabling the silhouette of the staircase to be visible from outside. Traditional materials such as slate, cherry veneer, granite and plaster have been combined using contemporary detailing to give this volume the necessary richness to perform the role of pivot for the building.

◀Staircase and extension volume　階段と増築部
Photo by Richard Bryant

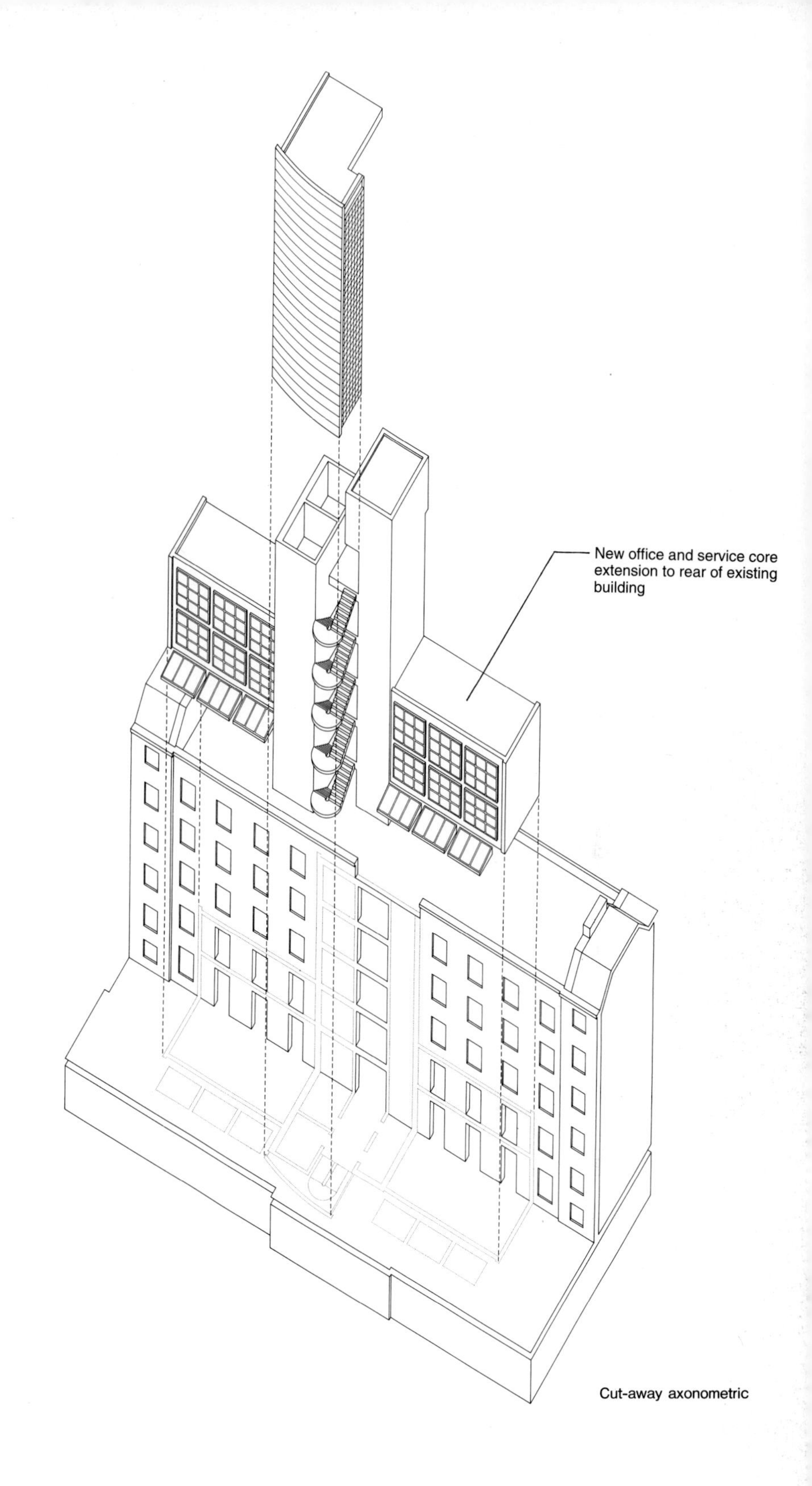

Cut-away axonometric

典型的なウエストエンドの通りに建つチャドウィックハウスは，今世紀初めに完成した保存グレード2にリストアップされている建物をオフィスに改修し，その後ろに新しい増築部分を加えて合計2,700㎡のオフィススペースをつくり出したものである．敷地周辺に呼応したデザインとしては，既存棟は石とレンガによる外観をできるだけそのまま保存し，新棟はそれとは対照的な仕上げとしている．この対比を強調するために，新棟は真っ白なコンクリートブロックとガラスブロック，白く塗装したカーテンウォールによる構成となった．

内部は，新旧の差を極力少なくしている．サービスコアを既存棟からなくして新たな建物に移し，建物全体をコンクリート・フレームで包んで安定させ，36m×10mのワンルームの大きなオフィススペースを確保している．古い建物の中にありがちな，ごく一般的な個室型でなく，よりモダンな事務空間となっている．天井高が低いという問題は，下に突出した天井梁から突き出す形で反射型の照明器具を内包した光天井を全面に取りつけることで解決している．このようにして一般的な吊り型の天井は避けられた．

建物全体の動線は既存のそれに呼応して計画された．中央の正面玄関がそのまま階段室に直結し，建物の両端には避難階段がある．玄関からの軸線上にあるエレベーターや階段室は新棟に収められた．階段室は彫刻的なコンクリートの表現で全6階分の床から床までキャンティレバー状に飛び出す形でつけられ，片方の全高18mをガラスブロック張りとして，外部から内部のシルエットが見えるようにしている．スレート，サクラのベニヤ，花崗岩，プラスターなどの伝統的な素材は現代のディテールと結合されて，建物の重要な表現要素となって，豊かな表情を付加している．

Rear extension　裏側増築部

Entrance detail at night　入口から内部をみる

Photos by Richard Bryant

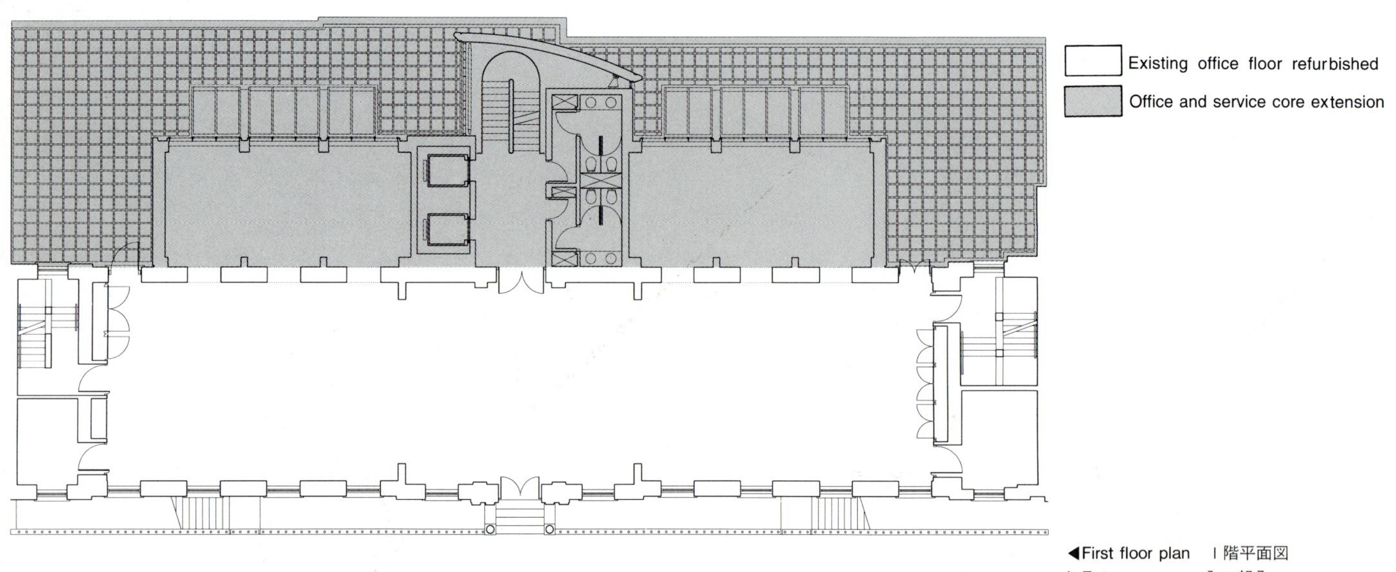

◀First floor plan　1階平面図
▶Entrance area　入口部分

Building FC3 Canary Wharf

London, England, 1992

キャナリーワーフFC 3 ビル

Entrance detail 入口詳細

Photo by John Miller

Troughton McAslan were the first British architects appointed to design an office building for the predominantly North American development on a derelict wharf at Canary Wharf where one million square metres of office space is being constructed east of the City of London. Their design marks a notable departure from the abstracted Classicism that has characterised the development to date.

The client, Olympia & York, asked for a building "modern but timeless and enduring, with a clarity of form and organisation", to which Troughton McAslan responded with a building wrapped in a sheer skin of steel, stone and glass, reflecting their interest in Owen Williams' 'Daily Express' buildings and Frank Lloyd Wright's Johnson Wax tower. It has a simple plan made up of two wings of offices linked by entrance spaces, reception areas and circulation. At ground floor level this central axis is developed to create a route from the street frontage to the waterfront promenade. To one side a lightweight canopy plays off the smooth facade, giving shelter to the adjacent quay.

The 40,000 square metre building adjoins the tower, Canary Wharf's centrepiece designed by Cesar Pelli, with which, in its finishes, it has some affinity. But where the tower is massive and dominating, Troughton McAslan's building is delicate and light, its pronounced horizontals offsetting Pelli's emphasis on the vertical. Troughton McAslan's design defers to Pelli's with the splays in its diagonals, but it holds its own amid its larger neighbours by virtue of its simplicity and restraint.

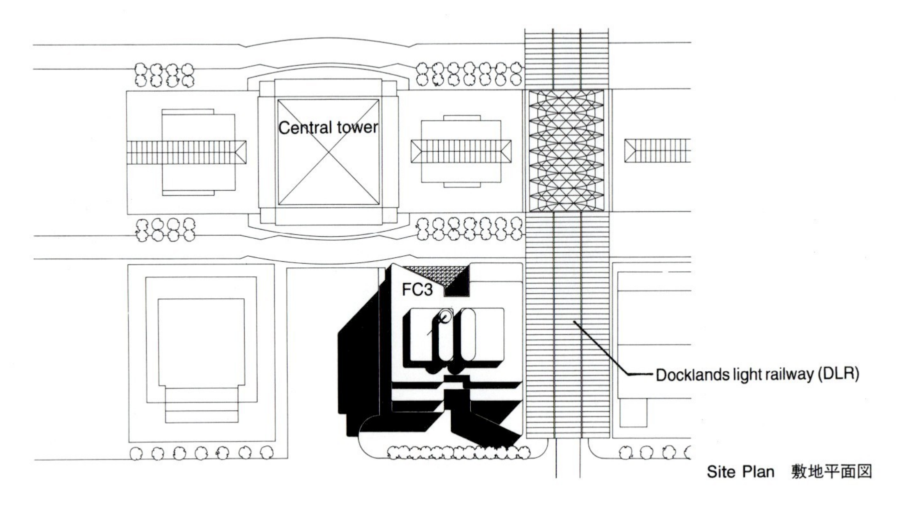

Site Plan 敷地平面図

▼Johnson Wax Tower as a design model デザインモデルとなったジョンソン・ワックスビル

Aerial view of Canary Wharf (and FC3) during construction　建設中のキャナリーワーフ(とFC3ビル)の鳥瞰　*Photo by Brian Harris*

トロートン・マッカーズランは，ロンドンの東にある，荒廃したキャナリーワーフ地区に約100万m²のオフィススペースを開発しようという，主に北米主導型のキャナリーワーフ開発計画の中で，英国人として初めて設計を依頼された．彼らの設計は，抽象的な古典主義が一般的である同開発計画の中で，そこからの明確な訣別を表明したデザインとなっている．

クライアントのオリンピア・アンド・ヨーク社は「モダンでかつ流行に左右されない，明快な形態と組織をもった建物」を要求していた．それに対してトロートン・マッカーズランは，スチールと石とガラスの薄い外皮に包まれた，オウエン・ウィリアムズのデイリー・エクスプレスビルやライトのジョンソン・ワックスビルを想起させるようなデザインを提出した．エントランス，受付，循環施設などからなるコア部分によって2つのオフィスウイングを結合したシンプルな平面である．1階では，この中央軸線は表通りからウォーターフロントのプロムナードにつながる散策路を形成する．一方埠頭に面する外壁にはシェルターとして軽量のキャンティレバー状の上屋がかかっている．

40,000m²のオフィスは，キャナリーワーフの目玉であるシーザー・ペリ設計の高層のオフィスタワーに隣接し，仕上げをこれと相似させている．しかし，タワーは量感があり，抜きんでているが，トロートン・マッカーズランの建物は繊細で軽快で，ペリのデザインが垂直を強調するなら，彼らのそれは水平を強調している．トロートン・マッカーズランのデザインはまた，ペリの対角線的な窓のスプレーとは異なり，シンプルで抑制の効いた独自のデザインで，巨大な近隣のスケールに対して独自性を保っている．

Mowlem

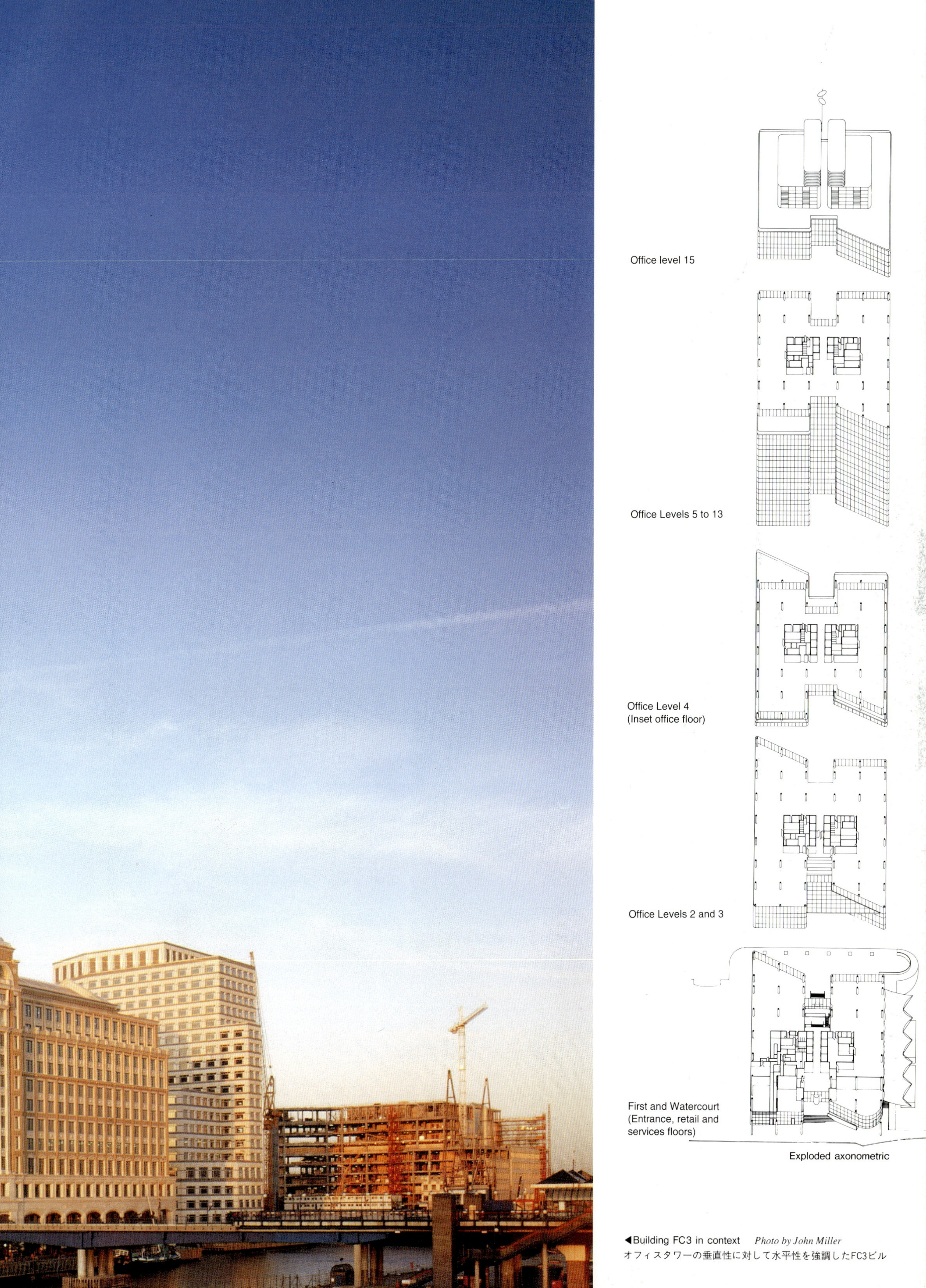

◀Building FC3 in context *Photo by John Miller*
オフィスタワーの垂直性に対して水平性を強調したFC3ビル

SB 368

Photo by John Miller

▲Building FC3 in context　ペリ設計のオフィスタワー（写真右）と仕上げを相似させている
◀Building FC3 in detail　*Photo by John Miller*

Rosebery Avenue and Hardwick Street
London, England, 1992

ローズベリー・アベニュー／ハードウィック・ストリート

Hardwick Street building elevation　ハードウィック・ストリートビル通り側ファサード

Photo by Peter Cook

This scheme is Troughton McAslan's first major office development on an urban site, but it embodies several themes developed on earlier projects. In particular it demonstrates at Rosebery Avenue lucid organisation in plan and elevation, and the practice's fondness for the light, orderly, sheer walled box offset by incidents of inventiveness and display. It also represents their most significant intervention to date on an existing building, with the attention to the existing Hardwick Street building.

Their response to an irregular site was to place the new building's office space in a rectangular block, fronting Rosebery Avenue with services and circulation in the residual spaces, thus making full use of the site without creating awkward or unworkable offices. This organisation informs the elevation, most of which is made up of the well proportioned glazing grid of the offices, supported on slender columns at ground level. Against this exercise in precision and order there is a play of stair and service towers and the deep eaved roof, which houses double height studio space. Out of a straightforward brief and the quirks of the site Troughon McAslan have created a complex and satisfying play of lightness and mass, sheer facades and deep shadows, horizontal and vertical, fantasy and restraint.

Hardwick Street is a separate but complementary project to the new offices on Rosebery Avenue and consists of the refurbishment and partial reconstruction of three linked buildings enclosing, with the new offices, an open planted courtyard. The refurbished building is designed to be let as separate light industrial units or to a single occupier. The existing exposed steel frame is retained. Adapting the strategy of the new building, services, circulation and entrances are concentrated in a fully glazed link between the two principal existing blocks.

With a structural and organisational approach common to the refurbishment and the new building, an irregular site has been unified by a consistency of intention.

Photo by Robin Barton

Construction photograph of both buildings　ハードウィック・ストリート側ビル(左)とローズベリー・アベニュー側ビル(右)の建設風景

トロートン・マッカーズランにとって，都心部に建てる初めての本格的な，かつ当初からいくつかむずかしい問題をもったオフィスビル計画である．新しい建物であるローズベリー・アベニュー側は，プランやエレベーションの明快な構成，軽快で秩序立った，薄い壁で被われた箱という，これまでの設計の集大成を示している傑作である．また，既存のハードウィック・ストリート側の3つの建物の改修に対する配慮は，これまでの既存の建物への介在という手法を結集した代表的な作品といえる．

不定型な敷地に対する彼らの解答は，新しい建物のオフィススペースをローズベリー・アベニューに面した長方形部分に置き，残りのスペースにサービスや循環動線部分を配置するという方法であった．このように極力デッドスペースをつくらないようにして，敷地をフルに活用している．新しい建物は，地上階の細い柱に支えられたグリッド状のガラス張りのエレベーションである．正確な秩序立ったこのエレベーションに対して，階段やサービスタワー，2層分のスタジオスペースを内包する深い庇状の屋根などが外観に変化をつけている．四角い敷地と変形な敷地という対比的な扱い以外にもトロートン・マッカーズランは，軽快さと重厚さ，透き通った薄いファサードと深い陰，水平と垂直，ファンタジーと抑制といった対比をうまく複合して使っている．

ハードウィック・ストリート側は3つの折れ曲がって接続する別棟で，ローズベリー・アベニュー側のオフィスビル新築を機に改修あるいは必要最小限の改築が加えられて，新たなオフィススペースが生み出された．これら4つの建物に囲まれた中央には植栽のあるオープンな中庭がつくられた．既存棟は，それぞれ軽工業の作業場あるいは単独のテナントに貸し出されている．既存のスチールフレームはそのまま活用された．新しい建物の戦略は既存棟にも応用し，サービス，循環動線，玄関などは2つの既存棟に挟まれたガラス張りの接続空間にまとめて配置されている．

改修棟，新築棟両方に共通の手法である構造的かつ組織的なアプローチによって，不定形な敷地は同じ内容をもつ建物で一体化された．

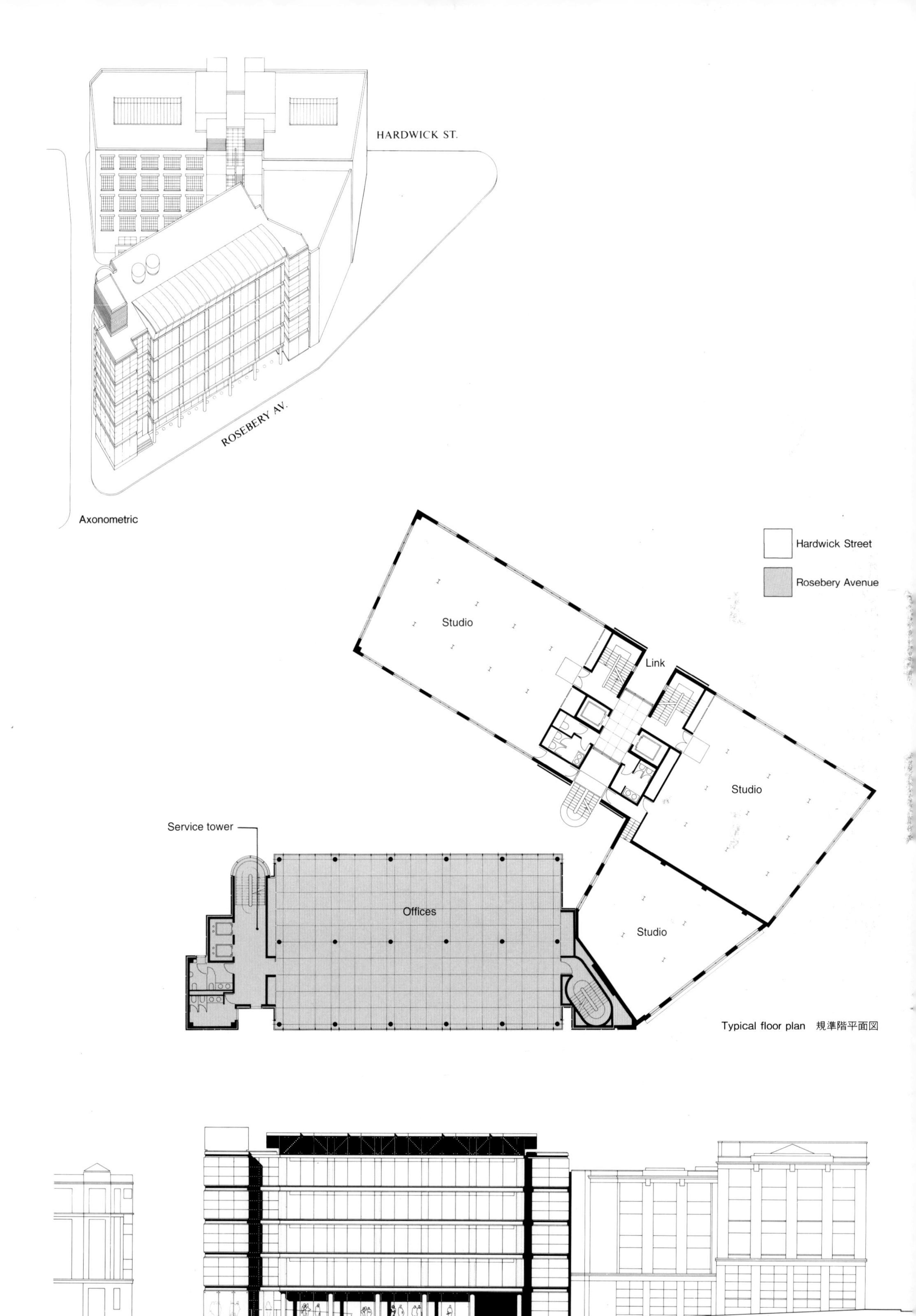

Axonometric

Typical floor plan　規準階平面図

Rosebery Avenue elevation　ローズベリー・アベニュー側立面図

All photos by Peter Cook

Typical studio, Hardwick Street building　ハードウィックストリートビル内の標準的なスタジオ

◀Rosebery Avenue building street elevation
ローズベリー・アベニュービル通り側ファサード

◀Entrance View, Hardwick Street building
ハードウィックストリートビル入口
▶Hardwick Street building link
ハードウィックストリートビル中央の接続部
All photos by Peter Cook

Hardwick Street building courtyard elevation 中庭からみたハードウィック・ストリートビル

▶Rosebery Avenue courtyard elevation 中庭からみたローズベリー・アベニュービル
All photos by Peter Cook

Middlesex House
London, England, 1993

ミドルセックスハウス計画

Troughton McAslan has been involved in the phased renovation into offices of this four floored substantial industrial building in west London since 1985.

New entrances have been formed and vertical circulation systems upgraded, each level has been renovated on a floor by floor basis, and the principal service systems renewed.

トロートン・マッカーズランは，ウエストロンドンにある4階建ての既存の工業建築を，段階的にオフィスに改造していく計画に1985年以来関与し，完成を見た．

新たにエントランス部分が設けられ，垂直動線がグレードアップされ，各階ごとに順に改修が進められ，主要設備はすべて新しくやりかえられた．

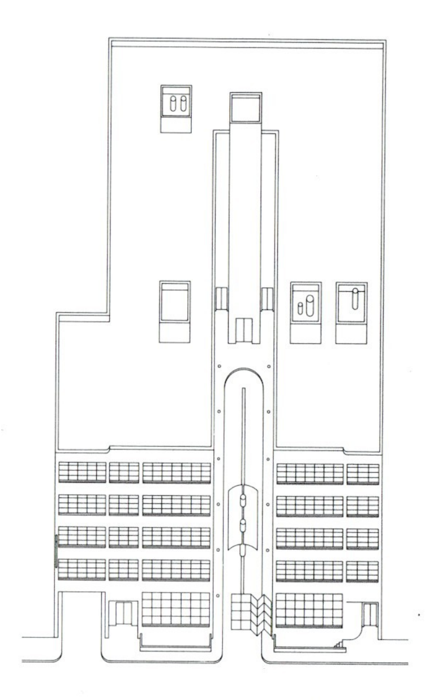

Axonometric

Photo by Robin Barton

Exterior view　外観

Typical entrance area to a refurbished office floor *(photo by Peter Cook)* 一新されるオフィス階のモデルとなる典型的な入口部分

SSAFA Building
London, England, 1993

SSAFA(陸海空軍人遺族会ビル)計画

This new office building on the edge of Shad Thames in London's Docklands extends Troughton McAslan's principles of urban integration. The building does not imitate the Victorian offices or the derelict warehouses nearby, but abstracts their brick facades and engineering quality. The main block of office accommodation stands five storeys tall, with a flush street elevation and stepped profile to the rear respecting the scale of the surrounding buildings. The concrete frame of the building is expressed externally and infilled with solid and glazed panels. The junction with the existing SSAFA headquarters building is articulated by a glazed service core housing stairs, lifts and toilets in an expressive manner.

ロンドン・ドックランドのシャド・テームズの端に建つ新しいオフィスビルは，トロートン・マッカーズランの都市施設の統合の手法を発展させたものである．建物はビクトリア風のオフィスや，また周辺にある荒廃した倉庫建築の模倣ではなく，それらのレンガのファサードや技術的な特徴を観念的に抽象化した建築である．オフィスのメインブロックは5階建て，表通りに面しては平らなエレベーションをもち，後ろ側では周辺の建物環境に合わせてセットバックしている．コンクリートフレームが外側に露出し，ガラスパネルがはめ込まれている．既存のSSAFA本部棟とは，階段，エレベーター，トイレなどを収容する表情豊かなガラス張りのサービスコアを介して接続している．

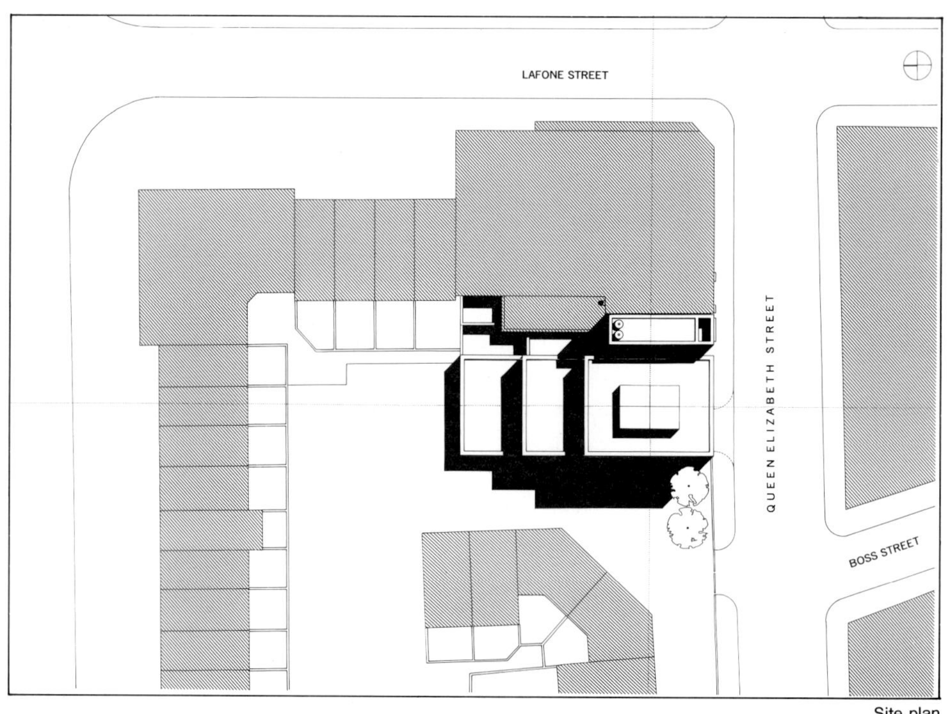

Site plan

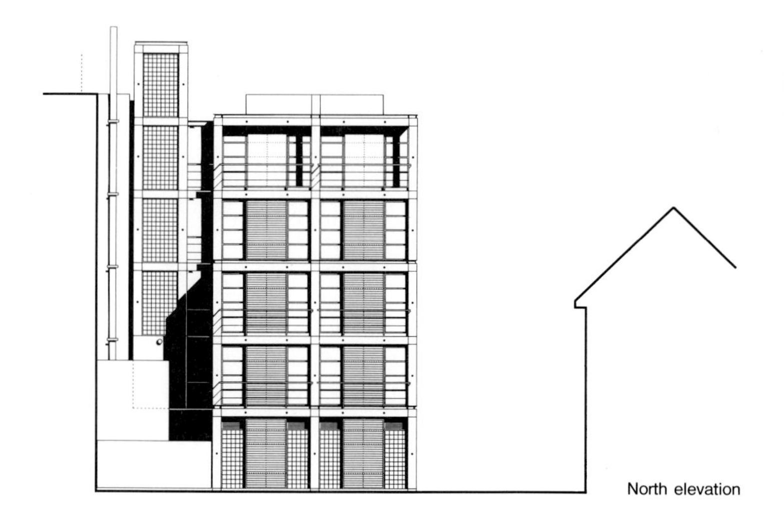
North elevation

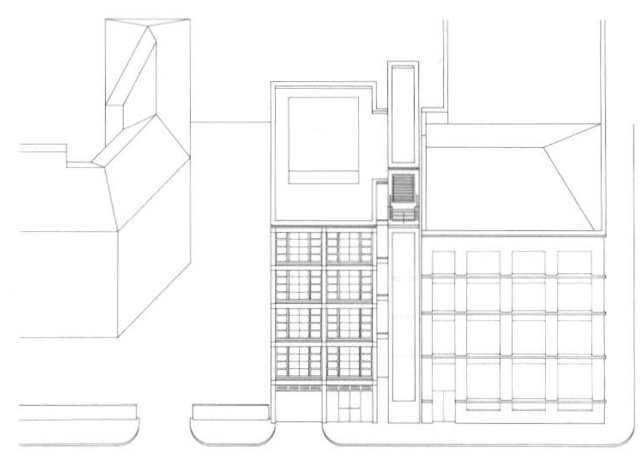
Axonometric in context

South elevation

Christopher Place
London, England, 1993

クリストファープレイス計画

This modestly sized new office building in Camden Town is to be inserted into a site defined by three existing party walls, maximising the internal floor area, with service spaces to the rear and access stairs to the sides. Its concrete frame construction is expressed externally, infilled with stainless steel and glazed panels, the sheer facade being offset by sculptural staircases at either end.

Despite its scale, this building will respond to its enclosed urban context in a confident contemporary manner.

カムデンタウンに建つ，ほどよい大きさの新しいオフィスビルである．建物は3方を既存の境界壁に区画された敷地にあるため，サービススペースを後ろ側にまとめてとり，アクセスのための階段を両脇にとって，床面積を最大限に確保している．コンクリートフレーム構造が外部にそのまま表現され，ステンレスパネルとガラスパネルがはめ込まれた薄い外皮の外観は，建物端の彫刻的な階段部分とうまく調和している．

周辺の都市の文脈に，現代的な感覚でしっかりと融合しつつ呼応する建物となっている．

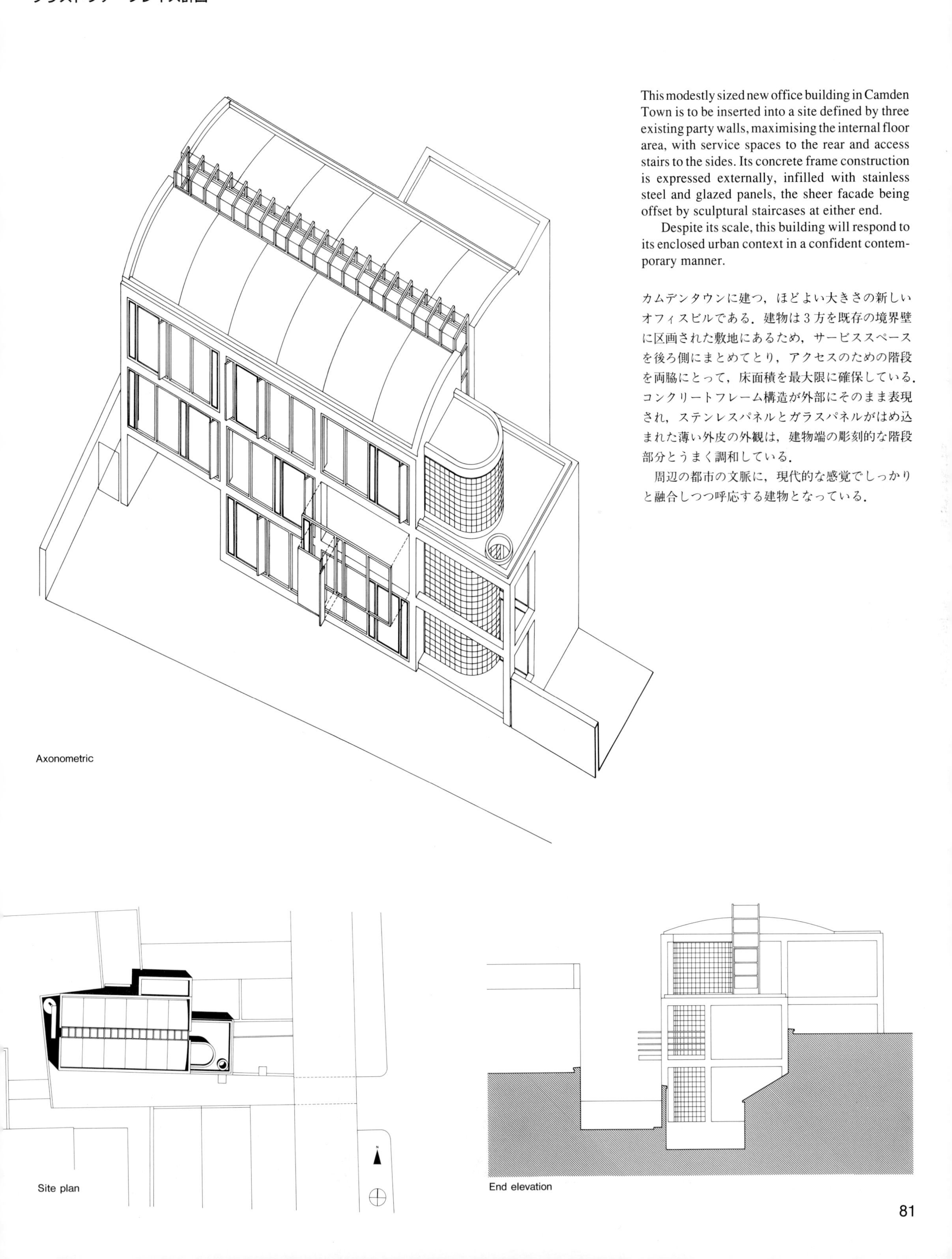

Axonometric

Site plan

End elevation

Docklands Office Building

London, England, 1994

ドックランド・オフィスビル計画

Although on a far more intimate scale than Canary Wharf, Troughton McAslan's international competition winning scheme for a mixed use development for the London Docklands Development Corporation occupies a key site in Docklands. At the junction of several busy roads, it acts as gateway to the most concentrated areas of development on the Isle of Dogs, and is located at a point where the dense traditional city meets the grander gesture of the docks.

Constrained by roads and existing buildings, the site is more urban than is typical of Docklands, and Troughton McAslan's success lay in resolving the site's difficulties and contributing to the surrounding townscape, with the confidence and optimism that marks the best Docklands architecture.

The project is in three parts. To the rear a listed building is retained and refurbished as offices, and on East India Dock Road an existing terrace is terminated with a three storey retail building that acts as a "bookend"; but the centrepiece is a new office and retail block on the apex of the junction. Here the lift tower and the prow of a curved glass wall establish not only an entrance to the building but also to the Isle of Dogs Enterprise Zone beyond.

In addition, the building steps back from the street at this point, to create a public space that relieves the narrow pavements enclosing the site. Inside a long atrium articulates and connects the interior, while the curved wall and the bookend building give form to Amoy Place, a small but historic pedestrian street running through the site.

The building works at several scales: at that of Amoy Place, of the large roads to either side, of the centre of Limehouse of which it is a part, and at the scale of the docks as a whole. Fundamentally, it demonstrates that regeneration need not mean either insensitivity or pastiche.

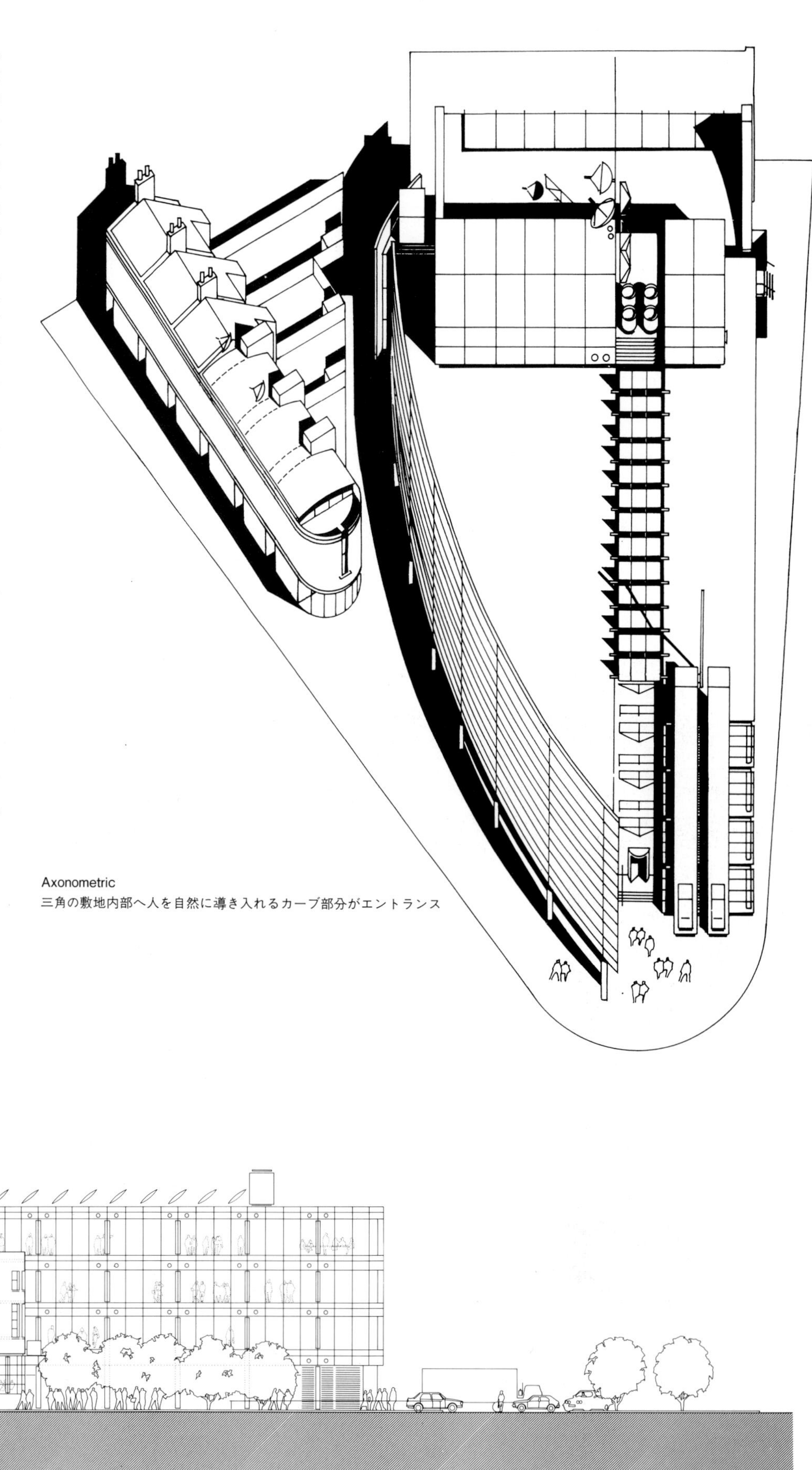

Axonometric
三角の敷地内部へ人を自然に導き入れるカーブ部分がエントランス

East India Dock Road elevation　イースト・インディア・ドック道路側立面

キャナリーワーフより一層小規模な計画ではあるが，トロートン・マッカーズランのこの計画は，ロンドン・ドックランド開発公社主催の国際コンペで入選したもので，ドックランドの重要な位置に建つ多目的施設開発計画である．数本の交通量の多い道路の交差点に位置し，ドッグズ島に集中した新しい開発地へのゲートウェイ的な役目を果たすと同時に，この地域は，既存密集市街地と規模の大きい新しく開発されたドック地域との接点でもある．

道路や既存の建物で規制された敷地は，ドックランドの他の計画の敷地に比べると，市街地に建てるのと同じ状況といえる．こうした敷地のもつ困難な条件を逆に利用して，周辺の街並みづくりに貢献し，ドックランドの建物の中でも最高ののといわれるだけの自信と楽天主義で設計していることが，トロートン・マッカーズランの提案の成功の鍵といえる．

計画は3つの部分からなる．敷地の奥には保存リストに挙げられた建物があり，これはそのままオフィスに保存改修される．イースト・インディア・ドック道路に面しては，3階建ての既存の小売店舗棟が，ちょうどブックエンドのように建っている．そして中央の部分が新しいオフィスと小売店舗からなるブロックである．三角の頂点に当たる部分にはエレベータータワーがあり，船のへさきのようなカーブしたガラス壁のエントランスが建物への玄関であると同時に，ドッグズ島全体への玄関の役目も果たしている．

加えて，建物は通りからセットバックさせて，歩道や歩行者空間の少ない周辺地域にパブリックスペースを提供している．内部の細長いアトリウム空間がインテリア空間を分節し，かつ接続している．カーブした壁やブックエンド状の既存棟は，敷地を貫通，する狭いが歴史的な歩行者用の道路であるアモイプレイスに形態を関連づけている．

建物はいくつかのスケールが混在している．アモイプレイスに合わせたスケール，両側の広い道路に合わせたスケール，中央のこの建物と一部が一体化しているライムハウスに合わせたスケール，そして全体としてはドッグズのスケールに合わせている．基本的には，周辺への無関心でもなければ，単なるつぎはぎでもない，真正の再生計画である．

Existing site　計画前の風景

Perspective view of the proposal　計画案・様々なスケールの建物を使い，計画前の景観にイメージを合わせている

RESIDENTIAL

Most "housing" - the term is significant - is not designed by architects. As much could be said in the USA, Japan or France as in Great Britain. The speculative house builders have created their own styles, independent of the world of architecture. In Britain, the role of architects has declined along with that of public housing - indeed, the failure of some large post-war housing schemes has contributed to the general public's disillusion with old-style Modernism.

What is most obviously lacking in Britain, however, is the one-off house or apartment, designed for a discriminating client. Although Troughton McAslan has designed one or two small extension schemes and a single apartment tower, they have yet to be asked to build significant residential schemes beyond these.

In the last decade or so, nonetheless, a small number of genuinely interesting and original residential developments have been completed for enlightened developers - the riverside projects by Foster and Rogers, Farrell and Grimshaw's Regent's Park block, various schemes by Jeremy Dixon and Ian Ritchie's Roy Court at Limehouse, East London, are examples.

London Docklands saw intensive residential development during the 1980s - part of a development process which equally encompassed Canary Wharf and other commercial schemes. Dixon built here, as did Ritchie and Richard MacCormac (his Shadwell Basin is a good example of the "wharfist" style), but the majority of the new housing was of no special interest. Indeed, Docklands planners tended to prefer a coy red-brick vernacular style, generally applied to small scale terraces of houses which look lost alongside the vastness of the Thames.

McAslan's design for the riverside Prince's Tower in Rotherhithe is an exception. It is anything but "Vernacular" - it is sharp, sleek, stylish, streetwise. Planning permission might have been refused had it not been for the support of the Royal Fine Art Commission and SAVE, plus enthusiastic words from several critics. The inspiration of the building is obvious: the 1930s and Mendelsohn in particular. During construction there were problems with the developer and some of the details were subjected to economies - facetted glass substituted for curved panes, and the elevations are constructed in applied rendered panels rather than being traditionally rendered.

Problems and defects apart, the building is a minor triumph and a landmark on London's river. No other project so fully expresses the firm's intelligent historicism and good humour. ***—Kenneth Powell***

Baitlaws Conservatory　バイトローズ温室

住居施設

ハウジングとは重要な言葉であるが，ほとんどの集合住宅は建築家によって設計されていない．英国だけでなく，アメリカでもフランスでも日本でも事情は同じである．投機的な住宅産業界は，建築界とは異なる世界で，独自のスタイルをつくり出している．英国では，公共住宅の分野における建築家の役割は衰退してしまった．実際，戦後のいくつかの大規模な住宅地計画の失敗によって，古いスタイルのモダニズムに一般の人たちは幻滅を感じてしまったのである．

英国には，いいものを識別できるクライアントのために，きちんと設計された住宅やアパートが最も欠けているのである．トロートン・マッカーズランは，1つか2つの小さな増築計画や単独の高層アパートを設計したが，それ以上の本格的な住宅計画はまだ依頼されていない

しかし1980年代以降，いくつかの本当に興味深い，独自の住宅開発が，啓発されたディベロッパーのためにデザインされた．フォスターやロジャースによるリバーサイド・プロジェクトやファレル・アンド・グリムショーによるリーゼントパーク地区計画，ジェレミー・ディクソンとイアン・リッチーによるライムハウスのロイコートやイーストロンドン計画などがその好例である．

1980年代にはロンドン・ドックランド地区において，キャナリーワーフや他の商業施設計画を含む開発のプロセスの一環として集合的な住居施設の開発が唱えられていた．ディクソンは，リッチーやリチャード・マコーマック（彼のシャドウェル・ベイスン計画は，ワーフスタイルの典型）同様に，ここに建物を設計している．しかし，新しい集合住宅の主流は，まだ大して面白くもないデザインのままである．事実，ドックランドの計画家たちは，個性のない赤レンガのバナキュラーなスタイルを好み，広大なテムズ川沿いに建ち並ぶ，ごく普通の小規模なテラスハウスを建て続けている．

マッカーズラン設計のロザーヒースの川沿いのプリンスタワーのデザインは例外である．決してバナキュラーでなく，シャープでこぎれいで，スタイリッシュでストリートワイズなデザインである．王立美術委員会やSAVE，何人かの批評家の強力な支持がなかったならば，おそらく計画は拒絶されただろう．建物のイメージは明らかに1930年代の，特にメンデルゾーン風のデザインである．建設中にディベロッパーと意見の相違があり，ディテールのいくつかは経済的な理由に従属させられた．カーブした壁面のガラス材は単なるパネルに変更させられ，エレベーションは伝統的にきちんと設計された原案から，表面的に描かれた仕上げで建設された．

しかし，こうした問題と欠点は別のものである．建物は小さな勝利を手にし，ロンドンの川筋におけるランドマークとなった．他のいかなる計画より以上に，トロートン・マッカーズラン事務所の知的な歴史主義やグッドユーモアをこれほどうまく表現した作品はない．

Riverside Apartments
London, England, 1990

リバーサイド・アパートメント

The building viewed from across the Thames at Wapping Pier　ワッピング・ピアからテムズ川を通してみる．川に突き出た居間のベイウィンドウの右にカーブしたバルコニー，その奥にスリット状の浴室窓が見える　*Photo by Robin Barton*

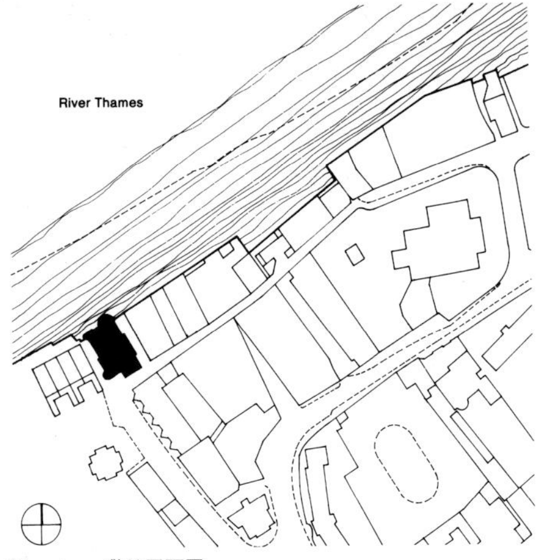

Site plan 敷地平面図
1. Living Room 居間
2. Bedroom ベッドルーム
3. Entrance hall 玄関ホール
4. Parking 駐車場

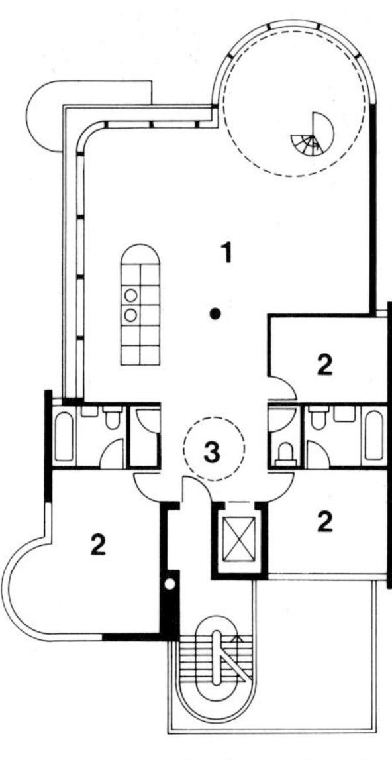

Penthouse floor plan

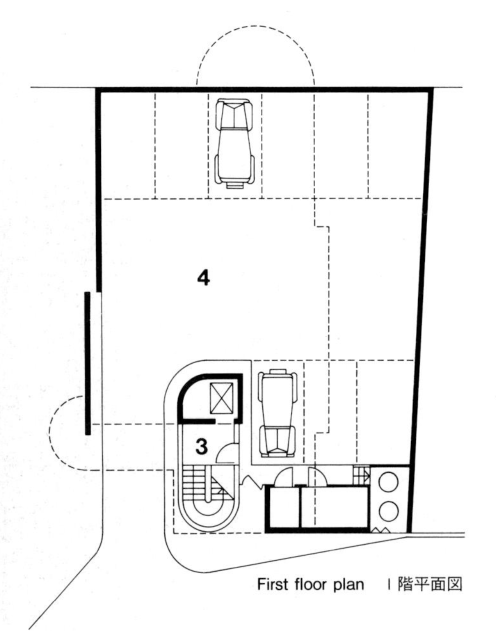

First floor plan 1階平面図

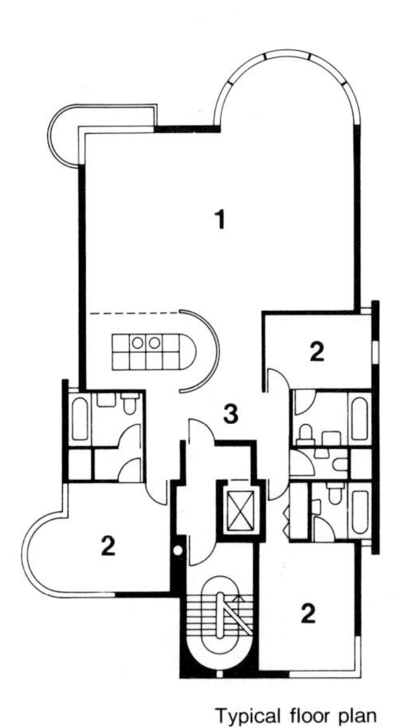

Typical floor plan

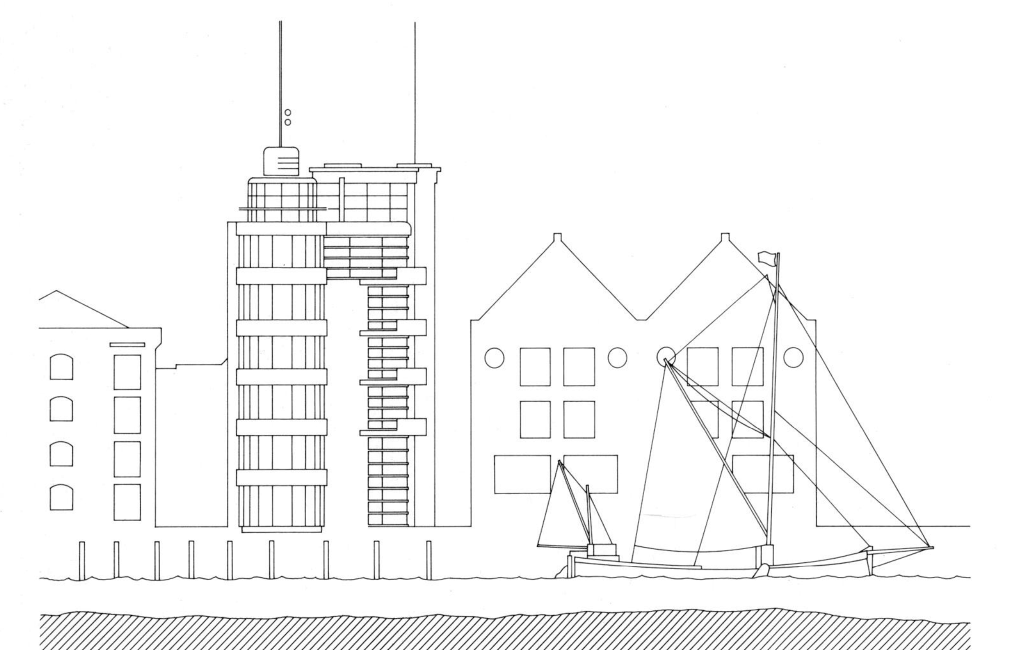

River elevation 川側立面

In common with other innovative young practices in the mid-80s, Troughton McAslan reacted decisively against the excesses of Post Modernism with a return to the clean lines and austere forms of the 1920s and 30s. However, this did not stop them inheriting from Post Modernism a more relaxed attitude to architectural style, which enabled them to see early Modernism less as polemic, more as inspiration and as a source of ideas. They are of a generation well versed in historical precedents, of which interwar Modernism is one among many.

Riverside Apartments, completed four years after it was designed in 1986, is an example of this new attitude to the Modern Movement.

Sadly, Troughton McAslan were not involved by the scheme's developer beyond the design stage and consequently much of the detailing in the completed building is poor and the quality of construction uneven.

With Riverside Apartments Troughton McAslan also found themselves in conflict with the prevailing planning orthodoxy, that fundamental social changes in the London Docklands should be concealed behind weak, imitative facades.

The most apparent inspiration for Riverside Apartments is Erich Mendelsohn's De La Warr Pavilion at Bexhill-on Sea, perhaps the most spectacular example of that white, nautical version of Modernism that took so well to English seafronts. At Riverside Troughton McAslan felt that its robust waterfront setting on the south side of the Thames called for the revival of such architecture. They also found that the style had a capacity for picturesque informality, which allowed them to juggle a complex mixture of different sized flats without straining the integrity of the design. The projecting bays give river views to rooms at the rear, while staggered flank walls allow residents to also see the river from their baths. Meanwhile the client's request for a penthouse could be amply satisfied with the added benefit of an observation turret and roof terrace.

Troughton McAslan's boldness found them support from unexpected sources, and created paradoxical inversions. The Royal Fine Art Commission and conservation bodies such as SAVE and the Thirties Society backed the scheme while the LDDC (who were to permit so many immodest schemes) initially held out for a more retiring design. In the event, in a relatively rare triumph for innovation, Troughton McAslan won through.

▶Landside detail of the tower *Photo by Peter Cook*
陸側から見たベッドルームのベイウィンドウ

PRINCES
HOUSE

All photos by Peter Cook

Landside view　階段室部分は上部２層分がカーブしたガラス壁となっている

1980年代半ばの他の革新的な若手建築家と同様，トロートン・マッカーズランも，異常なポストモダニズムの過熱に対抗して，1920年代から30年代の明快なライン，簡素な形態への回帰という形を打ち出した．しかし，このことで，彼らが建築のスタイルを自由に気楽に使うというポストモダニズムの特徴を受け継がなくなるということではなかったので，初期モダニズムを単に議論の対象として見ず，インスピレーションやアイディアの源泉と見なすことが可能になった．彼らは歴史や先例を熟知している世代であり，彼らにとっては，戦中のモダニズムもその他の数多くの先例の１つにすぎなかったのである．

リバーサイド・アパートメントは，1986年に設計され，４年後に完成しているが，近代建築運動の新たな局面の１つを示している．

残念ながら，トロートン・マッカーズランはディベロッパーの都合により，設計しただけで，それ以降はタッチしなかったため，結果として実際に完成した建物のディテールの多くは貧相で，施工精度もよくない．

この計画でトロートン・マッカーズランは，当時一般に普及していた計画手法と真正面から衝突することになった．つまり，ロンドン・ドックランドにおける重要な社会変化が，見せかけだけの弱々しいファサードの陰に隠蔽されてしまっている周辺の街並みに挑戦したのである．

リバーサイド・アパートメントに最も大きな影響を与えたのは，ベックスヒル・オン・シーに建つエリッヒ・メンデルゾーンのデ・ラ・ワーパビリオンである．これは英国の海岸にふさわしい，真っ白な，海のモダニズムによる解釈の好例である．トロートン・マッカーズランにとっては，テムズ川左岸の荒々しい環境の中には，メンデルゾーンの作品のような建物のリバイバルが必要と感じられた．このスタイルはまた，全体のデザインを犠牲にすることなく，さまざまなプランやサイズの住戸を混在させることができる，ユニークな外観が可能となった．突出したベイウィンドウによって，室内からすばらしい川の眺望が開け，浴室のある側面の窓からも川が眺められる．クライアントのペントハウスという要望に対しては，展望塔と屋上テラスを付加することで十分に応えている．

トロートン・マッカーズランのデザインは，思わぬ反響を呼び，予期せぬ支持を得，矛盾した展開を見せた．つまり，王立美術委員会や，SAVE，30年代委員会などの保存団体が彼らの設計案を支援してくれたが，クライアントであるロンドン・ドックランド開発公社は，いつも不謹慎なデザインでも承認しているのに，トロートン・マッカーズランの設計をもっとおとなしいものにすることを強要してきた．しかし，比較的珍しいことであるが，革新が勝利を収め，トロートン・マッカーズランはこの局面をうまく切り抜けることができたのである．

◀Landside detail of the tower
川の反対側にあたる建物入口部分

Baitlaws Conservatory
Lanarkshire, Scotland, 1985
ラナークシャーのバイトローズ温室増築

One of Troughton McAslan's first completed buildings, this conservatory extension to a farmhouse illustrates the influence of both modern and 19th century metalwork constructions, reinterpreted to create something wholly new. It is raised to first floor level to make the most of spectacular views, and is surrounded by an external balcony. The play of lightweight steel and timber strip floors has since become a recurring theme in Troughton McAslan's work.

トロートン・マッカーズランの活動の初期に，実際に完成した建物の1つで，農家の温室部分の増築である．ここでは，全く新たに解釈し直されてはいるが，モダンからの影響と同時に，19世紀の鉄の建築の影響も見られる．温室は眺望を確保するために2階レベルに設けられ，外側をぐるりとバルコニーが取り巻いている．軽量鉄骨のフレームと細長い板材の床という組合せは，その後トロートン・マッカーズランの作品に繰り返し出てくる手法となった．

◀External detail　温室頂部
▶Exterior view　バルコニーがとりまく温室外観
Photo by Alastair Hunter

Il Molino

San Gimignano, Italy, 1992

イル・モリノ

All photos by Peter Cook

This conversion of an 18th Century mill into a private residence respresents Troughton McAslan's first built European project. The scheme involved the rebuilding of the stone and brick building with the introduction of modernist intervention and extensive external landscaping.

18世紀の工場建築を個人住宅に改造する計画で，トロートン・マッカーズランの自国以外のヨーロッパ地域で初めて完成した作品である．計画は，石とレンガの建物本体の建て直しから，モダニスト的な介在の導入および外側に広がるランドスケーピングまで含んでいる．

◀Backyard view from second floor
2階から中庭をみる
▶Backyard view at 中庭側夕景

TRANSPORT

Britain was the birthplace of the railway and its 19th century railway monuments form a significant part of the national heritage. The Victorian railway established a comprehensive design philosophy, which extended from the smallest country station to the grandest city terminus. During the inter-war years, London Transport was a world-leader in the design field, with the architecture of its stations matched by the quality of its rolling stock, graphics and fabrics. The architect Charles Holden was the kıngpin of LT's achievement in the 1930s - his personal style embraced Classicism and the Romantic Modernism of the Scandinavians.

Since the Second World War, public transport has been under-funded, but transport is now high on the political agenda in Britain. In London approval has been given to construct the first new Underground line for 30 years - the Jubilee line extension serving London Docklands, Canary Wharf and beyond from Westminster.

Troughton McAslan's Canning Town station will stand at a point where the new line links with British Rail and the Docklands Light Railway. There will also be a heavily-used bus station. This new interchange station will be, says Troughton "essentially an engineering structure" unifying the various facilities. The interchange sits on a massive but expressive concrete structure recalling the work of Nervi and, perhaps, Calatrava. The enclosures to these structures have a lightness which balances out this massiveness. At Stratford, on the very eastern edge of London, the new platforms for the Jubilee Line and DLR have to fit in with the operations of one of the busiest suburban interchanges in the capital. Again, the new structures will largely be a matter of engineering (in the Victorian tradition) but with the addition of a new sub-station and staff building which will provide the opportunityy to create an elegant architectural intervention and to lift the spirits of the traveller in a dreary location.

Redhill Station is located on the Network South East division of British Rail, to the south of London. The existing station was unremarkable - there were platforms and canopies, little else. Redhill was one of the stations identified by BR's Director of Design, Jane Priestman, as needing major improvement. Priestman was able to commission station designs from a group of interesting young practices and Troughton McAslan got Redhill.

The ticket hall at street level shows some Holden influence (not surprising given the firm's interest in the Romantic Modernists), though using materials more lightweight and consciously elegant in character than Holden would have adopted in the 1930s. The platform building has a same vocabulary , being slotted under the 19th century canopy. If anything, these buildings are perhaps a little too elegant for their purpose. In more recent work, Troughton McAslan have moved back decisively towards the toughness of earlier railway buildings.

Transport projects will provide a significant part of the office's workload in the '90s - another factor mitigating its "commercial" character in the '80s. It is a demanding area of design - very much linked to the needs of end-users and calling for a tough and expressive aesthetic with none of the superficiality which typifies some office design. Transport buildings, it is clear, inspire Troughton McAslan. ***—Kenneth Powell***

交通施設

英国は鉄道発祥の地であり，19世紀の鉄道モニュメントは重要な国家遺産となっている．ビクトリア朝の鉄道は，田舎の小さな駅から大都市のターミナルにいたるまでの，包括的なデザイン哲学を確立した．

２つの大戦間の時期は，駅舎の建物はもちろん，それに調和した全車両の質，グラフィックス，ファブリックスなども含めて，ロンドン・トランスポートが世界の鉄道施設のデザイン的なリーダーであった．建築家チャールズ・ホールデンはロンドン・トランスポートの1930年代の業績の中心人物であった．彼のスタイルは，古典主義と北欧のロマンティック・モダニズムで構成されていた．

第２次大戦以後，公共輸送施設は資金を抑制されたが，しかし輸送施設はいまや英国では，政治的に高い関心が払われている．ロンドン

Redhill Station レッドヒル駅舎
Photo by Robin Barton

では，30年振りに地下鉄の新規路線の建設が初めて承認された．地下鉄ジュビリー線の延長によって，ロンドン・ドックランド，キャナリーワーフ，そしてはるかウエストミンスターまでも接続されることになった．

トロートン・マッカーズランのカニングタウン駅は，地下鉄新線が英国国鉄およびドックランド新交通（ドックランズ・ライト・レイルウェイ）と交差接続する地点につくられる．そこにはまた，利用客の多いバス路線のターミナルもできる．この乗換駅はトロートンによると「本質的に技術的な構造」があらゆる施設を結びつけている．ネルビーやカラトラーバの作品を思わせるコンクリートのマッシブで印象的な構造体の上に載る，その上の架構は，マッシブにバランスする軽快さである．ロンドンの東端にあるストラットフォード駅では，ジュビリー線とドックランド新交通のための新しいプラットホームが，首都ロンドン郊外の中でも最も交通量の多い交差点にはめ込まれる．ここでも，施設はビクトリア風の伝統の上に立った技術的な表現の強いものであるが，しかし，新たな地下鉄駅や管理事務所の追加によって，エレガントな建築的介在を生み出し，旅行者にとってつまらない場所を興味深い場所に変換させる機会を提供することになる．

レッドヒル駅は，ロンドン南部の英国国鉄のネットワーク・サウスイースト線に位置している．既存の駅舎はプラットホームとキャノピー上屋があるだけの，ごく普通の施設である．レッドヒル駅は，大改良を必要とするものとして，英国国鉄のデザイン部長であるジェーン・プリーツマンの指揮の下で進められている計画の１つである．プリーツマンは，駅舎のデザインチームとして，いくつかの興味深い若手建築家のグループを編成し，その中でトロートン・マッカーズランはレッドヒル駅を担当することになった．

道路レベルにある出札ホールは，マッカーズランのロマンティック・モダニズムへの関心を受けて，ホールデンの影響がはっきりと出ている．しかし，素材としては，ホールデンが1930年代に使ったものより軽いものを採用して意識的にエレガンスを表現している．プラットホーム部分もボキャブラリーとしては同じで，19世紀のキャノピーの下に細長い穴が横たわる形をとっている．少し問題があるとすれば，鉄道施設としてはエレガントすぎる点である．ごく最近の作品では，トロートン・マッカーズランは，初期の鉄道施設のすばらしいデザインに確実に回帰しつつある．

交通施設計画は，90年代のトロートン・マッカーズラン事務所の仕事の重要な部分を構成するだろう．それは80年代の彼らのコマーシャル的な特質を軽減する．しかし，交通施設のデザインは注意を要する分野である．つまり，エンド・ユーザーのニーズに密接に係わるため，オフィス建築などに存在する特殊性は一切存在しないにもかかわらず，美的にすぐれた表情豊かなものが求められる．交通施設がトロートン・マッカーズランに少なからず影響を与えるのは明らかである．

Redhill Station

Surrey, England, 1990

レッドヒル駅

Ticket Hall at night　出札ホール夕景
Photo by Peter Cook

In Troughon McAslan's architecture it is possible to discern two complementary but distinct attitudes to the Modern Movement: Modernism as methodology and Modernism as style. At Acton, where the central problem is one of organisation, it is the former that dominates; at Redhill, where the organisation is largely predetermined, the latter is in evidence.

The brief for Redhill can be interpreted at different levels. At one level it is the phased refurbishment of a tatty surburban station, at another the creation of an important civic building. In turning this brief into architecture the principal inspiration was an architect on the fringes of orthodox Modernism, Charles Holden. With his Piccadilly Line stations he created a civic architecture of austere, simple forms which also reflected the industrial quality of the railways they served.

These are the qualities Troughton McAslan are reinventing at Redhill. Their steel and glass interventions, by virtue of their construction, belong to the world of the railway, and echo the station's existing structures. The first completed phase, the platform building and Ticket Hall, have the proportions, the direct, minimal detailing, and the rhythmic quality of a train. The same vocabulary, when applied to the ticket hall building, is heightened by deep eaves and the direct rhetoric of the circular form to create a landmark, a symbol for the town of Redhill and of the station's role in linking London and the south east. With its solid base and tall columns the ticket hall is almost temple-like, a quality offset by its lightweight construction.

By combining the clean lines of engineering with simple architectural gestures, a messy site is unified and a continuity is established between the functional world of the railway and the life of the town it serves.

The experience at Redhill has also served to prepare the practice for the design of the more complex interchange stations for the Jubilee Line Extension at Canning Town and Stratford, due for completion in 1996.

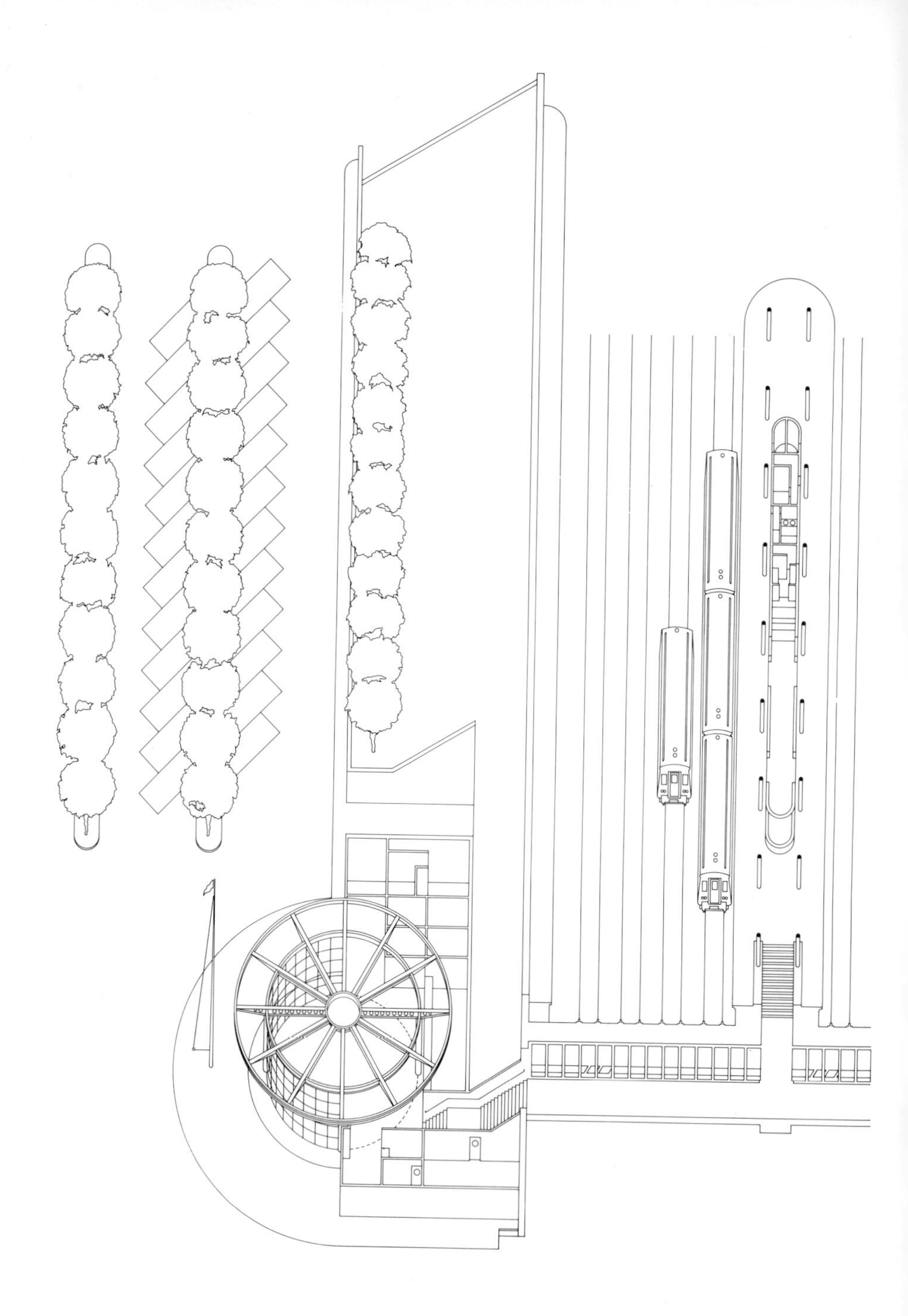

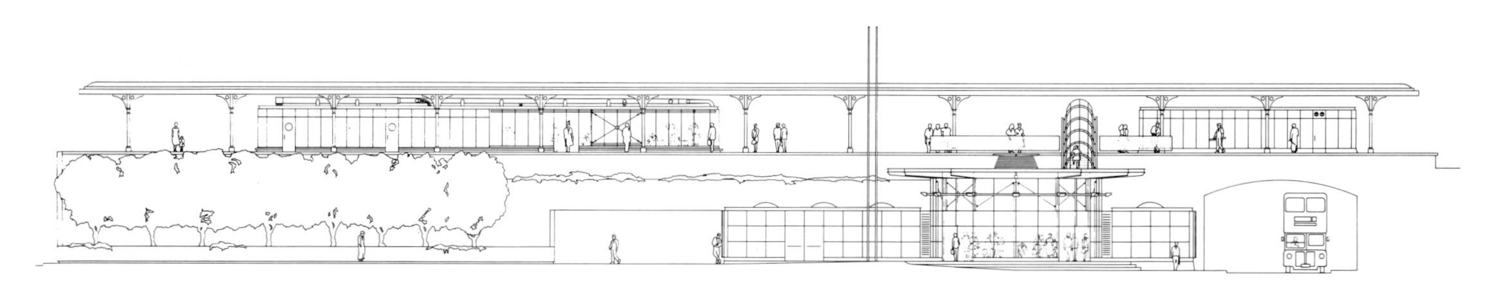

Ticket Hall elevation with the platform building beyond　出札ホールとその向こう側に見えるプラットホームの立面

Photo by Peter Cook

Exterior detail of Ticket Hall　出札ホールは軒の深い円形建物でシンボリックになっている

Photo by Peter Cook

Interior of Ticket Hall　出札ホール内部

Interior detail of Ticket Hall steelwork
細い柱による軽量鉄骨構造

Photo by John Donat

トロートン・マッカーズランの建築において，近代建築運動への補足的ではあるが明らかな姿勢が2つある．それは方法論としてのモダニズムとスタイルとしてのモダニズムである．アクトン地下鉄職員訓練所においては，中心課題は組織の構成であり，ここでは方法論としてのモダニズムが強く表われている．しかしレッドヒル駅では構成が基本的にすでに決定されていたため，スタイルとしてのモダニズムが顕著に表現されている．

レッドヒルの概略はいろいろなレベルに解釈できる．1つはうす汚れた郊外の駅施設の段階的な改修工事であるという側面，もう1つは重要な市民のための空間を新たに創出することである．この概略を建築化するために，主要な発想の根源となったのは，オーソドックスなモダニズムの淵にいた建築家であるチャールズ・ホールデンである．ピカデリー線の数々の駅舎において，彼は鉄道という工業的な特質を反映した，質素でシンプルな形態の市民のための建築をつくり出した．

レッドヒル駅でトロートン・マッカーズランが再生したのは，こうしたホールデンの建物のもつ特質である．レッドヒルでのスチールとガラスによって生み出された介在は，鉄道という分野に属し，かつ駅の既存の施設に呼応している．第1期工事で完成したプラットホームと出札ホールは，列車のプロポーション，方向性，ミニマル・ディテール，リズミックな特徴を有している．同じ特徴は，出札ホールの建物では軒の深い円形の建物というレトリックで強調され，ランドマークとなっている．また，レッドヒルの街のシンボルとなり，ロンドンとサウスイースト地区を結びつける役割を果たす．かっちりとした土台部分と細い柱による出札ホールは，まるで寺院建築のようであり，軽量鉄骨構造の特徴が余すところなく発揮されている．

技術的な清楚なラインと，建築的なシンプルさが合わさって，乱雑な敷地が一体化され，鉄道という機能的な世界とその街の生活との間に連続性を生み出している．

レッドヒルでの体験は，1996年完成予定のジュビリー線延長のカニングタウン駅やストラットフォード駅という，より複雑にいくつかの鉄道が交差する駅のデザインのために有効に役立ったのである．

Photo by Peter Cook

▲Interior of platform building　待合室内部

Platform Building cross section　プラットホーム断面

▶Exterior of platform building　待合室
Photo by Peter Cook

SouthEast

New Two Stations, Jubilee Line Extension
London, England, 1996

ジュビリー線延長新駅２題

Canning Town Station カニングタウン駅

Troughton McAslan were selected in June this year as Architects for two stations on the new £1 Billion Jubilee Line Extension for London Underground.

This line will link Westminster to East London and Docklands. The Jubilee Line extension is heralded as the most important and innovative engineering endeavour currently under development in Europe.

Completion is scheduled for 1996 in half the time normally anticipated for work of this complexity. The role of the Architects and Engineers is therefore exceptionally demanding.

Troughton McAslan's project for Canning Town comprising London Transport Bus, Jubilee Line and Docklands Light Railway stations will be a major transport interchange north-east of Canary Wharf.

Set in an uncompromising urban context, Troughton McAslan's design is in the tradition of great Victorian railway engineering with an architecture of strong structural expression generated by the stations' functional demands. The station plan comprises three parallel linear buildings located between the roads and railway lines serving the interchange, with each linked by an elevated public bridge running across the site.

The concept for a Jubilee Line and Docklands Light Railway stations was generated by the dynamic form of the escalators which in each case carries passengers from the upper level concourse to the platforms beneath. the inclined structural columns grouped around the escalators support a

トロートン・マッカーズランは1991年６月にロンドンの地下鉄路線のジュビリー線の延長計画，10億ポンド・プロジェクトの中の２駅の設計者に選ばれた．ジュビリー新線はウエストミンスターとイーストロンドン，ドックランドを結びつける．このプロジェクトは，目下発展するヨーロッパの中で，最も重要で革新的な計画といえる．

完成は1996年の予定で，その期間の約半分がこの駅舎を取り巻く複合施設の建設期間と考えられているが，そこでの建築家および技術者の役割は非常に重要である．

カニングタウン駅はロンドン・トランスポート・バス，ジュビリー線，ドックランド新交通の３つの交通機関が交差するところで，キャナリーワーフの北東に位置している．

複雑な都市のコンテクストの中にあって，トロートン・マッカーズランのデザインは偉大なビクトリア風の鉄道技術の伝統に則り，駅という非常に機能的な要求のはっきりした構造を明快に表現した建物となっている．駅は３つの細長い建物が道路と線路の間に平行に並び，その両者の交点を構成し，敷地を横切る高架の歩道橋によってそれぞれ接続している．

ジュビリー線およびドックランド新交通の駅舎のデザイン・コンセプトは，いずれの場合も上階のコンコースから，プラットホーム上部のブリッジを支えるエスカレーターまわりの一群の斜めの構造柱の下にあるプラットホームに乗降客を運ぶエスカレーターのダイナミックな形態から導き出さ

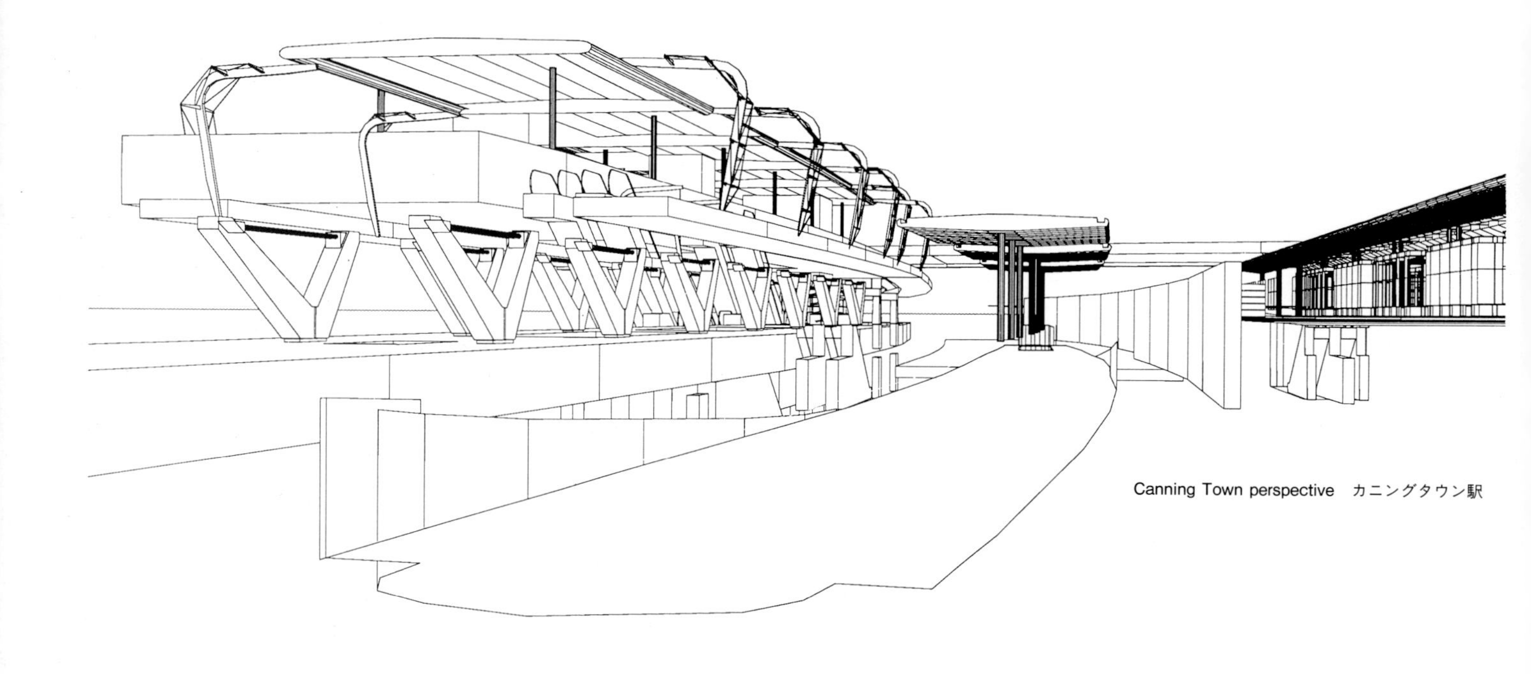

Canning Town perspective カニングタウン駅

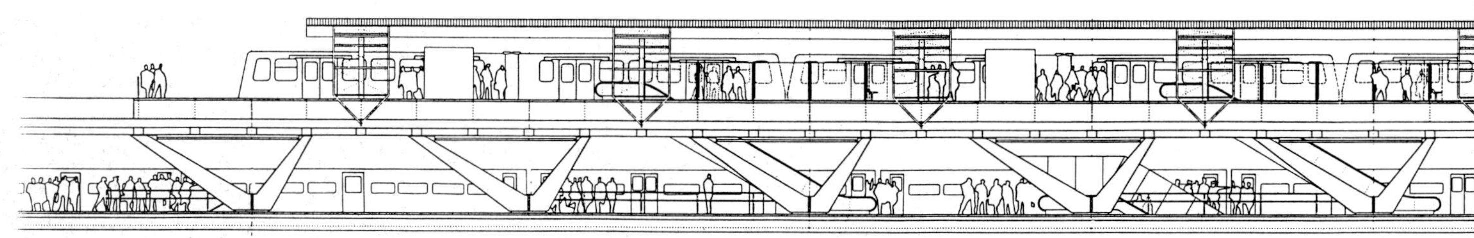

Canning Town elevation カニングタウン駅

bridge structure over the platforms. The platforms remain clear for passengers and an important visual link is maintained between the three parallel structure. The reinforced concrete bridge structures above support the main passenger concourse and the suspended service accommodation below.

Troughton McAslan's scheme is designed to emphasise the energy and dynamics which evolve from the nature of a new transport technology.

れている．プラットホームは乗降客にとって明快な空間とし，３つの平行する構造体相互の視覚的な関係を重視している．上部のRC造のブリッジがメイン・パッセンジャー・コンコースを支持し，サービス用の施設をその下に吊っている．

トロートン・マッカーズランの計画は，新しい輸送技術の特質から導き出されるエネルギーとダイナミズムを強調している．

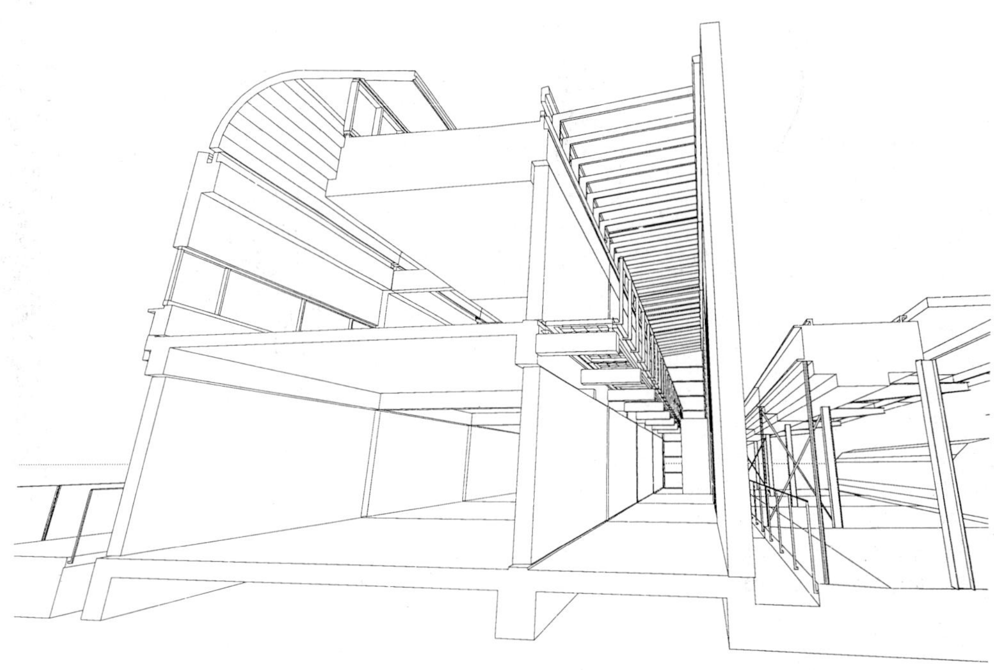

Stratford perspective　ストラットフォード駅

Stratford Station　ストラットフォード駅

The project for Stratford Station encompasses new platform accommodation for both the Jubilee Line and Docklands Light Railway together with a facility building for each line. Stratford Station differs from the other new stations, being both the end of the line and forming part of a projected overall re-development of the Stratford site by British Rail.

The project aims to assert the identity of both the new JLE and DLR lines while also being compatible with the new BR station concourse re-development. In addition the JLE and DLR station buildings located adjacent serve to celebrate Stratford as the East London "Gateway" to the new transport system and Docklands itself.

As with Canning Town Station a rich palette of natural materials is deployed giving clarity of structure and richness of form to all elements of the scheme. Smooth clad metal wings oversail the steel support structure for the canopies while the buildings consist of clad or infilled concrete framed structures offset against metal clad screen walls and glazed circulation zones.

As with the best railway architecture, simple, clear form and organisation combine to create a station which has the requisite dignity and purposefulness.

ストラットフォード駅は，ジュビリー線とドックランド新交通の駅，新しいプラットホームおよび管理施設をそれぞれ一緒に包含する計画である．ストラットフォード駅は，他の新駅と異なり，終点駅であり，また英国国鉄による敷地周辺の再開発計画の一部を形成する．

計画は，新たな英国国鉄駅コンコースの再開発計画に合致しつつ，新しいジュビリー新線およびドックランド新交通の両者の個性を形成するというものである．さらに，隣り合わせに建つ両新線の駅舎は，ストラットフォードが新交通やドックランドそのものへのイーストロンドンのゲートウェイ的役割も担うように計画された．

カニングタウン駅同様，ここでも自然の素材を取り混ぜて使用し，計画全体を通じて明快な構造，形の豊かさを表現している．建物はコンクリート・フレーム構造であるが，キャノピーのためのスチールの構造体の上の平滑な金属材によるウイングが，金属張りのスクリーン壁とガラス張りの階段・通路部分の外壁の表現に対応し，補足し合っている．

ホールデンなどの最良の鉄道施設と同様，この計画はシンプルで明快なフォームと構成によって，必要な品位と合目的性をもった駅を創出している．

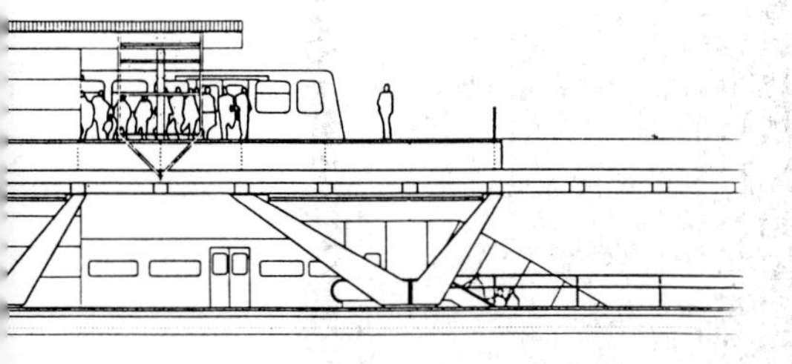

PUBLIC BUILDINGS

While commercial development boomed in the 1980s Britain, public building of every sort declined markedly. Many critics compared the United Kingdom unfavourably with France, where the "Grands Projets" of Paris were matched by new schools, housing and health buildings throughout the land. Young British practices thrived on commercial work, yet were deprived of the public dimension which had been the inspiration of some of the best firms of the 1950s and '60s.

In the absence of public commissions at home, British architects were driven towards international competitions (traditionally a proving ground for the young). In the two which Troughton McAslan entered (unsuccessfully in the event) the brief requirements lead to the design of a modern building which respected and reflected the traditions of other countries. The Indira Gandhi Centre competition came at a time when the practice was very young, with no experience of planning large buildings. The site in New Delhi was redolent with memories of Lutyens' attempts to merge Western Classicism and the Indian vernacular. John McAslan's entry, which he acknowledges owes a great deal to Aidan Potter's input, a key designer in the practice was shortlisted in the final twelve. The practice regards the competition as a landmark in its development, not least for the way in which it was obliged to look seriously at the implications of reconciling European Modernism and Eastern traditions. In the Nairobi High Commission entry, the problems were different. Where did the local "vernacular" lie? Could lessons be drawn from other countries - like Australia? The work of Glenn Murcutt has been a constant inspiration to McAslan over some years and came to the fore in the Nairobi scheme. The architecture of 19th century Kenya was studied, with the necessity to create a building suited to the climate of the country always to the fore. If anything, the resulting scheme was almost consciously anti-monumental - a complete abandonment of imperial swagger in an ex-colony. Perhaps the lack of monumentality was a mistake - the design has nothing about it which expresses "Britishness". But the competition, say McAslan, was another milestone in the practice's work. It was stimulating, he says, to respond to another culture in a modern, low-key way, appropriate to a country such as Kenya with its distinctive climate and lack of natural resources.

The competition to design a Museum of Scotland in Edinburgh - an extension to the 19th century Royal Scottish Museum in Chambers Street - generated much international interest amongst architects. Most of the 371 entries came from Britain and Troughton McAslan were amongst a group of rising British practices to enter and to be shortlisted. The existing museum building is internally spectacular, but externally rather severe and even drab. It lies near the University (with its fine original buildings by Robert Adam), but away from the Classical splendours of Prince's Street and the New Town and on the edge of the Old Town (which is essentially Gothic and Picturesque). Troughton McAslan had to respond to a brief which asked for a strategy rather than detailed designs, but they provided the "bones" of a building in their submission. Eschewing self-conscious picturesqueness they proposed a structure with classic modern qualities. The work of Louis Kahn has flavoured many of their projects but it was particularly relevant in this instance, with its insistence on the primacy of the street and the pavement - the Mellon Center at Yale is an obvious exemplar. Had it been built, the scheme would have added a distinctive, expressive and essentially non-deferential building to the streetscape of the Scottish capital. It was certainly amongst the more interesting of a number of distinguished entries to the competition.

The firm has yet to complete a public building in Britain; though it was recently selected from an open competition to develop proposals for the long term refurbishment of Eric Mendelsohn's masterpiece, the De La Warr Pavilion at Bexhill on Sea, Sussex. The choice of Troughton McAslan made sense - the practice has its roots firmly in the Romantic Modernism of the 1930s. Changing attitudes to public spending may rectify that omission in the next few years - already Troughton McAslan have benefited from a new concern to improve public transport with their designs for stations and Acton Training Centre. And the St Catherine' s College Kobe embodies many of the lessons learned in their competition entries over the last six years.

—Kenneth Powell

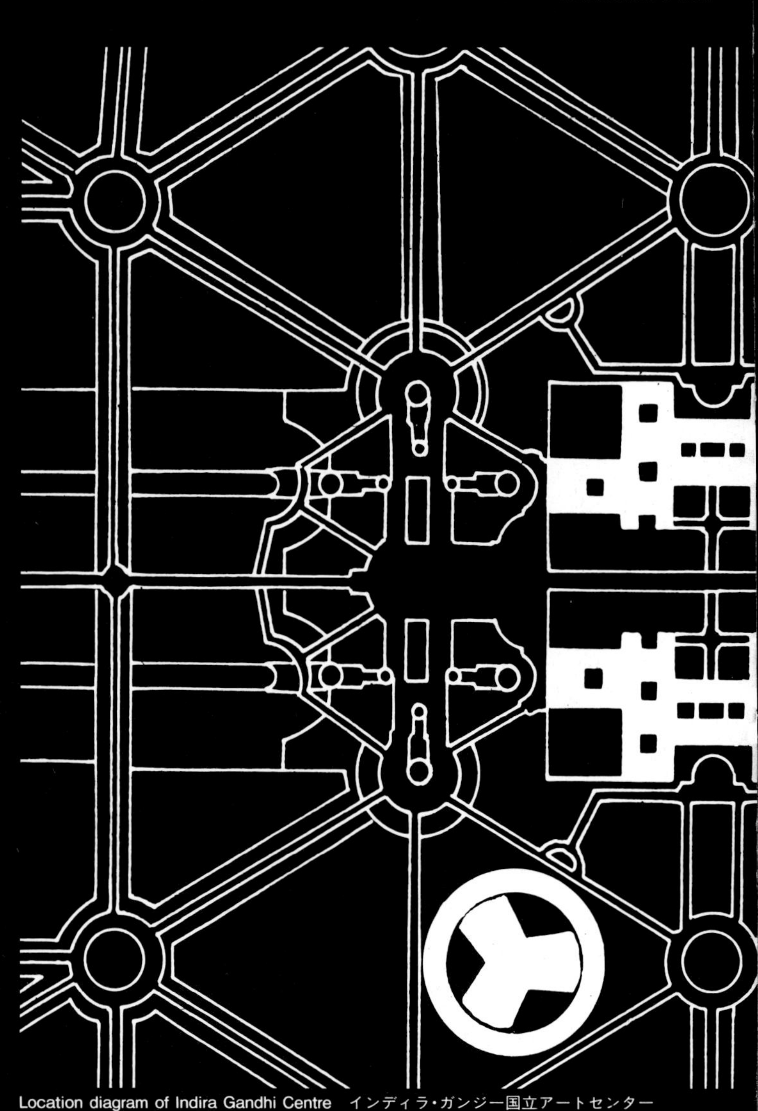

Location diagram of Indira Gandhi Centre インディラ・ガンジー国立アートセンター

公共建築

1980年代の英国では商業建築が主流を占める一方で，あらゆる公共建築は衰退の一路を辿っていた．フランスの「グラン・プロジェ」によって新しい学校やハウジングや健康施設などがどんどん整備されていくパリのそれと比較して，批評家の多くはこの英国の現状を批判していたのである．若手の建築家たちは商業施設によって成長していったが，反面，1950年代や60年代の優秀な設計事務所の創造の根本を構成していた公共的な仕事は存在しないままであった．

国内での公共的な仕事がないままに，英国の建築家は，いつの時代も若手建築家の登竜門である国際コンペによって外の世界で活躍を始めた．トロートン・マッカーズランの入選した２つのコンペ案は，残念ながら結局は実現されなかったが，それらのデザインは，他の国の伝統を尊重し，反映したモダンな建物であった．インディラ・ガンジー・センターのコンペ案は，彼らが活動を始めたばかりの，大きな建物の設計の経験がまだなかった頃の作品である．ニューデリーの敷地は，西欧の古典主義とインドのバナキュラーの両方の特質をもった，建築家エドウィン・ルチエンスを想起させる環境であった．マッカーズランの提案は，この計画の中心的なデザイナーであるアイダン・ポッターの支持に負うところが大きいのだが，最終12案の中に残った．計画に際して，彼らはこのコンペを開発のシンボルととらえ，ヨーロッパのモダニズムと東洋の伝統を調和させるということに真っ正面から取組むという方法は採用しなかった．

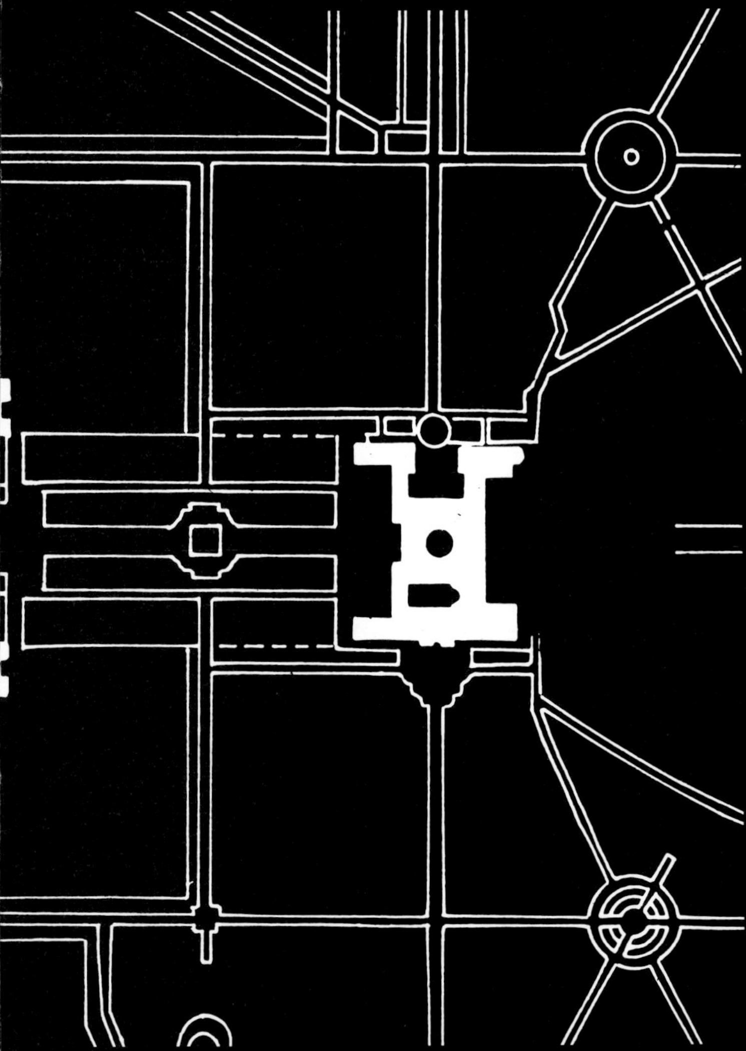

ナイロビ高等弁務官事務所のコンペでは事情は違っていた．地域のバナキュラーをどこに求めるのか，たとえばオーストラリアなどの他国に見習うべき前例があるのかといったことが問題としてあった．この計画の時期にはマッカーズランのイメージの中にはグレン・マーカットの作品が常に存在しており，ナイロビ計画ではそれが前面に出ている．いつも問題になることであるが，その国の気候に合った建物をつくり出すために必要なこととして，19世紀のケニアの建築がスタディされた．その結果，計画案は意識的にアンチ・モニュメンタルなもので，以前の植民地に支配国の力を誇示するようなデザインは一切排除されている．多分，モニュメンタリティの欠如は間違いだったのかもしれない．英国らしさを示すものはなにもなかったのである．しかしマッカーズランによると，このコンペは彼らにとって画期的な出来事であり，そのデザインは，特徴的な気候で，自然資源の乏しいケニアのような国にふさわしい，モダンで控え目に表現された，異なる文化に対応した刺激的なものであったという．

エジンバラのスコットランド博物館の設計コンペは，チェンバーズ・ストリートにある19世紀のロイヤル・スコティッシュ博物館の増築計画である．建築家の間で多くの国際的な関心と注目を集めた．371案のほとんどは英国の建築家のものであった．トロートン・マッカーズランはそれらの活発な建築家たちの中の１人として参加し，最終選考に残った．既存の博物館は内部空間は広々としているが，外観はどちらかというと地味で単調なデザインである．オリジナルはロバート・アダム設計の建物のある大学の近くに位置しているが，プリンス通りの古典主義建築の並ぶ地域やニュータウンや，ゴシックやピクチャレスク建築の残るオールドタウンなどからは少し離れている．トロートン・マッカーズランは，ディテールよりも戦略を必要とする状況に対応させて，建物の骨格を形成する案を提出した．自己満足的なピクチャレスク風を避けて，クラシック・モダンなデザインを打ち出した．ルイス・カーンの作品は彼らの仕事に多大な影響を与えているが，ここでは特にエール大学のポール・メロン・センターに見られる，通りや舗装を大事に強調したデザインとしている点を的確に参考にしている．完成すればこの計画は明快で，表情豊かな，そしてスコットランドの首府の景観にふさわしい風合いの建物となるだろう．数多くのすばらしいコンペ応募案の中でもたいへん興味深い提案であった．

トロートン・マッカーズランはまだ英国内では実際に公共建築を完成させていない．最近の公開コンペの結果，サセックスのベックスヒル・オン・シーにあるエリッヒ・メンデルゾーン設計の傑作であるデ・ラ・ワー・パビリオンの長期改修計画のためのプロポーザルが入選した．トロートン・マッカーズランがここでねらったのは感性の創出である．デザインは1930年代のロマンティック・モダニズムにしっかりと根ざしている．公共予算の配分変更によって，この計画が数年そのまま放置されている間に，トロートン・マッカーズランでは公共交通施設の改良のための新駅の設計やアクトン地下鉄職員訓練所計画などの設計が始まった．神戸のセント・キャサリン・カレッジ計画に，過去６年間，コンペ応募で学んだ数多くの教訓を活かして具体化している．

Indira Gandhi National Centre for Arts
New Delhi, India, 1986
インディラ・ガンジー国立アートセンター・コンペ案

The site for this major arts facility was on the Rajpath, the principal ceremonial route of New Delhi, at a point in Sir Edwin Lutyens' plan devoted to cultural institutions. The design was a response to the brief, the significance of the site and to the cultural diversity of India and of Delhi.

The five principal elements of the complex - administration block, art gallery, theatre, concert hall and research facility - were expressed as individual buildings, with four enclosing a raised piazza, and the fifth reached by a series of open and covered walkways at the end of a stepped garden. Within this plan public and private, and served and servant spaces were arranged into a clear hierarchy.

Elements of the scheme are reinterpretations of different periods of Delhi's architecture: its pitched walls and based on the Red Fort, and its elevated, open air exhibition walkway reinterprets the Chandhi Chowk bazaar. Connaught Place (the city's central commercial centre) becomes the southern arcade of the concert hall, the gardens are developed from Lutyen's gardens for the Viceroy's House, and the scheme's linear arrangement reflects that of the Rajpath. In this way the project becomes a reflection of Delhi's complex history and, by extension, that of India.

芸術活動の主施設となるこの計画の敷地は，エドウィン・ルチエンズ卿の計画では文教地区に割り当てられた地域にあり，ラジパス通りというニューデリーの主要な道路に面している．敷地の意味合い，そしてインドやデリーの文化的多様性といった概要に対応したデザインとなっている．

建物は管理棟，アートギャラリー，劇場，コンサートホール，研究棟の5つの主要素から構成される複合施設で，四周を壁で囲まれた広場と，4つの階段状の中庭，その向こう端に位置する，屋根つきの連絡通路によってアプローチする5つ目の広場をもつ，それぞれ独立した建物として表現されている．この平面計画によって，プライベートとパブリック，サービスする側とされる側の空間が明快なヒエラルキーに分割されている．

計画の構成要素は，デリーの建築における各時代の再解釈である．レッドフォートからの引用である傾斜のある壁面，高架の開放的な展示通路はチャンディ・チョーク・バザールの新解釈である．市の商業地区の中心であるコノート・プレイスはコンサートホール南側のアーケードになり，庭園はルチエンのバイスロイハウスの庭から引用された．全体の線状の配置はラジパス通りを反映している．このように，デリーの，あるいは拡大的にいえばインドの複雑な歴史を反映したプロジェクトとなっている．

Plaza level plan and site plan　プラザレベル平面

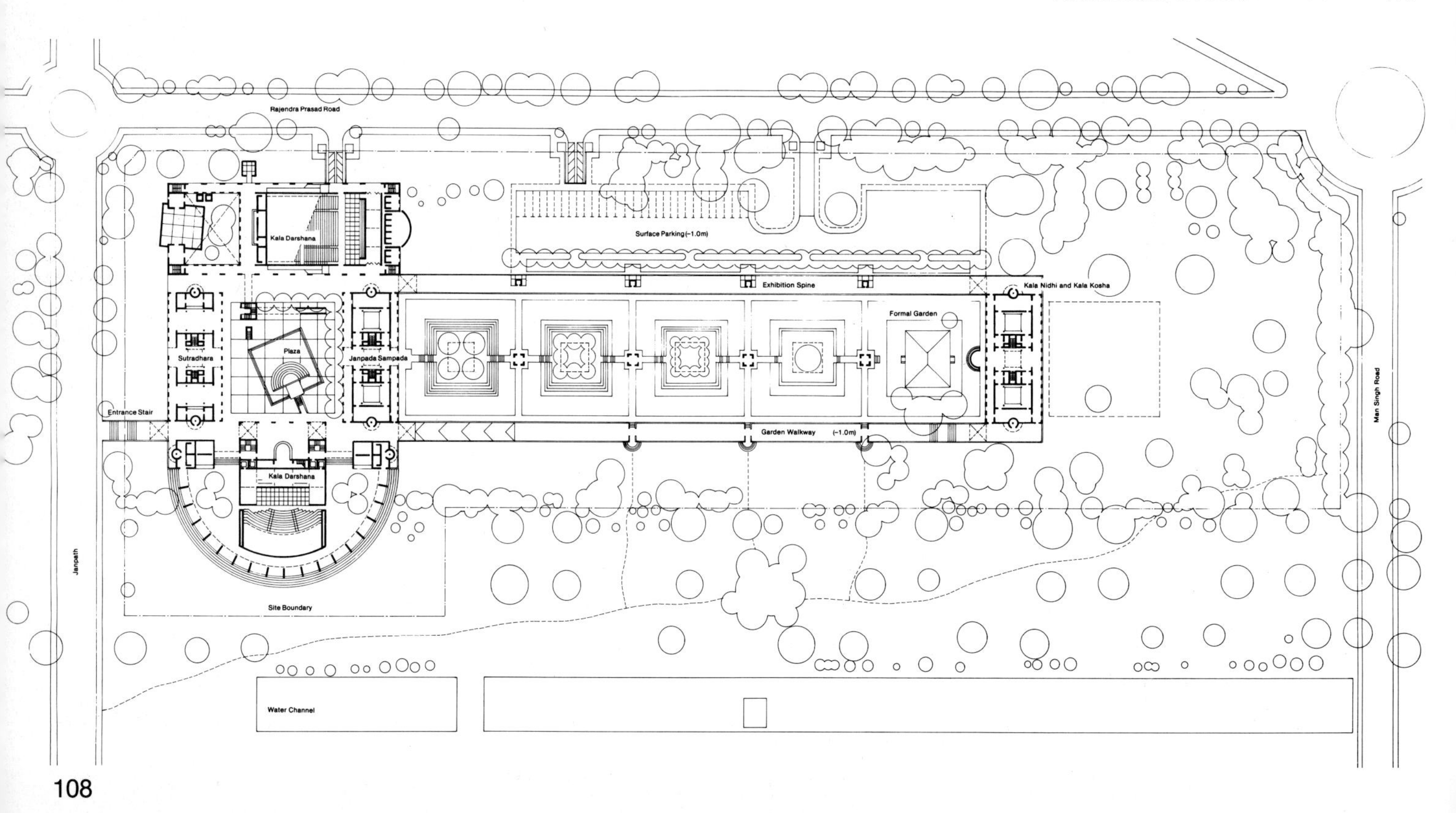

View of the model looking east 東側からみた計画案全体

Sectional elevation

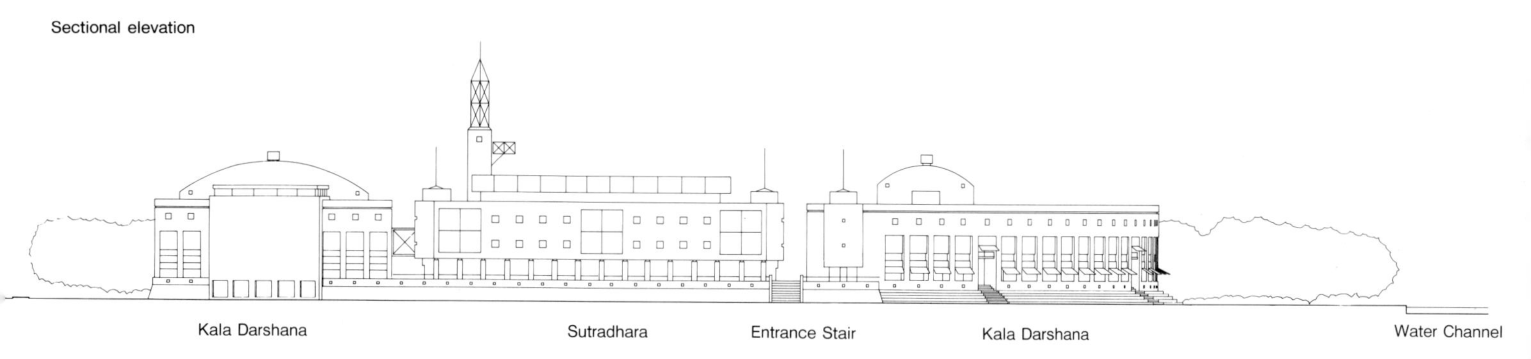

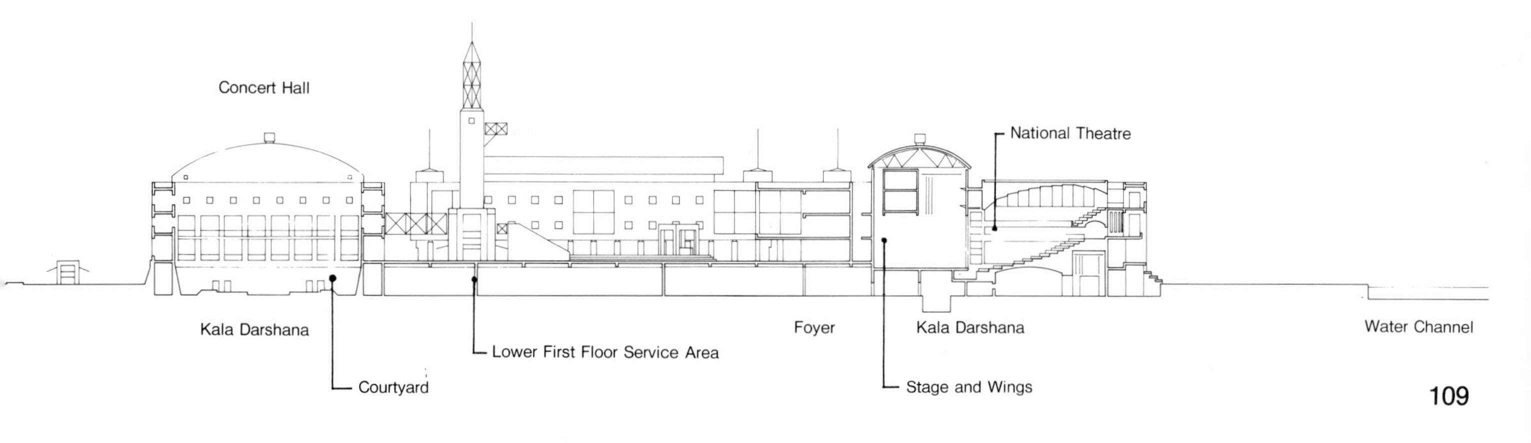

Offices for the British High Commission

Nairobi, Kenya, 1989

ケニヤ英国高等弁務官事務所

Perspective sketch from the garden　庭からながめたスケッチ

Troughton McAslan were one of three practices shortlisted to prepare designs for the proposed British High Commission building in Nairobi. The site is on a wooded hillside in a residential area overlooking the city.

The organisation of the project is simple: the diverse functions of the brief are represented by one larger building, the Chancery, and by three smaller buildings stepping down the slope towards Nairobi. All are designed using the same architectural language, modified to create major and subsidiary spaces, with the more formal, rectilinear entrance court giving way to a garden that retains existing contours and trees. The diversity of the spaces is given a consistency by the unity of treatment.

Rather than draw on Kenya's rather scanty architectural heritage, Troughton McAslan sought to create a more abstracted language that responded to climate, to local building conditions and to new technologies, and drew on both indigenous and European responses to hot climates. In particular, they were influenced by British colonial architecture, and by the work of Glenn Murcutt in Australia, Renzo Piano in Texas, and Charles and Ray Eames in California. In this way the design recognises the dual character of the High Commission as both a European and a local institution: its role is to represent the interests of the United Kingdom within the context of Kenya and East Africa.

The result is a series of concrete framed structures which could be readily erected by local contractors and infilled with glazed and timber panels manufactured off site. This simple system is then enlivened and modelled by aluminium louvres to deflect direct sunlight, and unified by deep eaved, curved roofs in lead coated stainless steel that float above the structure. The shallowness of the elevations is offset by heavy shadows and deep recesses for stairs and verandahs. The orientation and sections of the buildings are designed to make the best use of prevailing winds for cross-ventilation.

By basing the construction of the buildings on simple constraints, and using materials ranging from the crudest to the most refined, the design has a vernacular quality but is quite new. It achieves the dignity required of a diplomatic building, while remaining informal and without authoritarian overtones.

トロートン・マッカーズランは，このプロジェクトのデザインをまとめる3人の建築家の1人に選ばれた．敷地はナイロビの市街地を見下ろす住宅地で，木々の生い茂る丘の斜面にある．

構成はたいへんシンプルである．求められた多様な機能に対して，1棟の大きな建物である大法官庁と，ナイロビに向かって斜面を少しずつ下がる3棟の小さな建物から構成される．4棟はすべて同じ建築言語を用いてつくられ，既存の等高線や樹木を保護した庭を中心に，フォーマルで直線で囲まれた玄関前庭をもった，主従関係の明確な空間をつくり出している．これらの多様な空間が建築的な統一で調和を保っている．

ケニヤの乏しい建築遺産は直接は受け継がず，トロートン・マッカーズランは，この地方の気候や建築事情に見合った，そして新しい技術に呼応した抽象的な言語で，なおかつ土着であると同時に熱帯気候にふさわしいヨーロッパ建築の両者から引用してデザインすることを意図した．特に，英国の植民地建築，たとえばオーストラリアのグレーン・マーカット，テキサスのレンゾ・ピアノ，カリフォルニアのチャールズ＋レイ・イームズの作品に強い影響を受けた．このように，ケニヤおよび東アフリカのコンテクストの中で英国の権利を代表するという役割を含めて，高等弁務官のヨーロッパ風と地元の組織という両面性を象徴したデザインを採用している．

建物は地元の施工業者でもすぐに建てられるように，コンクリートのフレーム構造とし，工場生産のガラスおよび木製のパネルを外壁にはめ込んでいる．このシンプルなシステムに，直射日光を避けるアルミのルーバーが彩りを添え，深い軒の出，建物本体からは浮き上がった鉛引きのステンレスのカーブする屋根などによってさまざまな変化が加えられている．エレベーションの低さは階段部分やベランダがつくり出す深い影や凹みによって補完し合っている．建物の向きや断面は，建物間の風通しを考えて最も有効なデザインとしてまとめている．

建物の建設は簡単な制約の範囲内を基本として，また最も素朴な素材から，最も洗練された素材までを使い，結果としてデザインはたいへん新しい意味でのバナキュラー的な特質を有している．外交的な施設に要求される威厳をつくり出し，その一方でフォーマルでなく，権威主義的な行きすぎもなしに，うまくまとめられた．

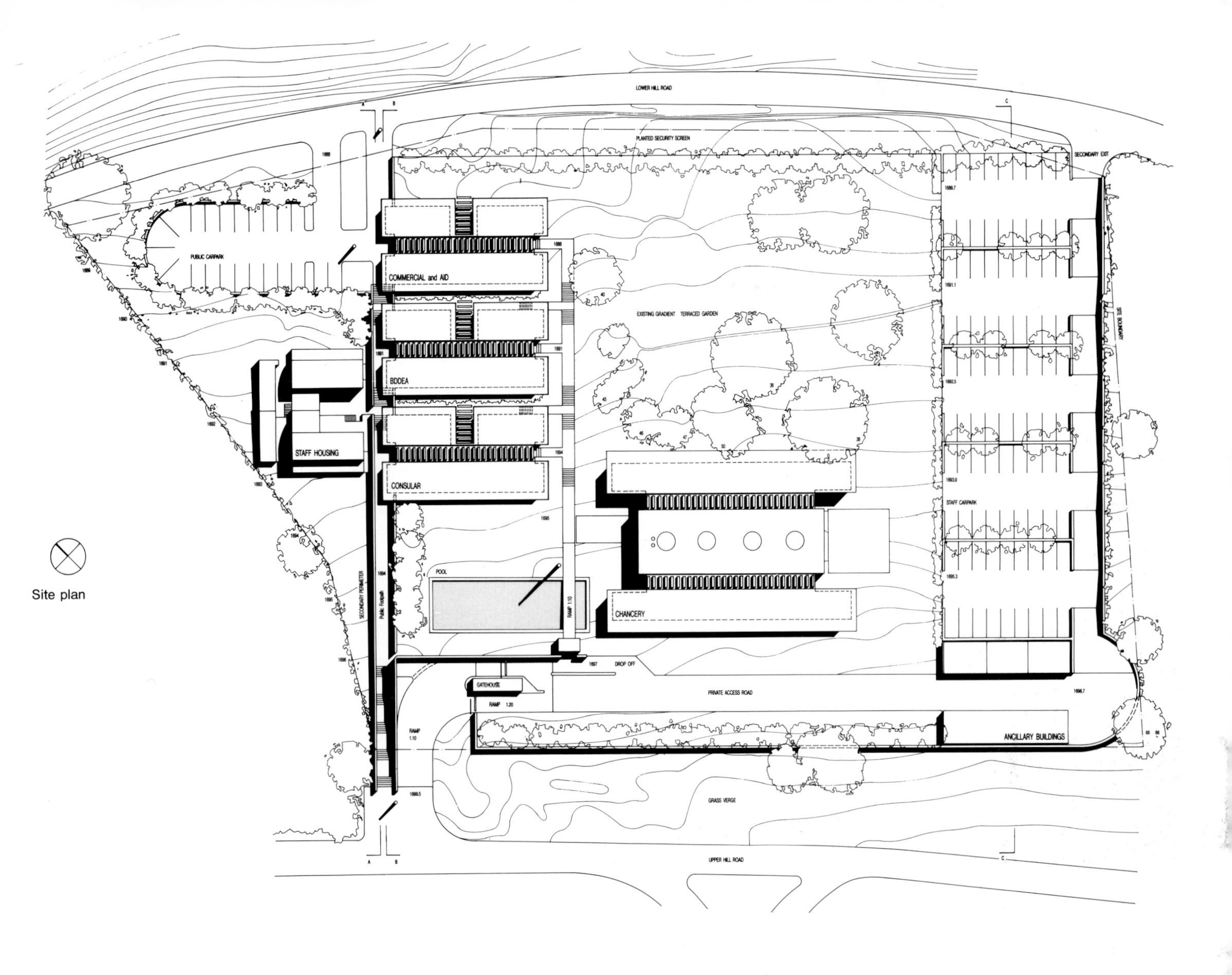

Site plan

Model view　手前段状になった駐車場　*Photo by Eamonn O'Mahoney*

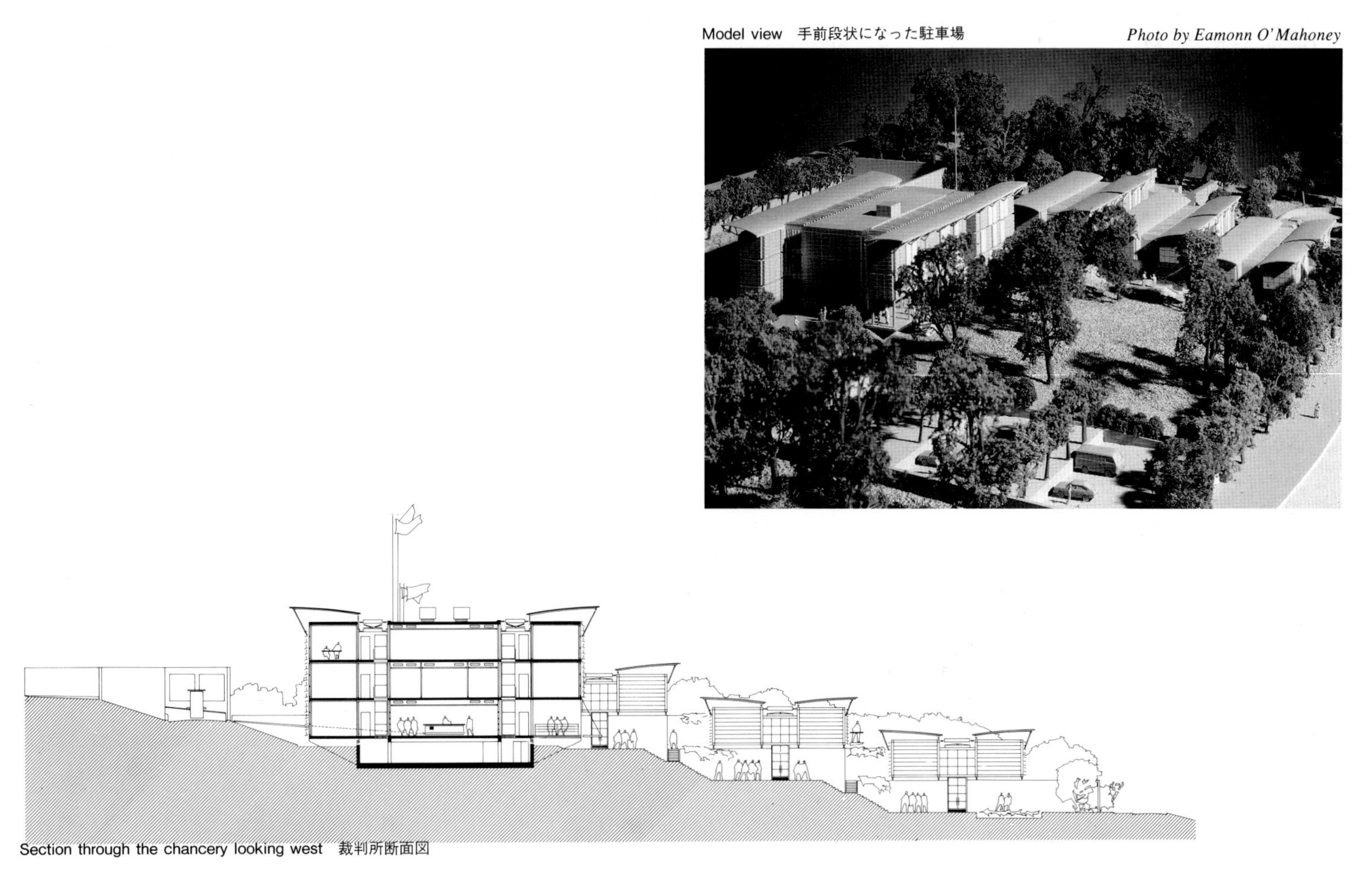

Section through the chancery looking west　裁判所断面図

De La Warr Pavilion
Bexhill-on-Sea, England, 1992
デ・ラ・ワー・パビリオン

The De La Warr Pavilion, Bexhill-on-Sea (1935) was designed by Erich Mendelsohn and Serge Chermayeff as an entertainments building, accommodating an auditorium seating 1,000, function rooms, library, restaurant, support facilities and extensive south facing external terraces.

The Pavilion is acknowledged as an important work in the history of the Modern Movement and was listed Grade 1 in 1986. With a structure of welded steel sections, the building was technically innovative and is one of the few surviving examples of Mendelsohn's work.

Over a period of fifty years the Pavilion has been modified, mainly internally, to meet changing demands. These alterations have never matched the quality of the original concept and as a result, the overall refurbishment and future use of the building have become matters for serious consideration.

The Pavilion Trust, formed in 1989 to assist in the conservation of the building, commissioned Troughton McAslan to prepare a Stage One report for the refurbishment of the Pavilion. Troughton McAslan's report suggests that the refurbishment of the building should take place over a period of years, returning the building to the quality of the original while incorporating a range of new uses.

ベックスヒル・オン・シーに1935年完成のデ・ラ・ワー・パビリオンは，エリッヒ・メンデルゾーンとセルジュ・シャマイエフ設計の1,000席のオーディトリアム，図書室，レストラン，管理諸室から構成される娯楽施設で，南面の広々としたテラスに沿って建っている．

パビリオンは，近代建築運動の歴史の中で重要な作品であり，1986年に第１級の保存すべき建物に指定されている．溶接スチール構造で，技術的にも非常に革新的で，現存する数少ないメンデルゾーンの作品の１つである．

50余年の間に，建物は主に内部が用途変更に伴ってつくり変えられていた．こうした変更はオリジナルのコンセプトには合わないものであったため，全体的な復元改修および将来的な建物の用途について，根本的に考え直す必要が生じていた．

建物の保存を支援するためのパビリオン・トラストが1989年に設立され，トロートン・マッカーズランはパビリオン改修の第１段階のレポート作成を依頼された．トロートン・マッカーズランは，この中で改修は長い年月をかけて，新しい用途に合わせつつも，建物本来の特質に引き戻すべきであると報告している．

Photo by RCHM

Building exterior 既存建物外観

Photo by RCHM

Photo by Martin Charles

Building interior 既存建物内観

Existing floor plans indicating the principal alterations since the Pavilion's completion in 1935

1 Lobby and hall altered and inner lobby screen added
2 Foyer altered and lift inserted
3 Temporary kitchen extension constructed
4 Cafeteria and restaurant altered.
5 Conference hall volume and interior altered to become Edinburgh Room, with offices added on second floor
6 Lounge and library replaced by bar and Elizabeth Room
7 Sun parlour enclosed to accommodate storage

1935年パビリオン完成時から現在に至るまでの主な改装

1. ロビーとホールが変更され，ロビースクリーンがつけられた．
2. ホワイエ変更．エレベーターを設置．
3. 臨時の厨房増築．
4. カフェテリアとレストランの部分的改装．
5. 会議室の大きさと内装を変え，3階に事務所をつけてエジンバラ・ルームとした．
6. ラウンジと図書室から，バーとエリザベス・ルームへ変更．
7. サン・パーラーを改装して倉庫を付設．

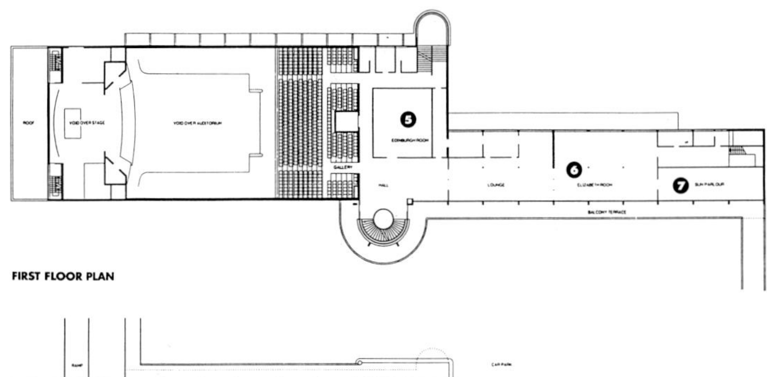

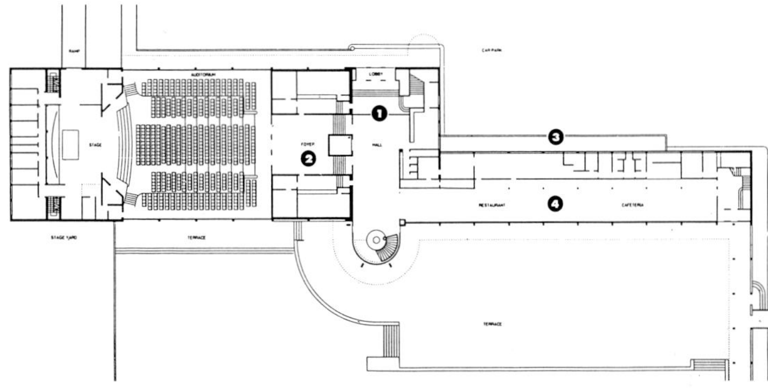

Proposed alterations to be investigated in Stage Two

1 Reorganise carparking, servicing and pedestrian access, improve external paving finishes, replace windbreak screen and orchestra stand, complete structural repairs, improve external wall finishes, reinstate original signage
2 Construct a two-level extension to provide additional kitchen space on the ground floor, offices and storage space on the first floor, and a secondary means of escape from the second –floor roof terrace. Remove offices from the second floor and storage from the sun parlour. Generally refurbish interiors to stairs and landings
3 Refurbish lobby and hall, remove inner lobby screen, restore entrance doors, provide new ticket and office areas
4 Refurbish foyer and relocate bar
5 Generally refurbish auditorium, replace seating, enlarge and improve stage and back–stage facilities, improve services
6 Refurbish restaurant and cafeteria
7 Reinstate sun parlour and relocate storange in first floor of proposed new extension
8 Refurbish Edinburgh Room and Elizabeth Room, remove suspended ceilings, improve services and reorganise partitions

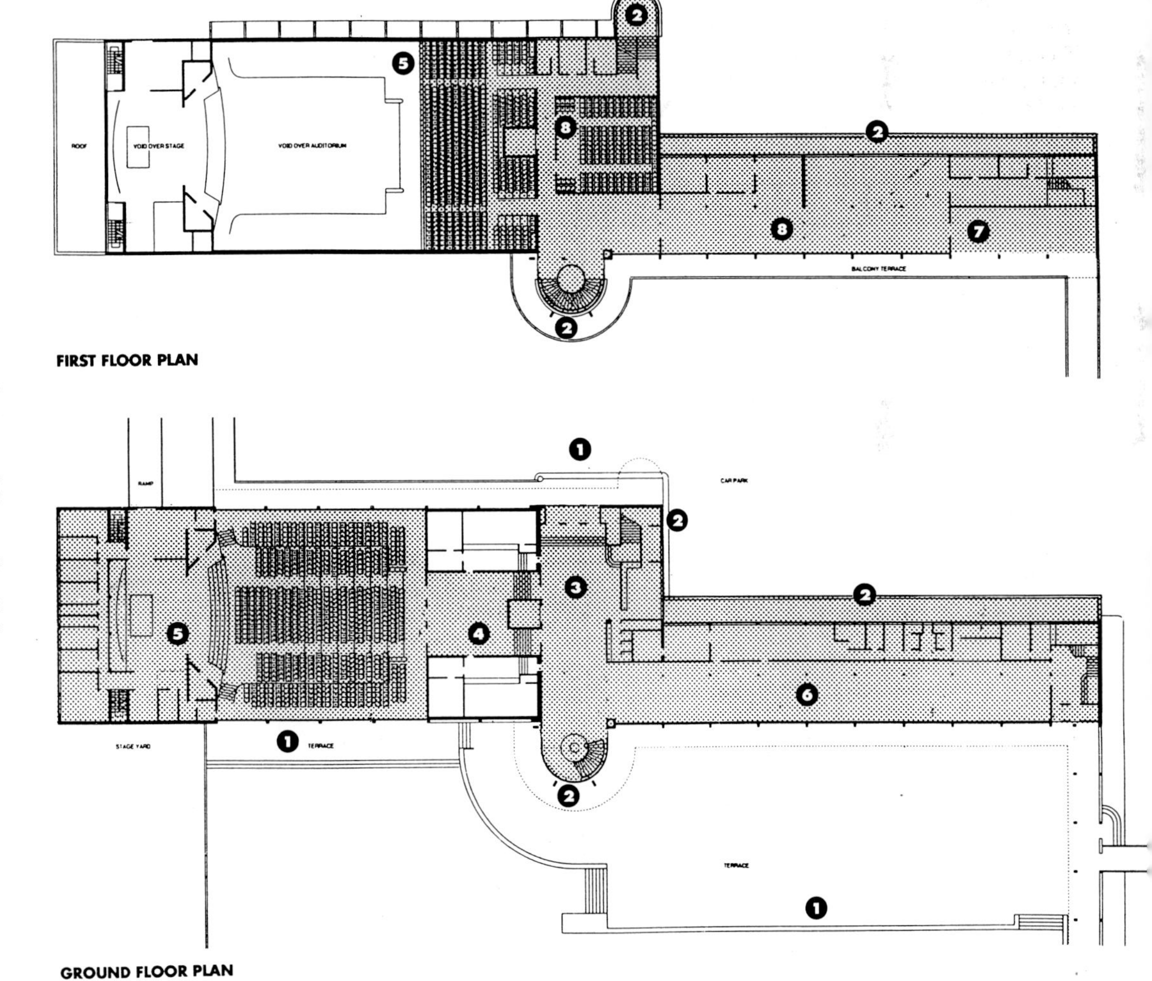

プロポーザルの概要

1. 駐車場，サービス，ペデストリアン・アクセスの再編制．外部舗装仕上げ改良．風除スクリーン，オーケストラ・スタンドの移動．構造体修復の完了．外壁仕上げ変更，オリジナルサイン全体の修復．
2. 2層分の増築によって3階のルーフテラスに避難口を設け，1階に厨房を新しくつくる．現在3階にある事務所とサン・パーラーにある倉庫を2階増築部分に移動．階段と踊り場の改装．
3. ロビー，ホール改装．屋内ロビーのスクリーンをなくし，入口ドア修復．新しくチケットカウンターと事務空間をつくる．
4. ホワイエ改装，バーの移動．
5. オーディトリアム改装，座席配置移動．舞台，舞台裏設備の拡張と再構成．サービス空間の整理．
6. レストラン，カフェテリアの改装．
7. サン・パーラー修復．2階倉庫を増築部分へ移動．
8. エジンバラ・ルームとエリザベス・ルームの改装．吊天井の移動，サービス，パーティションの再編成．

Museum of Scotland
Edinburgh, Scotland, 1991

スコットランド博物館・コンペ案

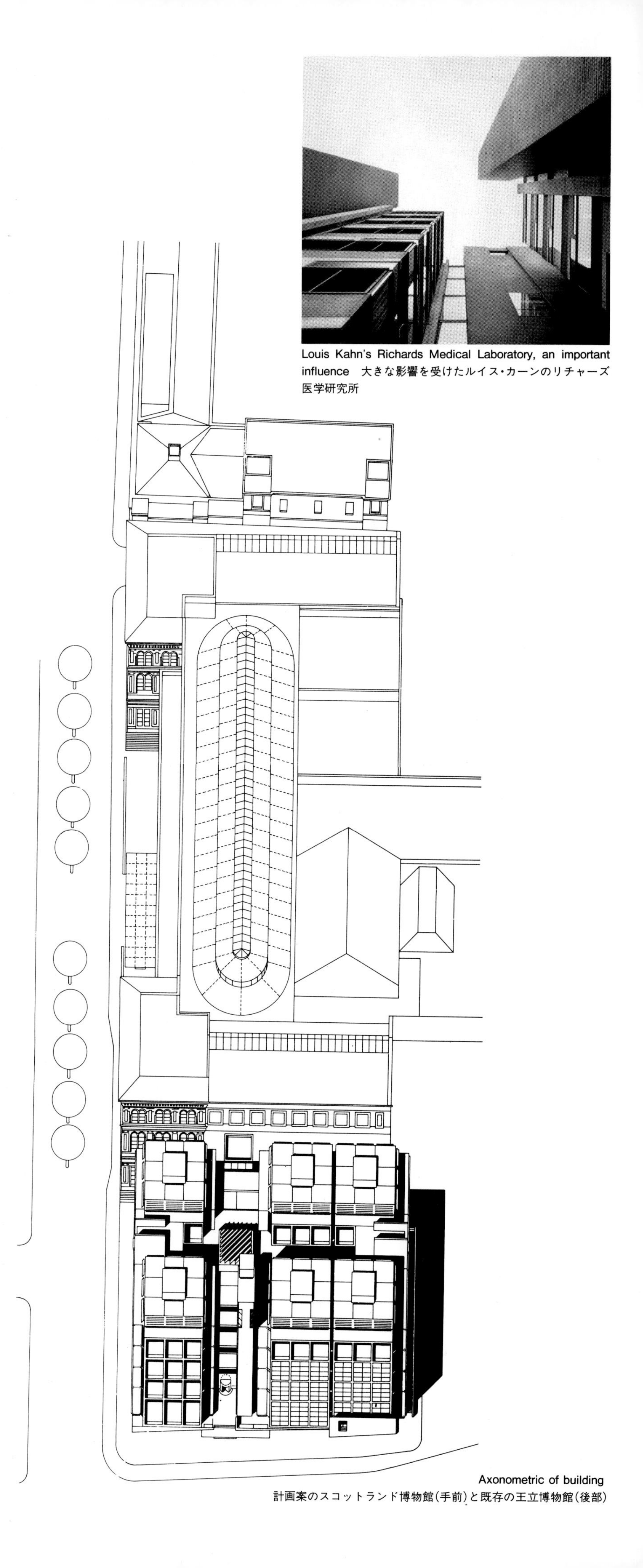

Louis Kahn's Richards Medical Laboratory, an important influence　大きな影響を受けたルイス・カーンのリチャーズ医学研究所

The existing building which houses the Royal Museum collection and onto which the Museum of Scotland will adjoin - was completed in 1861 and is listed grade "A". It is an engineer's building - with the "architecture" applied as a skin to the iron and glass structure which forms its core. Externally, it is a severe, factory-age version of the Renaissance palazzo. The magic is inside, in the form of the great central hall.

The site is beyond Robert Adam's Edinburgh University building, and is set apart from the "historic" Royal Mile; with an immediate context which is very mixed. Chambers Street has become a car-clogged enclave. South Bridge consists mostly of nineteenth century commercial buildings of no great consequence. There are dramatic views out from parts of the site - to the Castle and beyond.

Troughton McAslan's approach is akin to that of Asplund at the Gothenburg Law Courts or Connell, Ward & Lucas at The Firs, Redhill: a refusal to imitate the style of the existing building combined with a respect for its scale and form.

One radical move is proposed in the case of the existing listed building: the excision of the steep flight of steps to Chambers Street, currently flanked by murky parking places. A far more convenient and dramatic access is provided by entering the heart of the museum and taking a staircase into the centre of the main hall - with a directional thrust towards the new building. The latter is unselfconsciously, classically modern and represents a significant statement about the relationship between modern architecture and Scottish tradition which goes beyond the facile "Mackintosh: pioneer of modern design" approach.

The building echoes the economy of means and robustness of a traditional Scottish building, with a subtle bow to the tower-house form and to the trabeated progressive Classicism of the Glasgow school. The Museum of Scotland is a buiding for Scotland - it rightly reflects broad Scottish influences.

Like Louis Kahn's Mellon Art Gallery at New Haven, Troughton McAslan's building is streetwise: it squares up to the street and pavements and there is considerable potential for creating views through and into the structure from the street. Rigorously planned and taking its cue from Fowke, the building makes dramatic use of natural light inside and culminates in a top-lit cortile on the axis of the Fowke hall.

In a scene dominated by nostalgia, the building makes a bold statement about the possibilities of a new Scottish architecture. Its materials are durable, varied, appropriate. In its tight urban setting the romantic modernism of the architecture seems entirely at home. The new building responds to the site and adds a new dimension to the definition of Scottishness in architecture.

Axonometric of building
計画案のスコットランド博物館(手前)と既存の王立博物館(後部)

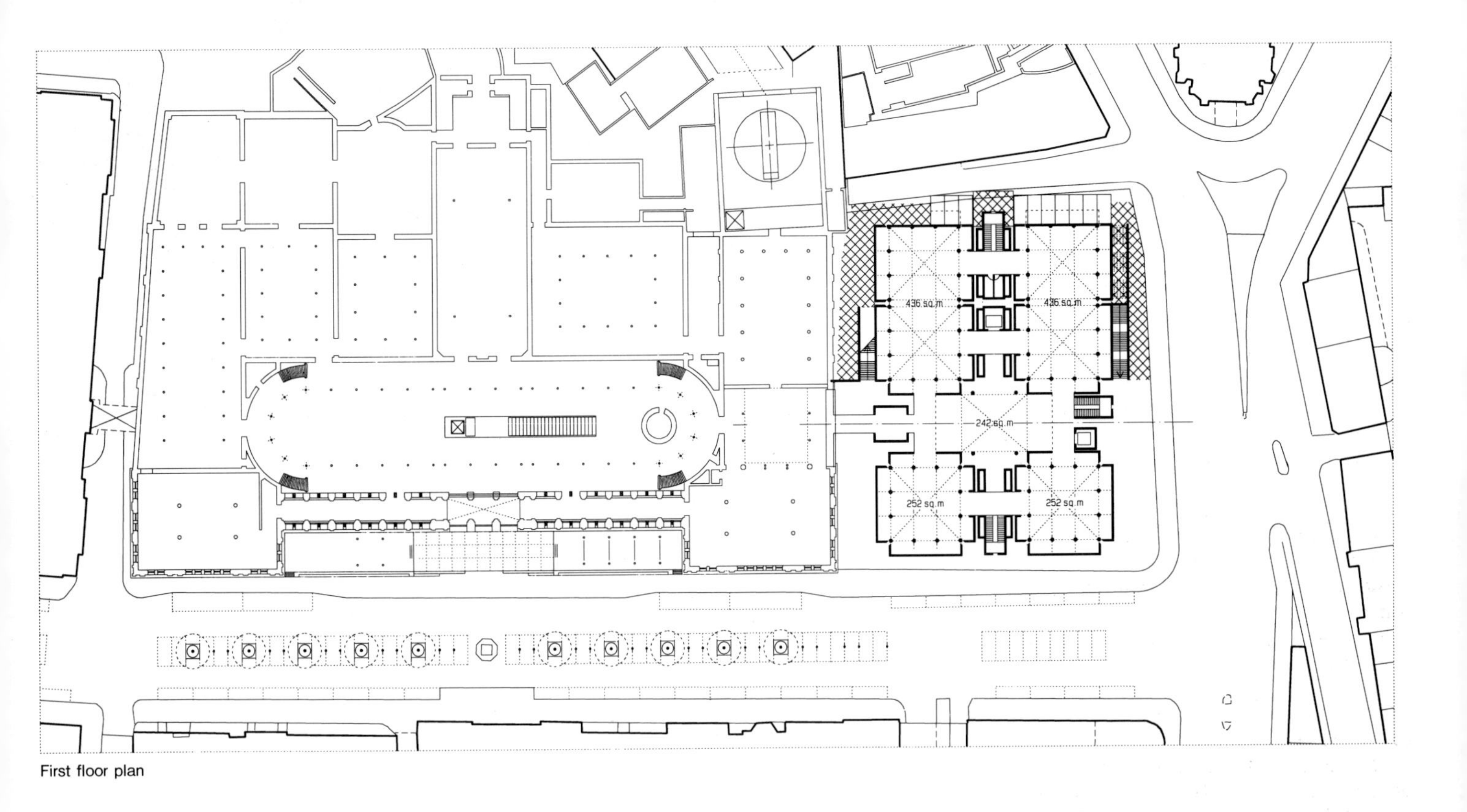

First floor plan

Street elevation in context with the existing Royal Museum
既存の王立博物館(左)とつながる計画建物

Sectional elevation

既存の建物は1861年に完成したもので，王立博物館のコレクションを収蔵し，Aクラスにランクされている重要な建築遺産である．ここにスコットランド博物館が隣接して建てられることになった．鉄とガラスによって建物コア部分を構成する，建築家ではなく技術家の手による傑作である．ルネッサンスのパラッツォをもっと質素にした工場のような外観に比して，内部の大きな中央ホールはまるでマジックのようである．

敷地はロバート・アダムのエジンバラ大学の先にあり，歴史的なロイヤル・マイルが一際目立って建っている．周辺は非常に混在したコンテクストの地区である．チェンバーズ・ストリートは交通量の多い通りで，サウスブリッジ地区は，それぞれなんの関係もない19世紀の商業建築が密集して建っている．ここからは，エジンバラ城の方向にドラマチックな眺望が開けている．

トロートン・マッカーズランはまず，アスプルンドのグーテンベルク裁判所やコーネル，ウォード・アンド・ルーカスのレッドヒルに建つザ・ファーを参考にしてアプローチした．すなわち，既存の建物のスタイルを，そのスケールや形態において踏襲することへの拒絶である．

ただ1つ，既存の保存建物に対して，うす汚れた駐車場にとり囲まれて現存する，チェンバーズ・ストリートに面した急勾配の階段を取り除くことを提案した．そして，もっと使いやすくドラマティックな導入部を提示した．それは，新しい建物に直接とりつく形で，博物館の中心に直接入り，メインホールの中央まで階段を使ってアプローチするものである．これは，無意識ではあるがクラシック・モダンの様相を呈し，モダンデザインのパイオニア，マッキントッシュの軽快なアプローチにもまさるモダンとスコットランドの伝統の結合への新しい提案である．

また，この建物はグラスゴー派の塔状の形態や，まぐさつきの進歩的な古典主義に対して敬意を表しながら，伝統的なスコットランド風の建物のもつ質素さや力強さを反映している．

ルイス・カーンのニューヘブンのメロン・アートギャラリーのように，トロートン・マッカーズランの建物は周辺環境にふさわしいもので，通りから四角く建ち上がり，見通しがよく，表通りから内部の様子を伺うことができる．厳密に計画され，フォークに見習った建物は，内部に自然光をドラマティックに導入し，フォークホールの軸線上に位置するトップライトのある内庭でその頂点に達する．

郷愁ということでいえば，この建物は新しいスコットランド風建築への大胆な提案といえる．素材は耐久性があり，多種多様で，それぞれふさわしい．密集地という周辺環境に対して，ロマンティック・モダニズムの建築がぴったりの場を得ている．新しい建物は敷地周辺に呼応し，建築のスコットランドらしという定義に新しい側面を加えることになった．

MASTER PLANNING

Troughton McAslan fully share in the New Modern concern for urban values - the campaign to repair historic British townscapes damaged by insensitive post-war development is not just a priority for Post Modernists of the Terry Farrell school. Reclaiming the street matters to Troughton McAslan.

The practice has itself had to respond to the masterplans of others on previously featureless sites like Stockley Park and Canary Wharf on the fringes of London without being able to influence the overall character of those developments. However with recent schemes in Liverpool and Edinburgh, they have been able to develop urban masterplans from the outset. Both cities have enormous - though very different - character. In both, there are great opportunities to repair the urban damage of the past.

Liverpool has become a byword in Britain for economic decline and the social problems which are its inevitable consequence. However, major steps have been taken in recent years to counteract the steady rundown of the city, once one of the greatest ports in the world. The regeneration of Albert Dock as offices, shopping, museums, apartments and leisure facilities was a notable achievement - this is probably the finest group of historic dock buildings in the world.

North of Albert Dock and of the imposing group of buildings at the Pierhead lies Prince's Dock, where only the "listed" 19th century walls and gates survive. Within them, everything had been cleared. A competition was held to determine the future form of the site. The aim was to reintegrate the Dock into the city centre (close at hand, but currently utterly isolated from it). There were monuments to relate to - the Pierhead and the old church of St Nicholas, for example. The practice proposes a landmark tower to add a new element to the city skyline. A congress hall will form the focus of a commercial development of the land, and a series of phased commercial buildings placed either side of the dock walls.

In Edinburgh, the railway carved its way through the valley below the Old Town and New Town in the mid 19th century and Waverley Station grew into an enormous complex under its spreading glass and steel roofs. The station is a vast and impenetrable barrier in the city, ill-planned and unsightly. British Rail has been considering a redevelopment to unlock the commercial potential of the site and rationalise railway operations. McAslan was concerned to put forward a positive proposal for Waverley - his intention to avoid placing a major new commercial development across the valley as a physical barrier and to initiate a dialogue in the city about the future of this historic site.

Both these schemes illustrate the ambitions of Troughton McAslan to work on a wider canvas - beyond the design of individual buildings - and their rejection of many current planning orthodoxies. The rigour and imagination of their buildings needs to be seen on an urban scale. ***—Kenneth Powell***

リバプールは英国の経済衰退の地として，またその必然的な結果としての社会的問題の多い都市として悪名高い．しかし，昨今はかつては世界一の港湾都市であった市の減退を跳ね返し復興させるための確実なステップが踏み出され始めている．その目玉となるのが，アルバートドックをオフィス，ショッピング，美術館，アパート，レジャー施設などからなる複合施設に再生する計画である．アルバートドックは，世界の歴史的なドック施設の中でもおそらく最もすばらしいところである．

アルバートドックの北，ピアヘッドに堂々と建ち並ぶ建物の北側にプリンスドックがある．ここには，保存対象に挙げられた19世紀の壁とゲートだけが残っている．内部はなにも残っていない．この敷地の将来計画についてのコンペが催された．市中心部の近くでありながら，現状では隔離されて全く孤立化しているドック地区を，再び一体化することが目的であった．ここには，ピアヘッドや聖ニコラス教会などの歴史に関連の深いモニュメントがあった．トロートン・マッカーズランは，この敷地に市のスカイラインの新しい要素としてのランドマークタワーを加えることを提案している．会議場がコマーシャルな開発計画の中心施設となり，ドックの壁面に沿って両側に商業施設が段階的に建設される．

エジンバラでは，19世紀半ばに新旧の市街地の間の谷間を貫いて鉄道が開通した．そしてウェイバリー駅は，大きく広がるガラスとスチールの屋根に覆われてどんどん巨大化していった．市にとって駅は，実は通り抜けることのできない，計画のむずかしい，見通しの悪い巨大な障壁である．英国国鉄はウェイバリーの敷地の商業的な可能性を見つけ出し，開発することを考え始めた．国鉄側の設計意図としては，新たな商業施設が谷の反対側で展開されて別な障壁となるのを回避し，この歴史的な敷地の将来的展望として，市中心部を活性化したいということであった．

これらの計画は両者とも，トロートン・マッカーズランの，それまでの個々の建物のデザインという枠を超えて，さらに広いキャンバスでの仕事への熱意を誘い出し，現行の計画手法に対しての拒絶を明らかにさせた．彼らのデザインする建物の厳密さやイマジネーションは都市的スケールで眺めて，初めてよく見えてくる．

Waverley Station model photograph　ウェイバリー駅模型
Photo by Eamonn O'Mahoney

Waverley Station Redevelopment

Edinburgh, Scotland, 1992

ウェイバリー駅再開発計画

This prizewinning competition proposal is for the transformation of land between the Old and New Towns of Edinburgh, at present dominated by railway tracks and Waverley Station. Troughton McAslan envisage a "green valley", which would mediate the two halves of the city, emphasising their individual identities.

The new space, built above the railway lines, would recall the original, pre-industrial valley within the more ordered framework of a square, bounded by lines of trees. The scheme also proposes a major new development to the east of North Bridge built to fund the station works, and the transformation of the two arches of North Bridge into dramatic glass-walled public spaces. In the centre of the square Troughton McAslan propose a new steel and glass station building. To the east and west, the railway lines will remain uncovered, preserving the familiar views enjoyed by railway travellers.

With an unprejudiced combination of landscaping and carefully placed architecture, Troughton McAslan aim to preserve the existing character of the site, while recalling its past and creating a new public space at the heart of Edinburgh. Where the railway is at present wholly divisive, Troughton McAslan are proposing a more complex space, part natural, part urban, part engineering, that will both unify the city and define its dual character.

現存のエジンバラの新旧の市街地の間に横たわる鉄道の線路と駅舎を，新たな施設として開発する計画のコンペ入選案である．提案は，それぞれの個性を活かしつつ，二分された街を仲介する緑の谷間を創出することをねらった．

線路の上に構築される新しい空間は，広場や並木による秩序正しい構成で，元来の工業化以前の谷間を想起させる．同時に，駅施設建設資金を調達するために架けられたノースブリッジの東側を新たに開発し，橋の2つのアーチを印象的なガラスで囲われたパブリックな空間に転換することも提案された．広場の中央には，新しくスチールとガラスの駅舎が建設される．東側と西側では線路は露出したままに残され，旅行者に親しみのある光景を残す．

ランドスケーピングと注意深く配置された建物のバランスによって，トロートン・マッカーズランはエジンバラの中心に，過去を継承し，新たな公共空間を創出しつつ，敷地のもっている特性を保存することを目指した．現在は鉄道が障壁となっているが，トロートン・マッカーズランは，ある意味では自然で，かつ都市的・人工的，技術的な，より複合化した空間をつくることで，市を一体化させ，市のもつ二重の特性をよりはっきりさせることをねらった．

Aerial view of the site looking east　既存の駅を東からみる

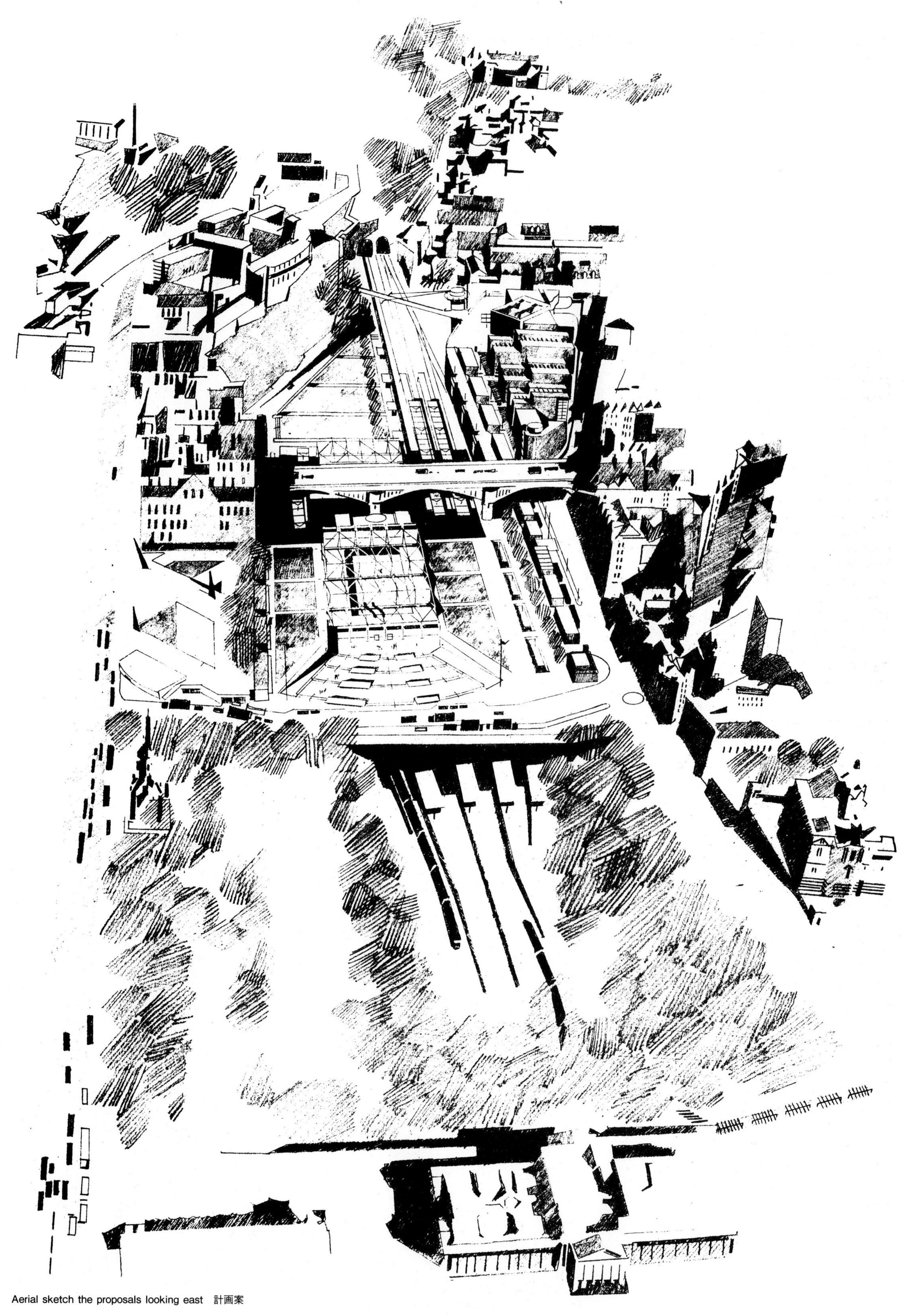

Aerial sketch the proposals looking east　計画案

Aerial model view

The city of Edinburgh in 1823　1823年のエジンバラの市街

Prince's Dock

Liverpool, England, 1991

プリンスドック

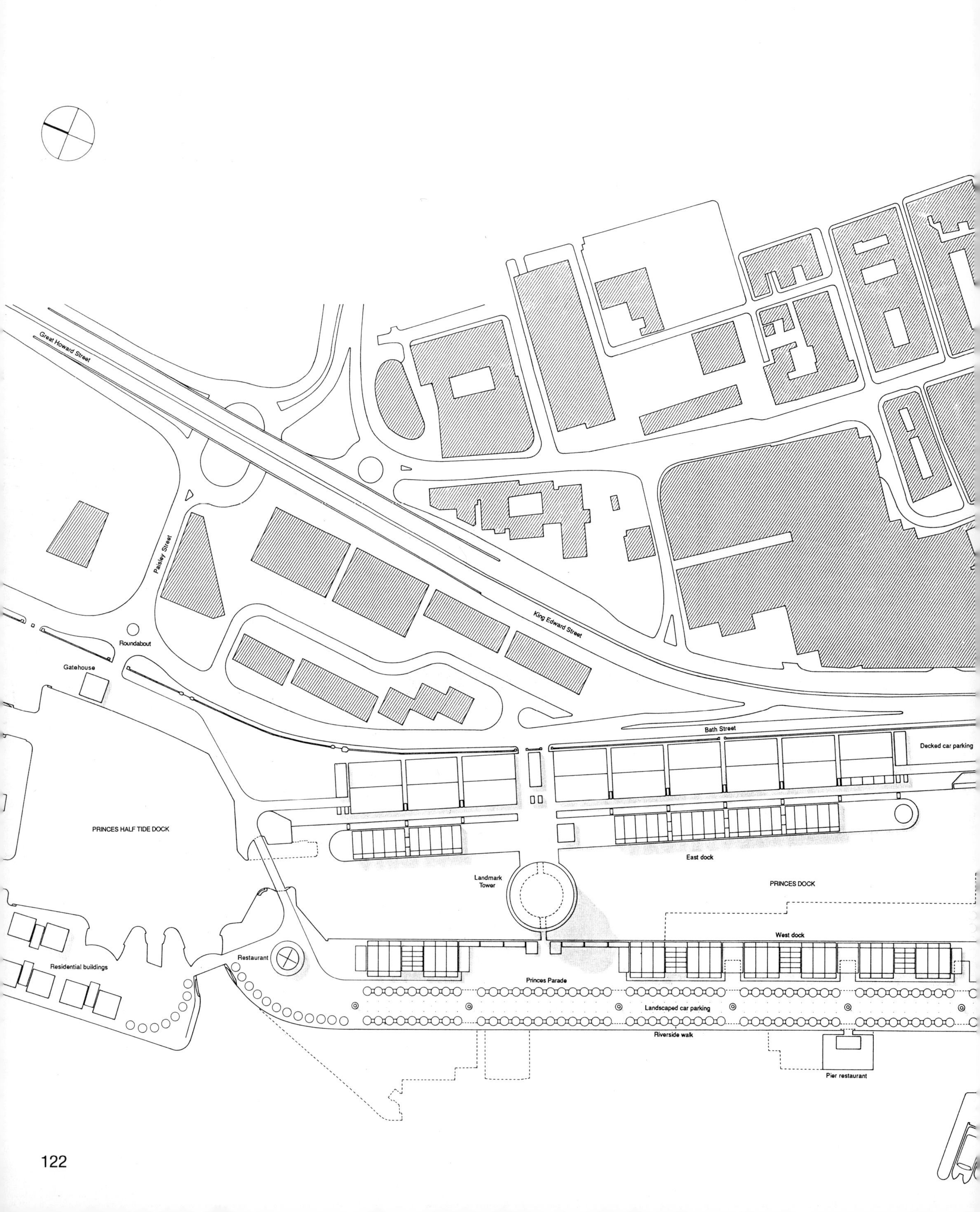

SCHEDULE OF ACCOMMODATION
Total office
accommodation / 48,850m² gross
(including 2,600m² ground floor
retail/leisure)

Retail/leisure
buildings / 840m² gross

Grade
car parking / 526 spaces

Car parking
structures / 1,080 spaces

MASTERPLAN DESCRIPTION

- The fully developed masterplan proposal for the Princes Half Dock and Princes Tide Dock is illustrated above.
- The strategy for the masterplan would need to remain flexible to allow options for phased development to occur, with the essential features of the design being apparent during each phase of the works.
- The principle elements of the masterplan are as follows:
- The grain of the City centre and Waterfront extend into Princes Dock.
- It is essential to preserve and express the historic features of the site; principally Dock walls and water and Dock boundary wall, while enhancing the environment adjacent to the Pierhead listed buildings and St Nicholas Church.
- The scale, orientation and sequence of buildings and landscape respond to the form of the Dock and Waterfront, and respect the protected views and axes of the Royal Liver Building, St Nicholas Church and Chapel Street.
- The 'fragile' office market in Liverpool increases the necessity for the development to respond to 'real' demand rather than speculative demand. This should result in the creation of a working community within Princes Dock, relating to its historic surroundings and existing City centre commercial areas, while taking particular advantage of the Waterfront location.
- It is important to improve pedestrian links to the site from the City centre and re generated Waterfront, and to provide arcaded pedestrian walkways around the proposed Dockside buildings.
- It is necessary to maximise the accessibility of the site, and in particular to link the northern part of Princes Dock to public transport facilities.
- It is necessary to minimise the visual impact of car parking and access roads on the site by the sensitive design of car parking structures, landscaped grade car parking, and by the use of qualitative materials.
- The landscape design extends the principles of the Pierhead proposals into Princes Dock, and should be visually complete during each phase of the development.
- The form and orientation of buildings and landscape respond to environmental conditions, and in particular protect pedestrians and building users from wind and sea spray, traffic noise, and direct or reflected glare.
- The masterplan responds to the particular features of the site's enclosure, The lower buildings to either side of the Dock might be solid in form, reflecting the scale and massing of the Albert Dock buildings. The Tower is conceived as a crystalline structure in constrast to the solidity of the Royal Liver Building and its Edwardian neighbours.

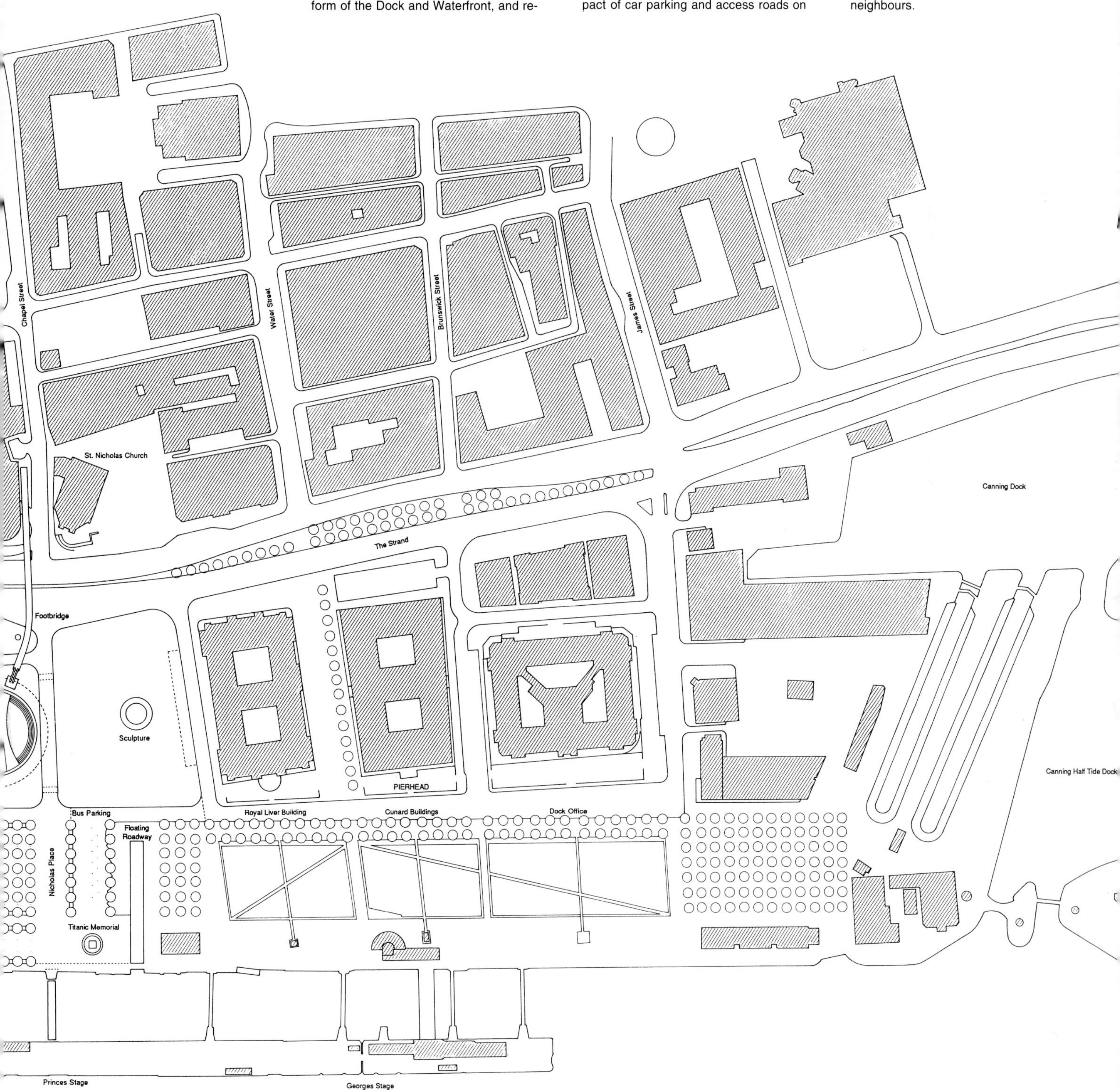

So far the renaissance of Liverpool's stupendous, but long neglected, network of docks has focussed on the area to the south of Pierhead - on the magnificent Albert Dock and, more recently, on Wapping Dock. With the revival of the Pierhead itself as a focus of the city, attention turns naturally to the northern docks.

Princes Dock, originally created in 1816-21 and reconstructed after 1860 by Jesse Hartley's successor, G Fosbery Lyster, is clearly a key element in that process.

At Albert Dock and Wapping Dock, the primary task was to bring the existing buildings back into use. At Princes Dock, the principal existing feature is the listed dock wall - itself, ironically, designed to isolate the docks from the city while the dominant concern today is to integrate docks and waterfronts into the life of Liverpool. Post war developments, including the King Edward Street and Great Howard Street dual carriageway, have actually increased the separation.

The group of commercial buildings at the Pierhead has long been ackowledged as a prime symbol of the city, rising out of the regular ranks of Victorian brick warehouses. Troughton McAslan's masterplan for Princes Dock, centred around their proposed fourteen storey glazed tower, would create a late 20th century counterpart to the baroque exuberance of the Royal Liver Building and the Gothic elegance of Thomas Harrison's St Nicholas spire. But their proposals are essentially rooted in a respect of the rigourous classicism of the 19th century warehouse, with three and four storey blocks sitting along the dock water's edge.

The proposals confront the basic problem in the replanning of dockland areas - the conflict between integration and the need to preserve the special identity of the historic location while creating a new urban pattern appropriate to the new uses on the site. Eschewing picturesqueness, they have a basic rigour which is in tune with the 19th century engineering tradition (and in contrast to the visual anarchy of much post-war building in Liverpool) while allowing for the opening-up of the dock as a public domain. The established pattern of the docks is echoed, yet the spaces provide for a range of uses and are humanised by the variety of surfaces, by tree planting, and by the provision of pavilions and other small structures. A new square, with the Liver Building to the south and focussing on the proposed "congress hall" to the north, forms a climax for routes to the site from the city centre. Pedestrians approach the space via a footbridge from Chapel Street or across the Strand at Water Street and Brunswick Street - then link with an ambitious riverside walk passing through Pierhead to Albert Dock.

The scheme is ambitious. But a pragmatic approach to phasing makes it a viable proposal. The masterplan, which reflects a respect for history and community, accords well with this objective. The revived Princes Dock would underline the status of the Pierhead as a prestigious gateway and centrepiece of 21st century Liverpool. The city has spent too long rejecting its past. The last 20 years has seen a gradual change of heart, with conservation and reuse as central themes. Liverpool now has to come to terms with new design. Troughton McAslan's pragmatic, history-conscious plan could provide the context for Liverpool's new dockland quarter, part of the city's return to the river from which its international fame derives.

Model photographs

リバプールの，長い間見捨てられていた広大なドックの再生計画は，最初はピアヘッドの南側地区，すばらしいアルバートドックから開始され，近頃ではワッピングドックにまで展開してきていた．ピアヘッドが市の中心として復活したことによって，さらに北側地域が注目され始めたのは当然の成り行きであった．

元来は1816年から21年にかけて造成されたプリンスドックは，1860年以降にジェス・ハートレーの後継者であるフォスベリー・リスターによって再建され，この開発プロセスにおける重要な鍵になった．

アルバートドックやワッピングドックでは，既存の建物の再利用が主眼とされたが，プリンスドックでは，現存する保存構造物はドックの壁面だけである．これは皮肉なことに，当初は市街地とドックを隔離するために建てられたものであるが，今日ではドックやウォーターフロントをリバプールの市民生活に融合させることが考えられているのである．キング・エドワード・ストリートやグレート・ハワード・ストリートといった戦後の道路開発によって，市街地の分断が一層進んでしまっていた．

ピアヘッドの場合は，商業施設群は，規則正しく並ぶビクトリア風のレンガ倉庫からなり，長い間市のシンボルとして親しまれてきた．14層のガラス張りのタワーを中心に配置したトロートン・マッカーズランのプリンスドック・マスタープランは，ロイヤル・リバービルのようなバロックの豊穣，トーマス・ハリソンの聖ニコラス教会の尖塔のようなゴシックのエレガンスに対抗する20世紀後半の創造である．この提案は，基本的にはドックの水際に沿って３層または４層で建ち並ぶ19世紀の倉庫の厳格な古典主義に根ざしている．

しかし，敷地に求められる新しい機能に見合う新たな都市空間を創造する一方で，歴史的な地区独特の個性を調和させながら保存するという，ドック地域再計画の基本的な課題に直面した．奇抜さは避け，19世紀の技術の伝統に則った厳格さを基調にし，逆にリバプールの戦後建てられた無秩序な建物には対抗させながら，ドックを公共の土地として開放していく方向を打ち出した．ドックのもっていた既存のパターンは踏襲されるが，空間は用途にしたがって使い分けられ，植栽や小さなパビリオンや構築物を付加することで居心地のいい空間にしている．南にリバービル，北側には新しく建設される会議場施設が建つ間に位置する新たな広場は，市街地中心部から敷地へのルートのクライマックスを形成する．歩行者はチャペル・ストリートから歩道橋を渡って，あるいはウォーター・ストリートとブランズウィック・ストリートの交点を越えてアプローチし，ピアヘッドからアルバートドックを結ぶ川沿いの活気ある遊歩道に連なっていく．

企画は意気揚々としたものであるが，実現させるためには，実際の計画を段階的なものにしなければならない．地域の歴史とコミュニティの特性を反映したマスタープランは，これらの目的にうまく合致している．復活したプリンスドックは，21世紀のリバプールの選ばれたゲートウェイとなり，中心的な施設としてピアヘッドのステータスとなる．リバプールはあまりにも長い間その過去を無視してきた．この20年ほどは少しづつ意識を変え，保存や再利用に目を向けるようになった．そして，今日にいたってようやく新たなデザインが生まれるところまで来たのである．トロートン・マッカーズランの実際的で歴史を充分考慮したデザインは，リバプールのドックランド地区に新たなコンテクストを付加し，国際的な名声を引き出す川沿いへ市を引き戻すことに，大きく寄与することになるだろう．

Aerial views of site

EDUCATION BUILDINGS

Troughton McAslan's portfolio of work has been principally commercial in character, the outcome of a marked downturn in public sector building in Britain in the 1980s and not untypical of young British practices. In the 1960s, in contrast, the UK had expanded its education system rapidly and private sector architects found plentiful commissions for universities and colleges while local authority architects' departments were responsible for a large number of schools.

However, there is now a new emphasis on the need for education and training in Britain and the practice is well-equipped to participate in the task of providing new education buildings. Admittedly, Troughton McAslan's only experience in the field of strictly educational design in Britain to date has been their unbuilt project to refashion and extend 1960s buildings at the City University, London.

The ActonTraining Centre is a rather different (but, in many ways, a more demanding) proposition - a facility for training staff of the London Underground system in practical matters. The building will bring together a number of activities currently spread across London which demand spaces ranging in character from workshops to straightforward classrooms. In form, the building has a picturesque, accretive quality appropriate to its purpose, with an internal "street" at its core. A high degree of flexibility in planning

教育研修施設

トロートン・マッカーズランの作品を眺めると，1980年代の英国の公共建築分野の著しい沈滞の結果，圧倒的にコマーシャルの分野のものが多い．これはまた，若手の建築家には典型的なパターンでもある．これとは逆に1960年代の英国では，教育システムを急速に拡張したために，プライベートに活動する建築家にとっては大学や各種カレッジの設計の仕事，そして地方自治体などの公共団体に所属する建築家にとっては，多数の学校施設の仕事があったのである．

しかし今日では，また別な意味で英国の教育研修施設の必要性が生まれ，新たな教育施設を供給するために必要な知識が求められている．厳密な意味でのトロートン・マッカーズランのこの分野における唯一の経験は，ロンドン市立大学の1960年代の建物の改修・増築計画であるが，これは実際には実現しなかった．

アクトン地下鉄職員訓練センターは，いわゆる教育施設とは少し趣きが異なり，実際には大変注意を要する施設であるが，ロンドンの地下鉄システムのスタッフの実際の訓練施設である．建物は，ロンドン中に広がる地下鉄網における，さまざまな活動を対象とするために，ワークショップから直線的な教室(実際の鉄道や車両を使うわけであるから)にいたるまでのさまざまな空間が必要とされた．建物は中央に内部のストリートを有し，目的にふさわしい，魅力的で成長増大する形態となっている．平面計画における高度なフレキシビリティの確保は設計条件でもあった．トロートン・マッカーズランは常にフレキシブ

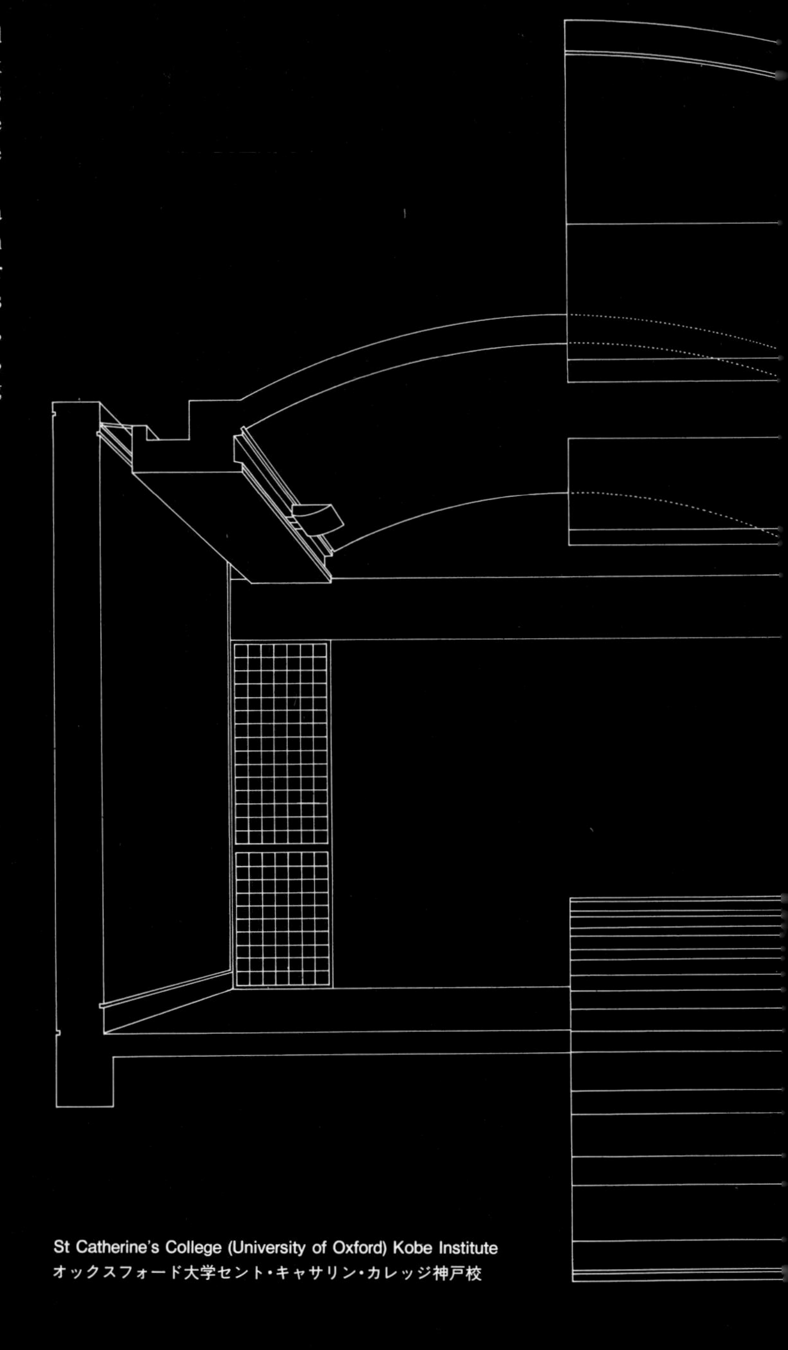

St Catherine's College (University of Oxford) Kobe Institute
オックスフォード大学セント・キャサリン・カレッジ神戸校

was also demanded in the Brief. Troughton McAslan have always rejected the inflexible megastructure, the monumental statement, in favour of buildings which contribute to and take their cue from the urban scene. The Acton Centre is in tune with that philosophy. It suggests that the firm could produce some very interesting schools and colleges given the opportunity.

This opportunity has arisen, ironically, not in Britain but in Japan, where the recently completed Kobe Institute for St Catherine's College, Oxford, represents one of the firm's most interesting designs to date. The Japanese sponsors had the sense to appreciate the qualities of Arne Jacobsen's original, 1960s college - an austere modern counterpoise to the lush romanticism of Oxford. An existing building had to be remodelled (a Troughton McAslan speciality) and the new blocks arranged so as to form a quadrangle. The form reflects the unusual character of the scheme : a Japanese outpost of a quintessentially English institution. The college with its dramatic site overlooking Osaka Bay manages to achieve a 1960s rigour with hints of Jacobsen's Scandinavian romanticism.

Acton and Kobe are worlds apart, but together they begin to suggest an approach to the design of educational buildings which contains the necessary qualities of a good education: flexibility and discipline, rigour and open-mindedness.

—Kenneth Powell

ルでない構成やモニュメンタルな造形を拒否し，周辺環境にふさわしい，そこになにかを寄与できるような建築を好んでデザインしてきた．アクトンセンターはこのフィロソフィに一致した計画である．このことからも，トロートン・マッカーズランは機会さえあれば，大変興味深いさまざまな学校施設を設計するだろうことが予測できる．

それは皮肉にも英国ではなく，日本において，絶好の機会がやってきた．オックスフォード大学セント・キャサリン・カレッジ神戸校が最近完成し，マッカーズランの今日までの代表作といえるものである．オックスフォードの華やかなロマンティシズムにバランスした清楚なモダン建築として，1960年代にアルネ・ヤコブセンが設計したキャンパスの建物を，日本のスポンサーが大変高く評価していた．この既存の建物はトロートン・マッカーズランの得意の分野であるが，改造され，新しいブロックが加えられて，四角く中庭を囲む形になった．最も英国的な施設の日本への移入である．大阪湾を見下ろすすばらしい敷地に建つカレッジは，ヤコブセンのスカンジナビア風のロマンティシズムを漂わせながら1960年代の清楚さをもって建っている．

アクトンセンターと神戸の作品は，全く異なる場所にあるが，両者ともにすぐれた教育に必要とされる特質，つまりフレキシビリティ，秩序，簡素，そして開放性といったものを包含した教育施設のデザインのあり方を示唆している．

St. Catherine's College (University of Oxford), Kobe Institute

Kobe, Hyogo, Japan, 1991

オックスフォード大学セント・キャサリン・カレッジ神戸校

View looking north 北側からの眺め
Photo by Hiroyuki Hirai

The Kobe Institute of St Catherine's College Oxford (the first ever overseas branch Institute of any of the Oxford Colleges) represents the meeting of two powerful cultures: of Japanese industry with a European university. This duality is reflected in the architecture: the brief is for a traditional Oxford college in miniature, with housing for students and tutors, teaching and administration space, library, dining hall and common room; but the site could hardly be more remote from Oxford. Perched on a steep wooded hillside on Rokko Mountain, it commands an impressive view of Kobe and Osaka Bay beyond.

Offering one-year courses taught in English, the Kobe school is the first such project by an Oxford college outside the city of Oxford, and Troughton McAslan's task was to reinterpret the essential qualities of the Oxford college in response to the wholly new setting.

In this they could draw on the precedent of St Catherine's which, built in 1963 by Arne Jacobsen on a semi-rural site, is itself untypical.

The design responds to the narrow site with a linear, rhythmic quality that is reminiscent of Jacobsen, as well as drawing more directly on traditional colleges. Like these, it is centred about a quadrangle which focusses and mediates the varied functions of the college, each of which is clearly articulated. The quadrangle is formed by the remodelled existing building on the north side and the newly built lecture theatre and to the south by a row of connected new concrete framed and stone clad buildings containing student and tutors' housing recalling in their design both Jacobsen and the traditional college. To accommodate the site's magnificent views, the students' and tutors' housing blocks frame an opening on the south side that also admits views to the existing main building either side of a concrete framed clock tower.

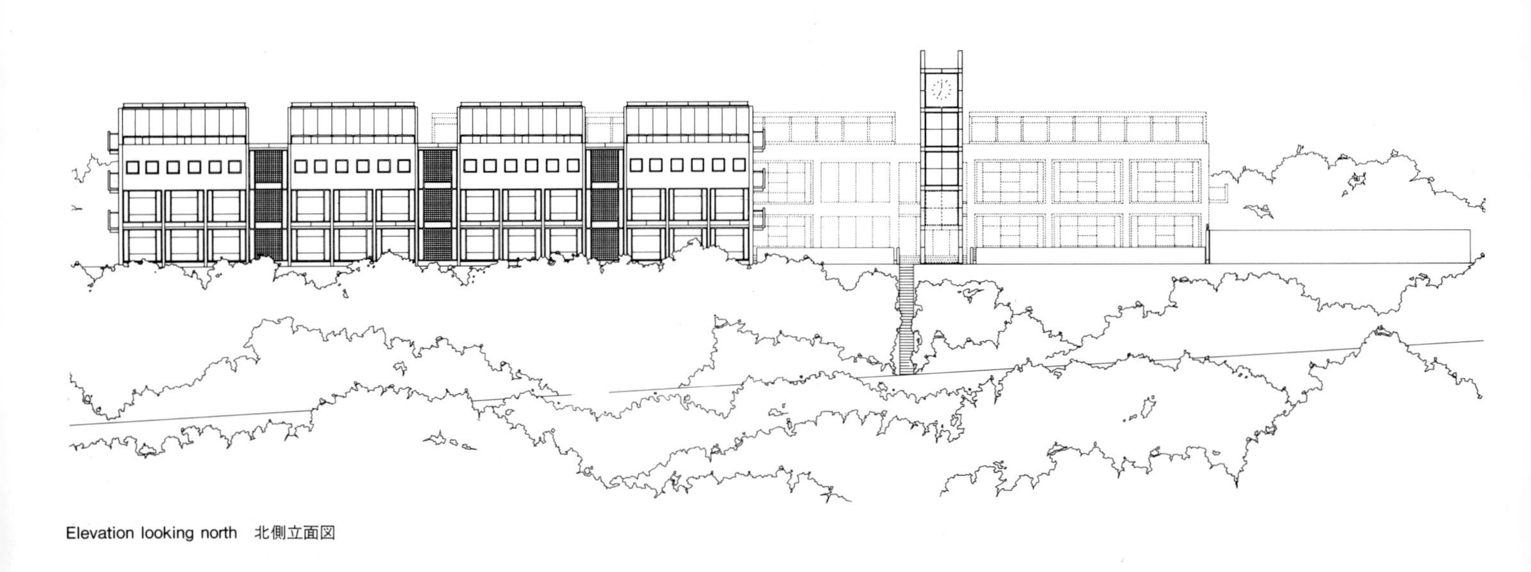

Elevation looking north 北側立面図

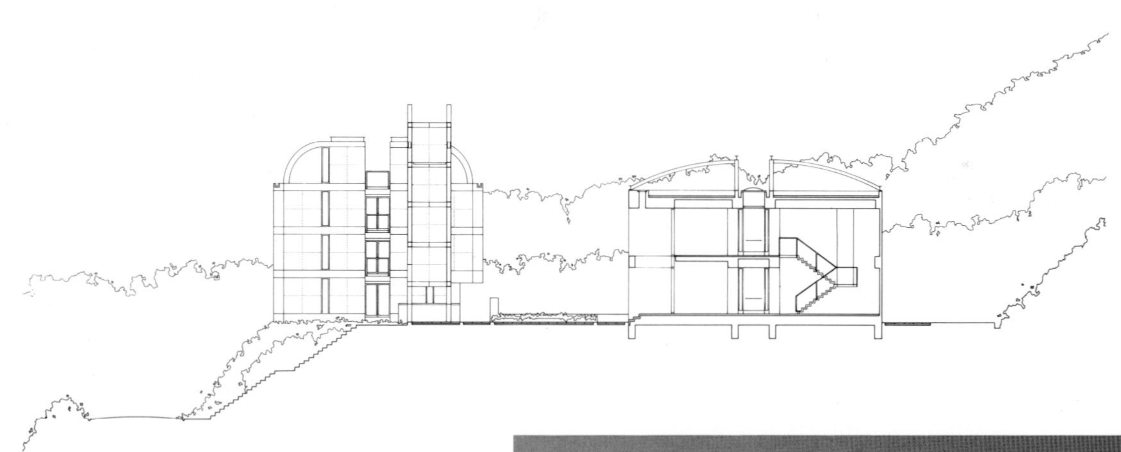

Section looking west 西側断面図

Photo by Hiroyuki Hirai

View of the Kobe Institute from the main entrance 神戸校正門

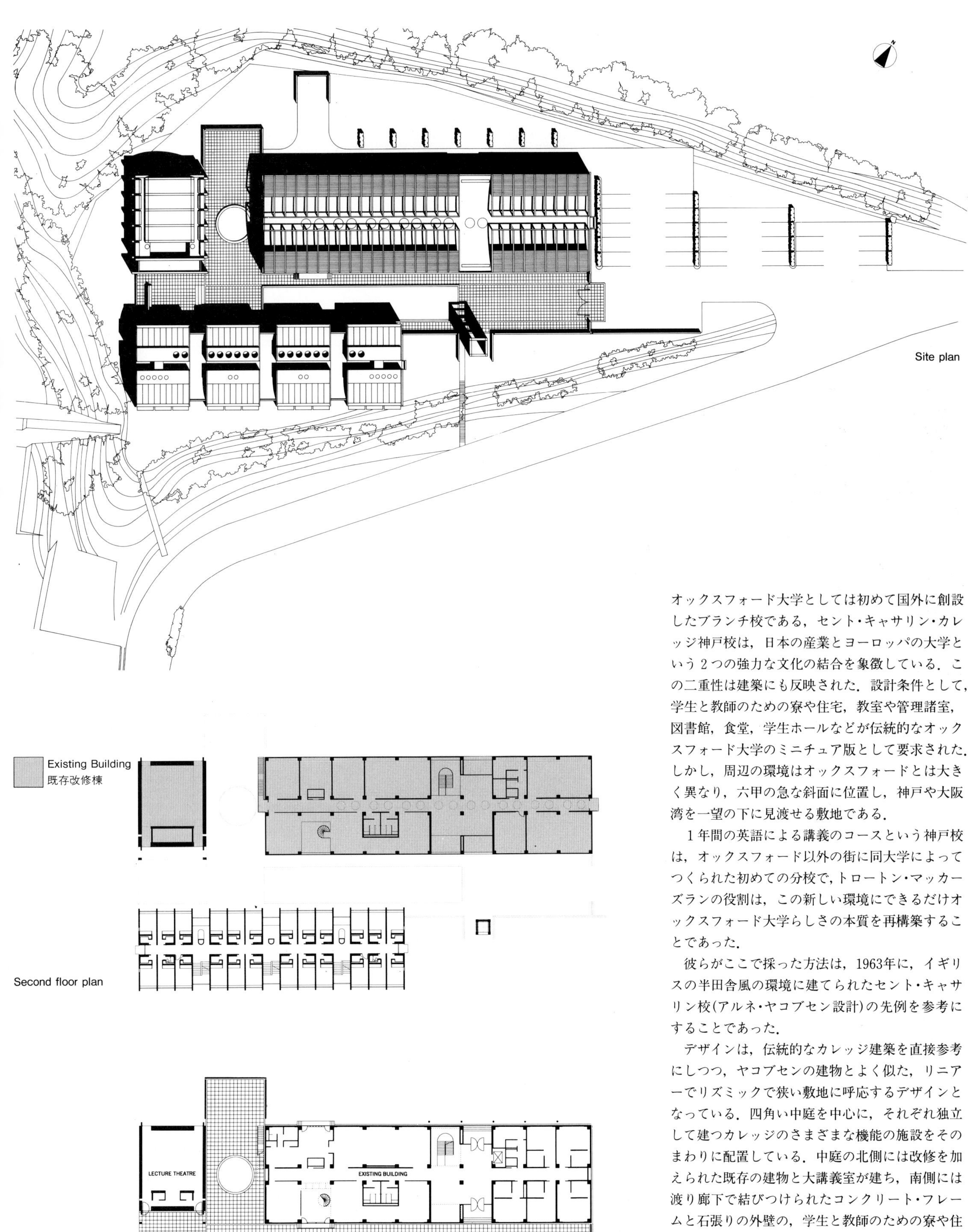

Site plan

Second floor plan

First floor plan

オックスフォード大学としては初めて国外に創設したブランチ校である，セント・キャサリン・カレッジ神戸校は，日本の産業とヨーロッパの大学という２つの強力な文化の結合を象徴している．この二重性は建築にも反映された．設計条件として，学生と教師のための寮や住宅，教室や管理諸室，図書館，食堂，学生ホールなどが伝統的なオックスフォード大学のミニチュア版として要求された．しかし，周辺の環境はオックスフォードとは大きく異なり，六甲の急な斜面に位置し，神戸や大阪湾を一望の下に見渡せる敷地である．

１年間の英語による講義のコースという神戸校は，オックスフォード以外の街に同大学によってつくられた初めての分校で，トロートン・マッカーズランの役割は，この新しい環境にできるだけオックスフォード大学らしさの本質を再構築することであった．

彼らがここで採った方法は，1963年に，イギリスの半田舎風の環境に建てられたセント・キャサリン校(アルネ・ヤコブセン設計)の先例を参考にすることであった．

デザインは，伝統的なカレッジ建築を直接参考にしつつ，ヤコブセンの建物とよく似た，リニアーでリズミックで狭い敷地に呼応するデザインとなっている．四角い中庭を中心に，それぞれ独立して建つカレッジのさまざまな機能の施設をそのまわりに配置している．中庭の北側には改修を加えられた既存の建物と大講義室が建ち，南側には渡り廊下で結びつけられたコンクリート・フレームと石張りの外壁の，学生と教師のための寮や住宅棟が並んでいる．彼らのデザインは両方ともヤコブセン風であり，かつ伝統的なカレッジの特質を有している．敷地からのすばらしい眺めを確保するために，学生や教師の住宅部分は南面して窓をもち，この窓は同時に既存の建物の眺めも手に入れている．また，コンクリート・フレームの時計塔が建物のどこからも眺められる．

Photo by Hiroyuki Hirai

Above: Detail of Arne Jacobsen's St Catherine's College, University of Oxford　(上)オックスフォードにあるセント・キャサリン・カレッジ(アルネ・ヤコブセン設計)
Left: Courtyard view　既存棟(左)と宿舎(右)
Bottom left: Courtyard view　計画にあたった宿舎(正面)，階段教室棟(右)と既存棟(左)に囲まれた中庭
Bottom right: Typical student bedroom
(下右)学生宿舎の部屋
Cpposite page : Residential building
右ページ：宿舎の階段室

Photo by Hiroyuki Hirai

Photo by Hiroyuki Hirai

Opposite photo by Hiroyuki Hirai

◀Main building entrance staircase detail
中央棟エントランスの階段

▶Lecture Theatre perspective
階段教室パース

Main building entrance unit and stairscase　中央棟入口ユニットと階段

▶Detail of the Residential building staircase　学生・教員宿舎棟の階段

All photos by Hiroyuki Hirai

Entrance area of the Main building at night　中央棟入口
All photos by Hiroyuki Hirai

Lecture theatre interior　階段教室内部

Acton Vocational Training Centre

London, England, 1994

アクトン地下鉄職員訓練センター

The brief for the Acton Vocational Training Centre is complex: 20,000 square metres of workshops, classrooms, administration and back-up facilities, and a simulated working station for the training of London Underground staff. The surburban setting is typical of its kind, part residential, part industrial, with the site bounded on one side by the backs of houses, on the others by railway lines and yards.

The brief and site called for a building that is responsive and sensitive, but simple and clear. With their breadth of experience and influences, Troughton McAslan, who won the commission following a single stage competition, are well equipped to realise such a building. As at Alexander House the context requires care, without giving the architect all the answers. As at Apple, modern materials and techniques are called for, but employed pragmatically and without dogma.

The training centre will be a structure considerably more distinguished than any that surrounds it, but it is careful to take its cues from its context. To the west the more enclosed, cellular accommodation is contained in a long, two-storey frontage interspersed with well planted courtyards, interpreting the houses and gardens opposite in an ordered and elegant way. The courtyards break down the scale of the training centre and give a sense of local identity within a larger whole. To the east the long span barrel vault roofs clearly belong to the industrial world of railways, sheds and open spaces in which the building will sit but, again, designed with precision and care. Its edge is more irregular, in response to the haphazard yards and sheds it will face.

The two sides are mediated by an internal street, a larger and enriched development of a similar idea at Apple. In plan it echoes the residential roads to the west, but it is covered by a linear barrel roof. The internal street, based in part on the study of the RATP training centre in Paris and Henning Larsen's university building in Trondheim, will focus the disparate elements at the Acton site, and encourage the users to communicate and exchange ideas. Glass walls will allow views across the street to all parts of the building.

The construction strikes one most forcibly as a confident display of structure and of modern materials, but it is designed to cope with the varied and changing demands of the centre. It is principally composed of barrel roofs and a concrete frame system, with only simple connections made on site. The frames will carry demountable panels that can be altered at will in response to the bulding's varied requirements for enclosure, natural lighting and environmental control. The building's section is designed to make the best use of natural ventilation, while the internal street's glass roof will exploit passive solar gain in winter.

The training centre reinterprets urban spaces such as courts and streets, and is informed by a very low-technology wish to make the most of natural resources and to minimise machinery and plant. It is governed less by a single, pervasive idea, more by a set of flexible and varied responses unified by strong planning principles. The complexities of brief and site are brought together and mediated by a construction sufficiently adaptable to cope with both, but sufficiently self assured to exceed either.

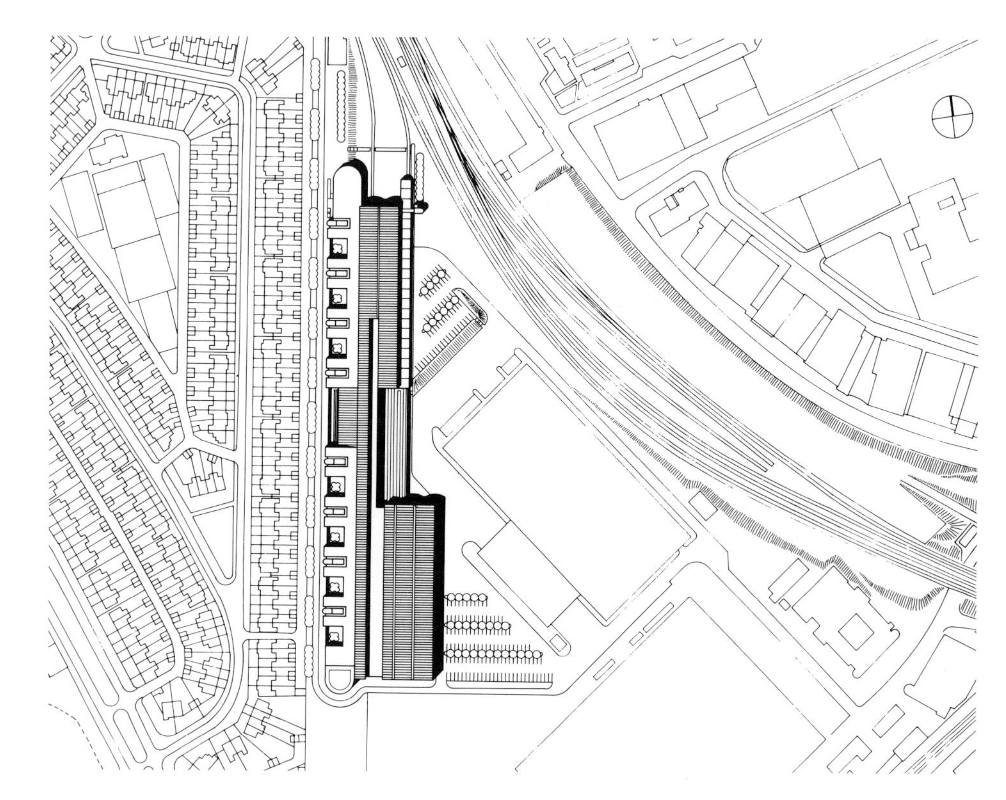

Henning Larsen's Trondheim University which has influenced the design by its treatment of the internal street　ヘニング・ラーセン設計のトロンドハイム大学．この内部ストリートの処理からデザインのヒントを得る

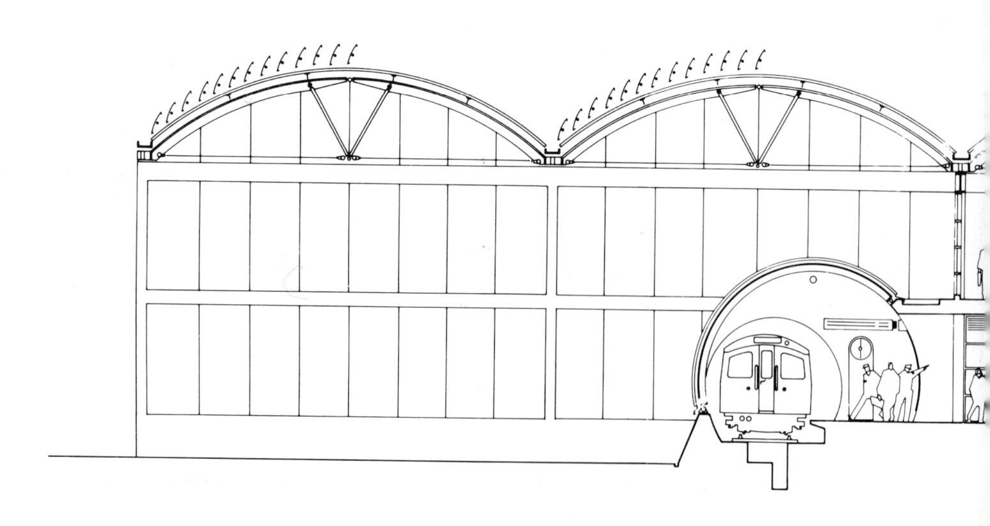

アクトン地下鉄職員訓練センターの設計条件は複雑であった．全体で20,000㎡のロンドン地下鉄のスタッフ用のワークショップ，教室，管理・設備諸室，そして実践訓練ステーションが要求された．この種の施設用地としては，敷地の片方が住宅地で，もう一方は鉄道線路とその構内という，半住宅地，半工業地の郊外という設定が一般的である．

設計条件や敷地の状況から，建物は柔軟で繊細，かつシンプルで明快なものが求められる．幅広い経験と実績によって，トロートン・マッカーズランは1段階コンペに入選し，充分にそれらの要望に応えた．アレキサンダーハウス同様，ここでもコンテクストは建築家にすべての答えをくれるわけでなく，細心の注意を必要とした．アップル・コンピューター社の場合と同様，モダンな素材や技術が実用的かつ独断なしに採用されている．

トレーニングセンターは周辺のいかなる建物以上に目立つものであるが，しかし注意深く周辺に融合させる必要がある．敷地の西側には，小さな単位の研修室などを2層に，長く延びる建物にとりつく形で配置し，その間や外側に植栽のある庭を散在させ，さらに西側に規則正しく並ぶ住宅やその庭園に呼応させている．中庭はトレーニングセンターのスケールをブレークダウンし，大きな全体の中で個々の個性を表現している．東側には，ロングスパンの円筒ヴォールト屋根のかかる全く工業的な部分がある．ここには鉄道，車庫のほか，将来建物が入るであろうことから精度高く，注意深くデザインされたオープンスペースがある．施設の東橋は，その外側の鉄道構内の乱雑な建物形態にあわせて不規則な形となっている．

この東西の両施設を，内部のストリートが仲介している．これはアップル・コンピューター社の内部ストリートと同じアイデアであるが，より大きく，豊かな空間である．ストリート部分は平面的には西側の住宅地に呼応しているが，外観はヴォールト屋根のリニアーな建物である．内部ストリートは，パリのRATPのトレーニングセンターやヘニング・ラーセンのトロンハイム大学施設を研究した結果，導き出されたアイデアであるが，アクトンでは全く様子が異なり，研修生たちがコミュニケーションをもつ場となっている．ガラスの仕切り壁によって，内部ストリート越しに建物内部がすべて見通すこともできる．

建物は構造や新しい素材を際立つように使っているが，センターの多様な，変化の多い需要に合わせてデザインされている．構造は円筒・ヴォールト屋根とコンクリート・フレーム・システムを基本とし，すべて現場組立て施工である．フレームは，取り外し可能なパネルを支えている．このパネルは，用途や間取りの変更や，自然光や環境制御の変更にしたがって自由に移動が可能である．各室内は自然換気を最大限に活用し，また，内部ストリートのガラス屋根には冬期のパッシブソーラーのための集光器が取りつけられる．

トレーニングセンターは，中庭やストリートで都市空間を再現し，できるだけ自然の素材を用い，機械力による制御を極力少なくしてローテク建築にすることを目指している．たった1つのアイデアでまとめられたのでなく，フレキシブルで多様な要望への対応を，強力な計画原理の下に集結したものとなっている．設計条件と敷地の複合性は個々にそれぞれの機能を充足させつつ，両者が一体となって充分に機能することで調和が成立していくのである．

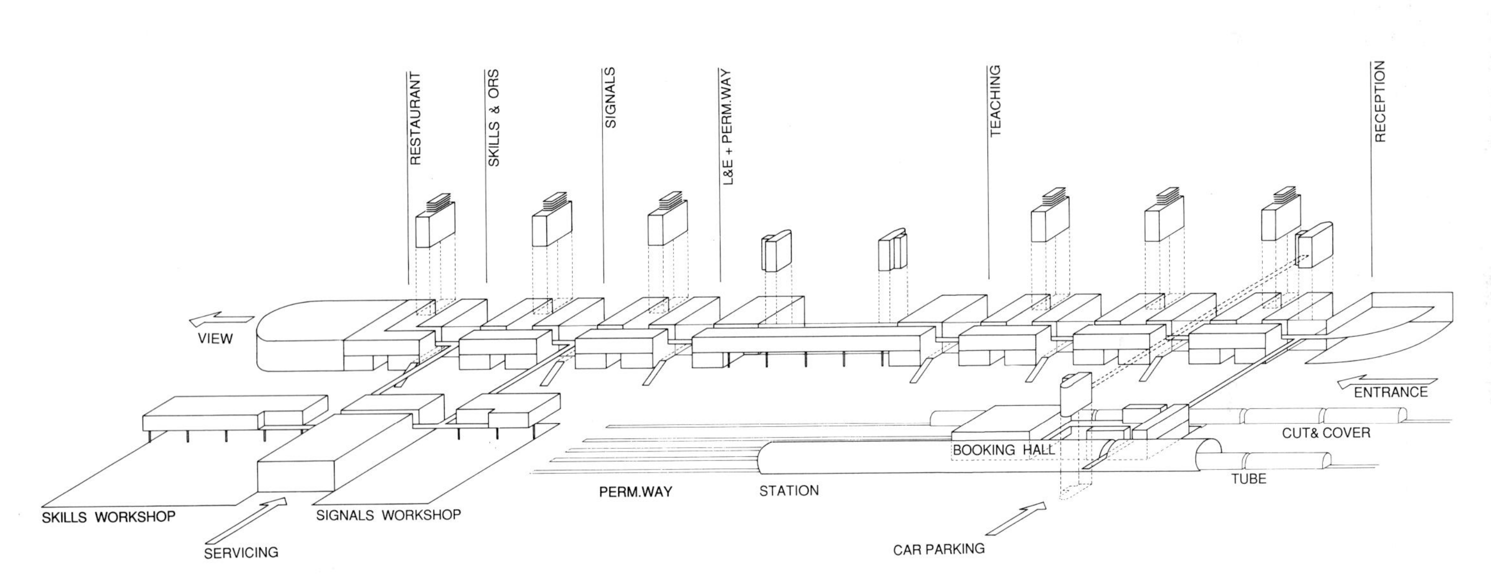

Massing diagram of the building 建物各要素のボリュームダイアグラム

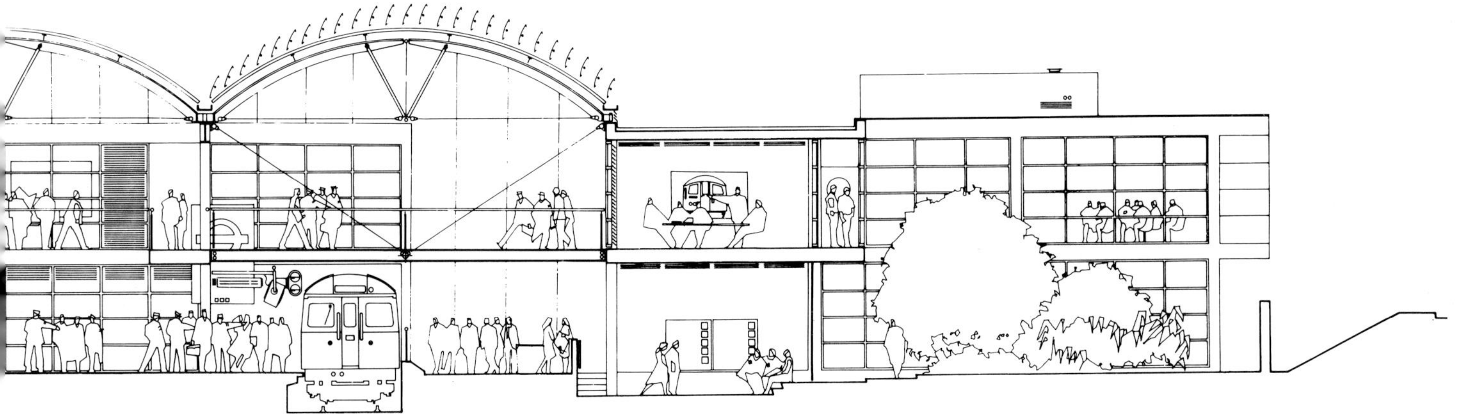

Cross section through the building, illustrating working station, internal street, teaching accommodation and courtyard ワーキングステーション，内部ストリート，教室，中庭を通した断面図

1	Reception/Display	12	Storage
2	Administration	13	Workshops
3	Training Management Accommodation	14	IMR/Control Room
4	Interview Room	15	Restaurant/Kitchen
5	Conference/Induction Room	16	Rig Rooms
6	Shop/Bank	17	Library
7	Waiting/Vending Area	18	Station Facilities
8	Courtyard	19	Multi-Gym
9	Classroom	20	Model Railway Room
10	WC/Plant Cores	21	Permanent Way
11	Restricted Area	22	Uniform Issue

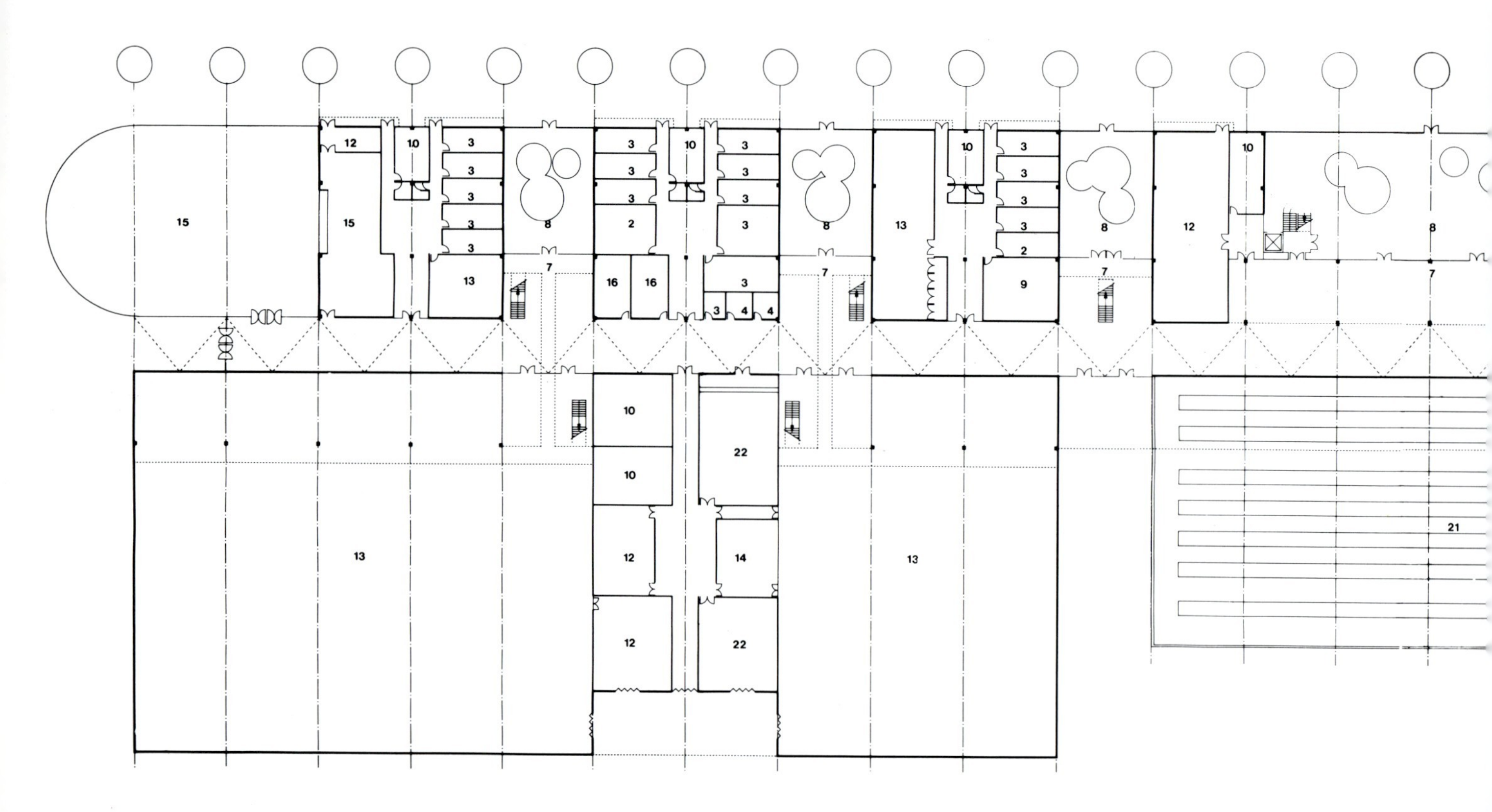

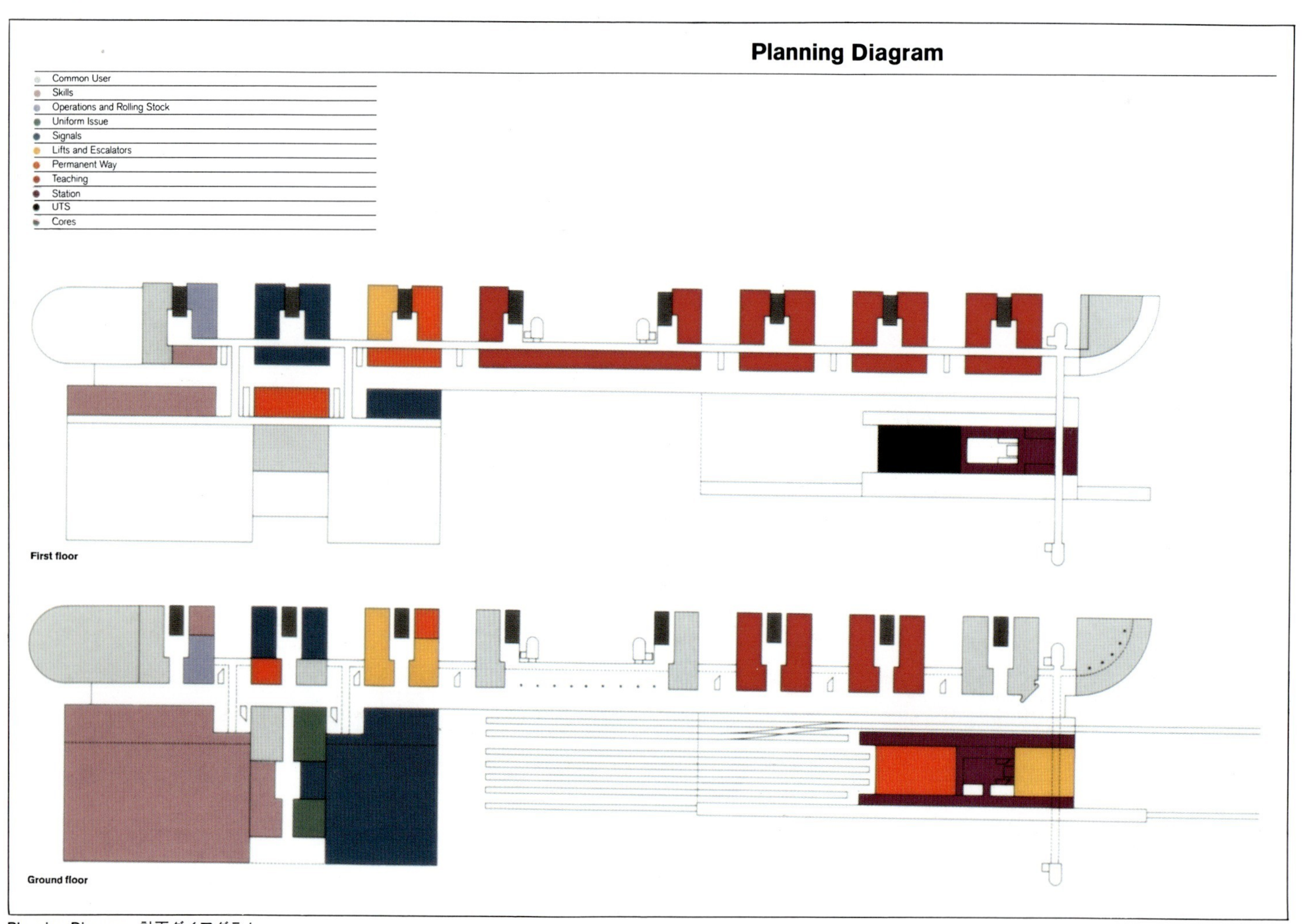

Planning Diagram　計画ダイアグラム

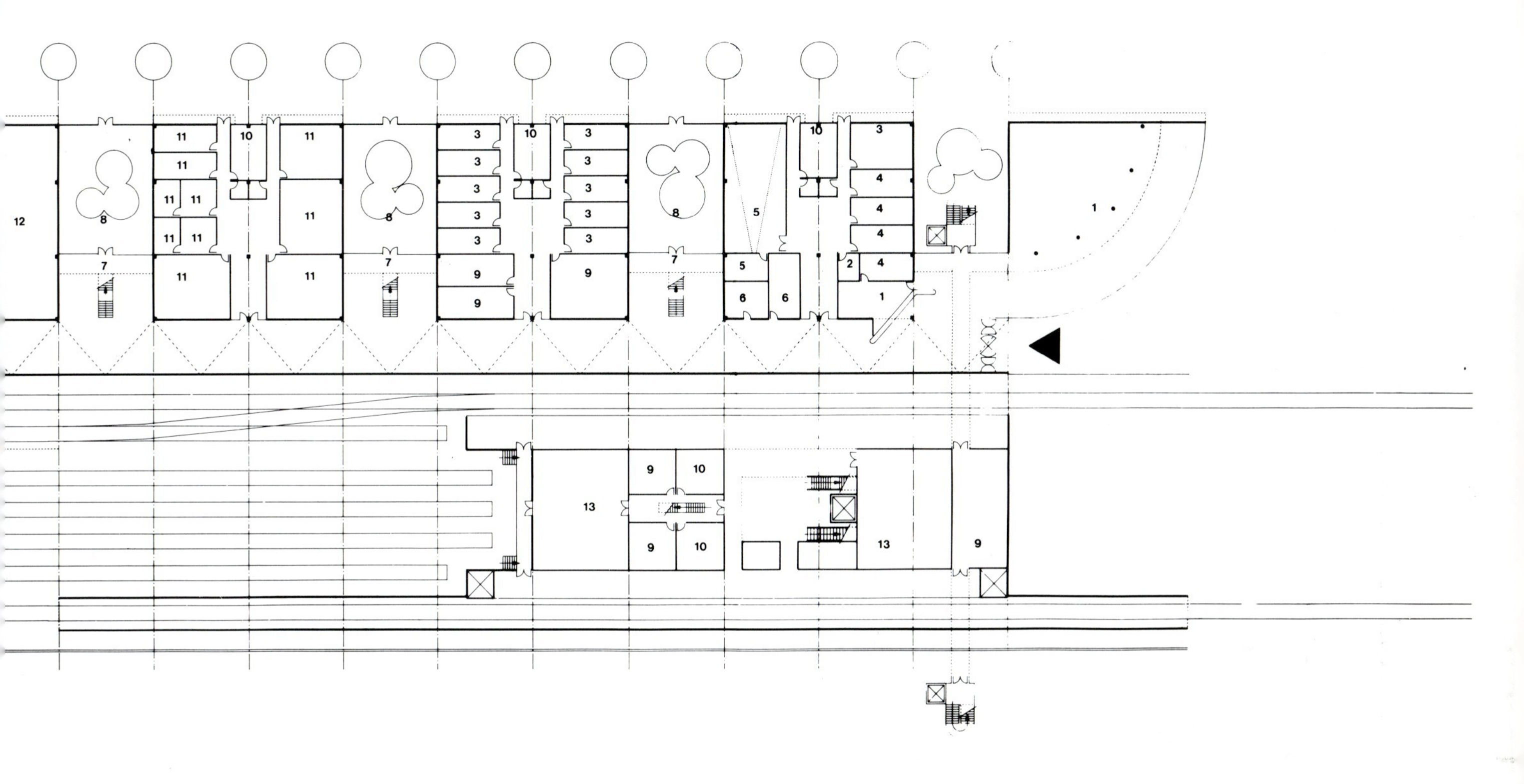

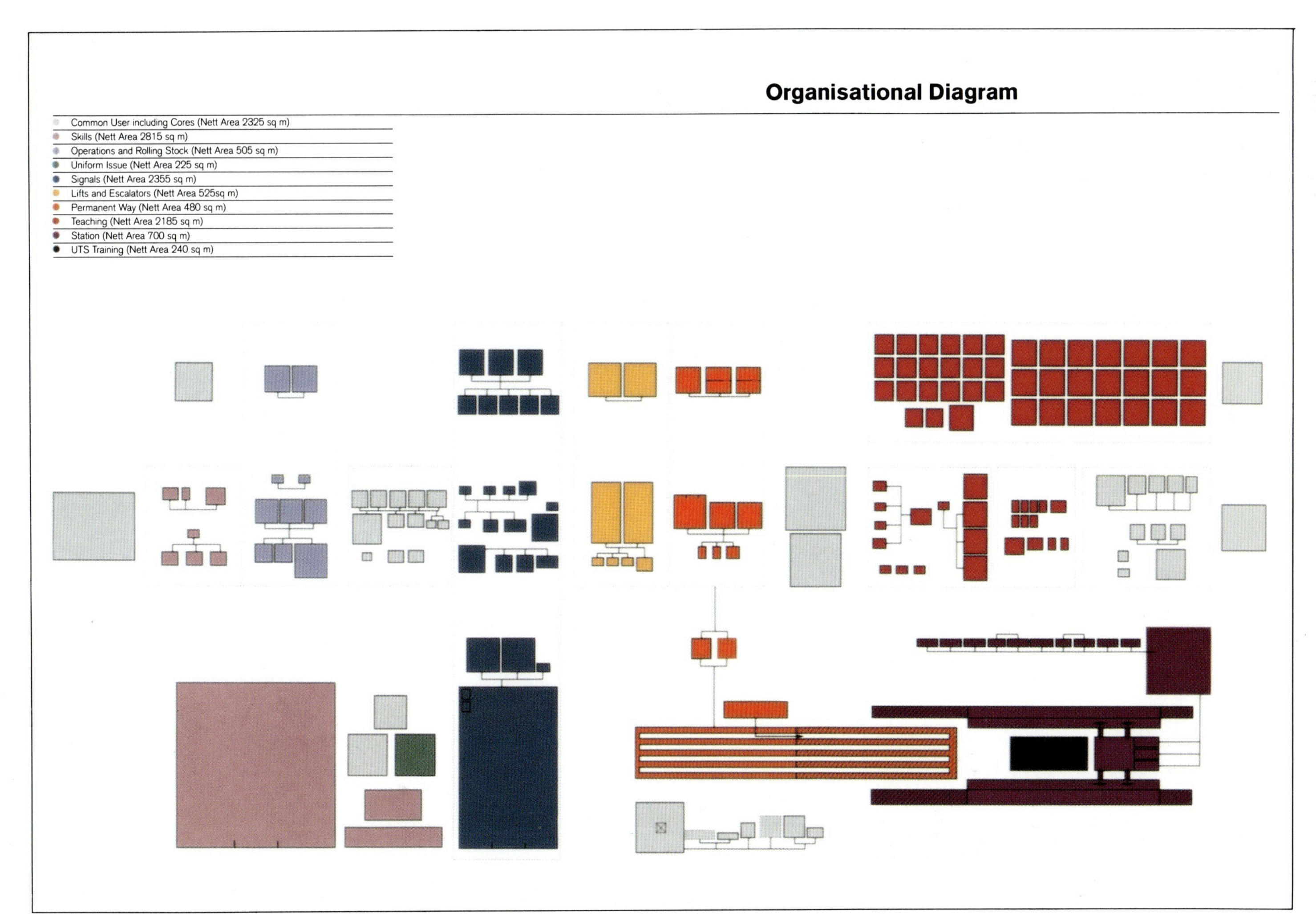

Organisational Diagram 組織ダイアグラム

Aerial view of the site model looking north, illustrating the new building
計画案の全体模型

Aerial view of the site model, illustrating the existing buildings which occupy the site
既存の全体模型

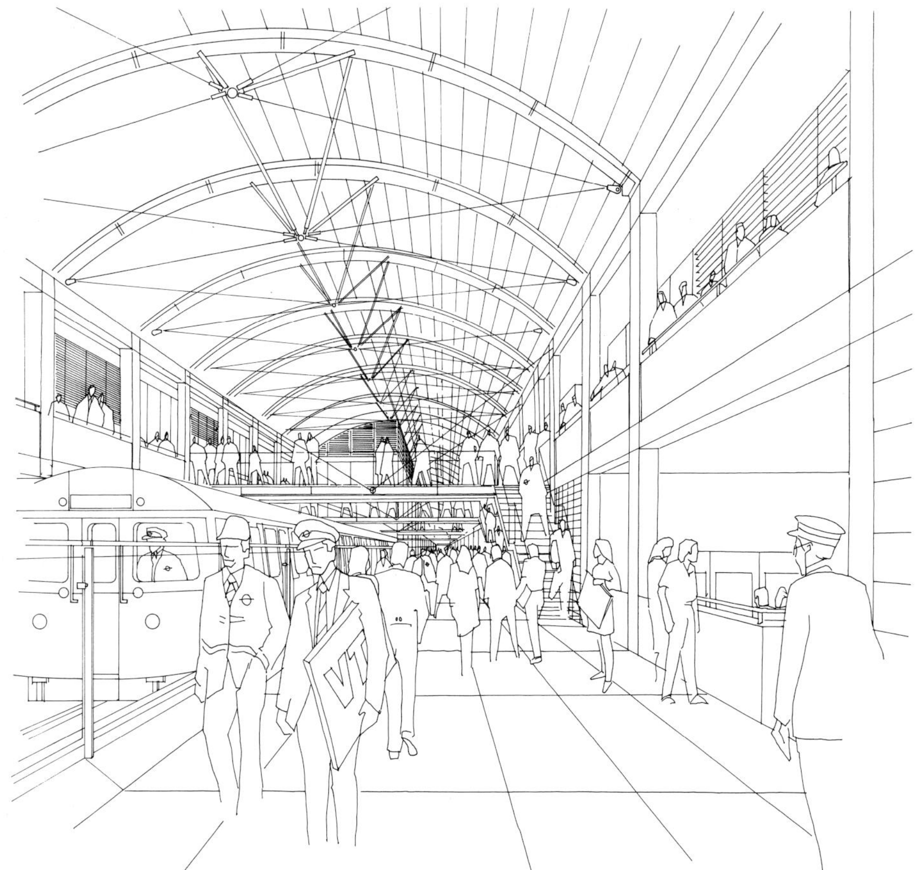

Perspective sketch of the internal street at first floor level
1階レベルの内部ストリート

APPENDICES

付記

Principal Buildings and Projects
作品リスト

1984

DESIGN HOUSE
London, England
Client: Design House Ltd
Collaborators: Ove Arup and Partners (Engineer), Barrie Tankel Partnership (Quantity surveyor)
Floor Area: 600m²
A garage showroom refurbishment into design studios on two levels enclosed within a glazed facade

デザインハウス／自動車のショールームをガラス張りの２階建てのデザイン・スタジオに改修.

1985

ALLIED BREWERIES HEADQUARTERS
Burton-on-Trent England (project)
Client: Allied Breweries Ltd
Collaborators: F J Samuely and Partners (Engineer)
Floor Area: 4,000m²
A headquarters building design on a riverside site.

醸造組合本部(計画案)／川沿いの敷地に建つ本部ビル

BAITLAWS CONSERVATORY
Lanarkshire, England
Client: Private
Collaborators: F J Samuely and Partners (Engineer)
Floor Area: ——
A raised steel and glass conservatory construction adjoining an existing farmhouse.

バイトローズ温室棟／高床のスチールとガラスの温室棟を既存の農家建築に増設.

LONDON HOUSE
London, England
Client: Local London Group Ltd
Collaborators: Jampel Davison and Bell (Engineer), Barrie Tankel Partnership (Quantity surveyor)
Floor Area: 2,000m²
A disused warehouse refurbishment into offices.

ロンドンハウス／放置されていた倉庫をオフィスに改修.

SHEPHERD'S BUSH STUDIO
London, England
Client: Design Group
Collaborators: John Savage Associates (Engineer), Boyden and Company (Quantity surveyor)
Floor Area: 3,000m²
A three storey concrete framed warehouse refurbishment into studio and office accommodation incorporating a triple height top-lit central volume.

シェパード・ブッシュ／３階建てのコンクリート造の倉庫をトップライトのある３層吹抜けの空間を中心としたオフィス兼スタジオに改修.

1986

INDIRA GANDHI NATIONAL CENTRE FOR ARTS
New Delhi, India (project)
Client: Government of India
Collaborators: Ove Arup and Partners (Engineer)
Floor Area: 50,000m²
An arts centre design in New Delhi incorporating concert halls, theatres, gallerys and research facilities.

インディラ・ガンジー国立アートセンター／インドのニューデリーに建つアートセンター計画. 音楽ホール, 劇場, ギャラリー, 研究施設から構成.

IXWORTH HOUSE
London, England (project)
Client: Imperial Land Ltd
Collaborators: John Savage Associates (Engineer), Boyden and Company (Quantity surveyor)
Floor Area: 1,500m²
An infill office building design in West London.

イクスワース・ハウス(計画案)／ウエスト・ロンドンのオフィス増改築計画.

1987

FARM PLACE
London, England
Client: Portmans Ltd
Collaborators: Cameron Taylor Partnership (Engineer)
Floor Area: 100m²
A three storey Georgian residential property refurbishment.

ファームプレイス／３階建てのジョージ王朝風の住宅の改修.

HILLINGDON STATION
London, England (project)
Client: London Regional Transport
Collaborators: Ove Arup and Partners (Engineer)
Floor Area: ——
The design for a new station incorporating a ticket office building bridging over the tracks and linking to the platforms beneath.

ヒリントン駅(計画案)／線路を跨いで建つ出札・改札部分が下階のプラットホームに連結.

RIBA GALLERY
London, England (project)
Client: Royal Institute of British Architects
Collaborators: ——
Floor Area: ——
The design of a single storey gallery adjoining the headquarters of the Royal Institute of British Architects in Central London.

RIBA展示スタンド(計画案)／プレハブ部材のガラス壁を組み立てて建てる展示スタンド.

RIBA EXHIBITION STAND
Birmingham, England (project)
Client: Royal Institute of British Architects
Collaborators: ——
Floor Area: ——
A glazed exhibition building erected from a kit of pre-fabricated glazed and solid screen components.

RIBAギャラリー(計画案)／ロンドン中心部のRIBA本部に隣接して建つ平屋のギャラリー計画.

1988

CAPABILITY GREEN
Luton, England (project)
Client: Lytgun Ltd
Collaborators: Alan Baxter Associates (Engineer), Howard Associates (Quantity surveyor)
Floor Area: 5,000m²
The design of a two storey office building in a linear arrangement.

Capability Green(計画案)／リニアーな軸線沿いに配置した２階建てのオフィスビル計画.

GORDON PLACE
London, England
Client: Private
Collaborators: ——
Floor Area: 180m²
The refurbishment of a nineteenth century residential property.

ゴードンプレイス／19世紀の住宅の改修.

PETERSHILL
London, England(project)
Client: MEPC Development Ltd
Collaborators: ——
Floor Area: 35,000m²
The design of a six storey office building adjacent to St Paul's Cathedral in London.

ピーターヒル(計画案)／セントポール大寺院の隣接地に建つ６階建てのオフィスビル計画.

POND PLACE
London, England
Client: Local London Group
Collaborators: Jampel Davison and Bell (Engineer), Boyden and Company (Quantity surveyor)
Floor Area: 300m²
The construction of a three storey concrete framed office building in a conservation Area.

ポンドプレイス／保存地区に建つ３階建てのコンクリート造のオフィスビル.

3 ST PETER'S STREET
London, England

Client: Derwent Valley Holdings plc
Collaborators: Jampel Davison and Bell (Engineer), Boyden and Company (Quantity surveyor)
Floor Area: 600m²

The refurbishment of a Victorian building to provide studio accommodation on two levels with a double height entrance area and remodelling of the front facade.

セント・ピーターズ・ストリート3番地／ビクトリア朝風の建物を，2階吹抜けのエントランス部分とスタジオに改造．正面ファサードも改築．

1989

ALEXANDER HOUSE
London, England

Client: Shilton plc
Collaborators: Jampel Davison&Bell (Engineer), Boyden&Company (Quantity surveyor)
Floor Area: 1,800m²

A double volume warehouse and distribution building and three storey office building in south London.

アレキサンダー・ハウス／サウスロンドンに建つ3層のオフィスと，その後ろの2層分の高さの倉庫・配送センター．

APPLE COMPUTERS' FACILITY PHASE 1
Stockley Park, England

Client: Stockley Park Consortium Ltd, Apple Computer UK Ltd
Collaborators: Ove Arup and Partners (Engineer), Davis Langdon and Everest (Quantity surveyor), Charles Funke Associates (Landscape consultant)
Floor Area: 5,000m²

A two storey headquarters building containing a central double height circulation space.

アップルコンピューター社第1期／中央に2層吹抜けの動線部分をもつ2階建ての本社ビル．

BRITISH HIGH COMMISSION
Nairobi, Kenya (project)

Client: British Foreign and Commonwealth Office
Collaborators: Davis Langdon&Everest (Quantity surveyor), Barker&Barton (Quantity surveyor), Whitby&Bird (Engineer), Max Fordham Associates (Environmental engineer)
Floor Area: 4,000m²

The design of new offices and varied accommodaiton in a series of pavilions located on a hillside site overlooking Nairobi.

ケニアの英国高等弁務官事務所(計画案)／ナイロビ市街を見下ろす丘の斜面に建つ事務所・宿舎などからなる建物群計画．

EMERSON VALLEY NORTH
Milton Keynes, England (project)

Client: Milton Keynes Development Corporation
Collaborators: ——
Floor Area: ——

The design of three villas located on a rural site.

エマーソンバレー・ノース(計画案)／自然の中に位置する3軒のヴィラ計画．

1990

1-3 COLEBROOKE PLACE
London, England

Client: Derwent Valley Holdings plc
Collaborators: Ove Arup and Partners (Engineer), Boyden and Company (Quantity surveyor)
Floor Area: 600m²

The refurbishment of a single storey Victorian building to provide studio accommodation.

コルブルックプレイス1-3番地／ビクトリア朝風の平屋の建物をスタジオに改修．

HUNTSWORTH MEWS
London, England

Client: Barrie Tankel Partnership plc
Collaborators: Jampel Davison and Bell (Engineer)
Floor Area: 500m²

A three storey office building situated on a narrow mews in central London.

ハンツワース・ミューズ／ロンドン中心部の狭いミューズに位置する3階建てのオフィスビル．

REDHILL STATION
Surrey, England

Client: British Railways Board
Collaborators: Alan Baxter and Associates (Engineer), Boyden and Company (Quantity surveyor)
Floor Area: ——

A new railway station south of London.

レッドヒル駅／ロンドン南郊の新駅．

RIVERSIDE APARTMENTS
London, England

Client: Private
Collaborators: Jampel Davison and Bell (Engineer), E C Harris and Partners (Quantity surveyor)
Floor Area: 1,100m²

An eight storey apartment building situated on the south bank of the River Thames.

リバーサイド・アパートメント／テムズ川南岸に建つ8階建てのアパート．

1991

APPLE COMPUTER'S FACILITY PHASE II
Stockley Park, England

Client: Stockley Park Consortium Ltd, Apple Computer UK Ltd
Collaborators: Ove Arup and Partners (Engineer), Davis Langdon and Everest (Quantity surveyor), Charles Funke Associates (Landscape consultant)
Floor Area: 6,000m²

A three storey office building forming the second phase of a development for the Apple Computer company.

アップルコンピューター社第2期／同社の本社整備計画の第2期工事として3階建てのオフィスビルを建設．

BOLSOVER STREET
London, England

Client: Great Portland Estates
Collaborators: Pell Frischmann Group (Engineer), Boyden and Company (Quantity surveyor)
Floor Area: 2,300m²

The refurbishment of a five storey Victorian building in central London to provide office space including the construction of a full height rear addition.

ボルソバー・ストリート／ロンドン中心部の5階建てのビクトリア朝風の建物をオフィスに改修し，さらに敷地後ろに新たな建物を増築したもの．

PRINCES DOCK
Liverpool, England(project)

Client: P&O Developments Ltd
Collaborators: ——
Floor Area: ——

The masterplan for the redevelopment of the Princes Dock in Liverpool.

プリンスドック／リバプールのプリンスドック再開発計画のマスタープラン．

ST CATHERINE'S COLLEGE (UNIVERSITY OF OXFORD) KOBE INSTITUTE
Kobe, Japan

Client: Kobe Steel/St Catherine's College
Collaborators: Takenaka Corporation (Production Information and Main contractor), Ove Arup and Partners (Engineer)
Floor Area: 4,000m²

A branch college of the University of Oxford, providing housing for students and tutors, teaching, administration and common area facilities,and a lecture theatre in three separate buildings organised around a central courtyard on a hillside site.

オックスフォード大学神戸校／オックスフォード大学のブランチ校．丘陵地に中央のリニアな中庭を囲むように教室棟，学生寮，教職員宿舎，本部棟，厚生棟などが3つの建物群を構成．

1 ST PETER'S STREET
London, England
Client: Derwent Valley Holdings plc
Collaborators: Jampel Davison and Bell (Engineer)
Floor Area: 80m^2
A two storey warehouse refurbishment providing studio space.

セント・ピーターズ・ストリート1番地／2階建ての倉庫をスタジオに改修.

1992

BUILDING FC3 CANARY WHARF
London, England
Client: Olympia and York Canary Wharf Ltd
Collaborators: Adamson Associates (Executive architect), Ove Arup and Partners (Engineer), Flack and Kurtz (Engineeer)
Floor Area: 40,000m^2
The construction of a sixteen storey office building forming part of the 500,000m^2 Phase One of the Canary Wharf development east of the City of London.

キャナリーワーフFC3ビル／ロンドン東郊のキャナリーワーフ開発の1つで16階建てのオフィスビル.

DE LA WARR PAVILION
Bexhill-on-Sea, England
Client: Rother District Council and Pavilion Trust
Collaborators: F J Samuely and Partners (Engineer), Ove Arup and Partners (Engineer), Davis Langdon and Everest (Quantity Surveyor)
Floor Area: ——
Masterplan proposals for the refurbishment of this Grade One listed modernist building designed by Mendelsohn and Chermayeff in 1935.

デ・ラ・ワー・パビリオン／1935年にメンデルゾーンとシャマイエフによって建てられた貴重な近代建築遺産の改修のためのマスタープランの提案.

HARDWICK STREET
London, England
Client: London Merchant Securities Group of Companies
Collaborators: Jampel Davison and Bell (Engineer), Boyden and Company (Quantity surveyor)
Floor Area: 5,000m^2
The refurbishment of three interconnected five storey steel framed buildings, for mixed studio accommodation.

ハードウィック・ストリート／3つの隣接して建つ5階建ての鉄骨造の建物を軽工業およびスタジオオフィスとして改修.

LEEDS CORRIDORS INTIATIVE
Leeds, England
Client: Leeds Initiative and Leeds City Council
Collaborators: Ove Arup and Partners (Engineer), Davis Langdon and Everest (Quantity surveyor), Landesign Group (Landscape consultat), Public Art Development Trust (Public Art consultant)
Floor Area: ——
Urban masterplan proposals for the redevelopment of the urban motorway approaches into and through the city of Leeds.

リーズ道路沿い再開発計画／リーズ市の環状および貫通の自動車路沿いの再開発計画のマスタープラン.

LEGAL AFFAIRS AND JUDICIARY BUILDING
Seychelles (project)
Client: Republic of Seychelles
Collaborators: Atelier One and Atelier Ten (Engineer), Barker and Barton (Quantity Surveyor)
Floor Area: 4,000m^2
The design of a two storey building housing the functions of the judiciary and legal affairs for the Republic of Seychelles.

セイシェルの裁判所・司法事務所ビル／セイシェル共和国の2階建ての裁判所および司法関係の建物

IL MOLINO
San Gimignano, Italy
Client: Private
Collaborators: ——
Floor Area; 200m^2
The conversion of an eighteenth century mill situated in a valley in Tuscany, to provide design studio and living accommodation.

イル・モリノ／イタリア・トスカーナ地方の谷間の18世紀の水車小屋をデザインスタジオと住宅に改装.

ROSEBERY AVENUE
London, England
Client: London Merchant Securities Group of Companies
Collaborators: Ove Arup and Partners (Engineer), Walfords (Quantity surveyor)
Floor Area: 2,500m^2
The construction of a five storey concrete framed office building, adjacent to the Hardwick Street building.

ローズベリー・アベニュー／ハードウィック・ストリートビルに隣接して建つ5階建てのコンクリート造のオフィスビル.

ST CATHERINE'S COLLEGE
Oxford, England
Client: St Catherine's College (University of Oxford)
Collaborators: Davis Langdon and Everest (Quantity surveyor), Edmund Hambly Ltd (Engineer)
Floor Area: ——
The refurbishment of the entrance areas to St Catherine's College.

セント・キャサリン・カレッジ／英国オックスフォードのカレッジ本校の正面周辺の改修計画.

WAVERLEY STATION REDEVELOPMENT
Edinburgh, Scotland
Client: The Scotsman newspaper and Royal Incorporation of Architects in Scotland
Collaborators: Ove Arup and Partners (Engineer), Davis Langdon and Everest (Quantity surveyor), Ian White Associates (Landscape consultant)
Floor Area: ——
A design for re-vitalising Waverley Station and its surroundings in the centre of Edinburgh.

ウェイバリー駅再開発計画(計画案)／エジンバラ中心部のウェイバリー駅周辺の活性化計画.

1993

3-5 CHRISTOPHER PLACE
London, England
Client: Ross Jaye Ltd
Collaborators: Jampel Davison and Bell (Engineer), Boyden and Company (Quantity surveyor)
Floor Area: 300m^2
The design of a concrete framed three storey building located in a mews site enclosed by three existing properties.

クリストファー・プレイス3-5番地／3方を既存の建物に囲まれたミューズに建つコンクリート造の3階建てのビル.

4-6 COLEBROOK PLACE
London, England
Client: Derwent Valley Holdings plc
Collaborators: Jampel Davison and Bell (Engineer)
Floor Area: 450m^2
The conversion of a Victorian warehouse building to provide studio accommodation on two levels.

コルブルックプレイス4-6番地／ビクトリア朝風の倉庫を2層のスタジオに改装.

DOCKLANDS OFFICE BUILDING
London, England
Client: London Docklands Development Corporation
Collaborators: ——
Floor Area: 5,000m²
The design of a four storey steel framed office building.

ドックランド・オフィスビル／4階建ての鉄骨造のオフィスビル.

MIDDLESEX HOUSE
London, England
Client: Derwent Valley Holdings plc
Collaborators: Jampel Davison and Bell (Engineer), Boyden and Company (Quantity surveyor)
Floor Area: 4,000m²
The phased refurbishment of a five storey building in central London constructed during the 1930's.

ミドルセックスハウス／ロンドン中心部に位置する1930年代に建てられた5階建ての建物の段階的改修.

MONTERIGGIONI
Siena, Italy
Client: Comune di Monteriggioni
Collaborators: ——
Floor Area: ——
The design of an urban park in a medieval fortified hill town in Tuscany.

モンテリジオーニ／トスカーナ地方の中世の丘陵地にある城塞都市の都市公園再開発計画.

SSAFA
London, England
Client: Soldiers,Sailors and Airmens' Families Association (SSAFA)
Collaborators: F J Samuely and Partners (Engineer)
Floor Area: 1,100m²
The design of an infill office building.

SSAFA／オフィスビルの増改築のデザイン.

WATERLOO LINK
London, England
Client: British Railways Board
Collaborators: Kenchington Ford (Engineer)
Floor Area: ——
The construction of an elevated enclosed pedestrian link at Waterloo Station

ウォータールー・リンク／ウォータールー駅の高架の歩行者用の連絡通路.

1994

ACTON VOCATIONAL TRAINING CENTRE
London, England
Client: London Underground Ltd
Collaborators: F J Samuely and Partners (Engineer), Nigel Rose and Partners (Quantity surveyor)
Floor Area: 20,000m²
A training centre containing workshops, classrooms, administration and a simulated working station for the training of London Underground staff.

アクトン地下鉄職業訓練センター／ロンドン地下鉄のスタッフ養成用の教室，管理施設，実地訓練施設.

1996

CANNING TOWN STATION
London, England
Client: London Underground Ltd
Collaborators: Kenchington Ford plc (Engineer), E C Harris and Partners (Quantity surveyor)
Floor Area: ——
The design of an interchange station for the Jubilee Line Extension.

カニングタウン駅／ロンドン地下鉄の新しい延長ジュビリー線と従来の交通機関の交差駅
舎計画.

STRATFORD STATION
London, England
Client: London Underground Ltd
Collaborators: Kenchington Ford plc (Engineer), E C Harris and Partners (Quantity surveyor)
Floor Area: ——
The design of an interchange station for the Jubilee Line Extension.

ストラットフォード駅／ロンドン地下鉄のジュビリー線の終点駅のデザイン.

Awards and Distinctions
受賞リスト

Royal Academy of Arts, Exhibition, London, Three Projects Exhibited, 1992

Judiciary and Legal Affairs Building, Open International Competition, Prizewinner (2nd), 1992

Apple Computers Headquarters, Financial Times Awards, Finalist, 1991

De La Warr Pavilion, Limited competition, Winner,1991

Museum of Scotland, Open competition, Second Stage, 1991

Royal Academy of Arts, Exhibition, London, Model Exhibited, ——, 1991

Redhill Station, Structural Steel Design Awards, Prizewinner (Commended), 1991

Riverside Apartments, 3 St Peters Street, BBC Design Awards, Joint Finalists, 1990

'Lipstick' Site, LDDC International Design Competition for an office building, Winner, 1990

Waverley Challenge, Edinburgh, Competition, Prizewinner (3rd), 1989

Apple Computers Headquarters, Civic Trust Award to Stockley Park development, including Apple Computers Headquarters, 1989

Alexander House, Merton Road, Civic Trust Awards, Award winner, 1989

London Underground, Acton Vocational Training Centre, Limited Competition, Winner, 1989

Royal Academy of Arts, Exhibition, London, Drawing Exhibited, ——, 1989

"Latter Day Modernism" Exhibition, London, Work Exhibition, ——, 1989

3 St Peters Street, International Interior Design Awards (IIDA 1989), Prizewinner (2nd), 1989

"Process to Form", University of London, Lecture and Practice Exhibition, ——, 1988

"40 Under 40" Exhibition, RIBA, London, Work Exhibited, ——, 1988

"International Architects", Sydney, Austrailia, Exhibition and Lecture Series, John McAslan, Keynote speaker, 1988

Uplighter, Progressive Architecture, International Furniture Design Award, Prizewinner (Commended), 1987

Shepherd's Bush Offices, BBC Design Awards, Finalist, 1987

RIBA Gallery, Limited Competition, Prizewinner (2nd), 1987

Riverside Apartments, Limited Competition, Winner, 1986

Royal Academy of Arts, Exhibition, London, Model Exhibited, Prizewinner (Non-Members Award), 1986

Design House, Office of the Year Award, Prizewinner (Commended), 1985

"21 Young Architects" Exhibition, Design Council, London, Work Exhibited, ——, 1984

Published Work
作品掲載誌リスト

Project Name
Publication / Date/ Title or Comments

Alexander House
Architect's Journal (UK)/ 5 Apr, 89/ "Road Show"

Apple Computers' facility phase 1
Architecture Interieure Cree (France)/ Apr, 89/ Cover Story: "Architecture Facility"
Techniques et Architecture (France)/ Apr, 89/ "The Sunshade and the Parasol"
Architectural Review (UK)/ May, 89/ Recent Building
Baumeister (Germany)/ May, 90/ Cover Story: "Stockley Park in London"

Baitlaws Conservatory Lanarkshire
RIBA Journal (UK)/ Nov, 85/ Cover Story: "Conservatory in the Border Country"

Canary Wharf, Building FC3
The Independent (UK)/ 1 Apr 92/ "At last, its in sight"
Building Special Issue (UK)/ Oct, 91/ 25 The North Colonnade (FC3)

De La Warr Pavilion
The Independent (UK)/ 11 Dec, 91/ "Bexhill's Bauhaus-on-Sea"

Design House
Architect's Journal (UK)/ 25 Jan, 84/ Cover story: "High Tech turns the Corner"

Kobe Institute (St Catherine's College)
Architect's Journal (UK)/ 7 Nov, 90/ "St Catherine's at Kobe"
The Sunday Times (UK)/ 11 Nov, 90/ "Dons go east to built new Oxford St Catherine's College in Japan"
The Architectural Review (UK)/ Nov, 91/ "Importing Cats"
Kenchiku Bunka (Japan)/ Nov, 91/ St Catherine's College Kobe Institute
The Independent (UK)/ 13 Nov, 91/ East meets West in Japan's university challenge"

Lipstick Competition
Architect's Journal (UK)/ 1 Aug, 90/ "West Gate win at Isle of Dogs"

Pond Place
RIBA Journal (UK)/ Nov, 88/ "Taking on the Planners"

Practice Profile
Baumeister (Germany)/ Mar 92/ Cover story: "Bauten von Troughton McAslan"
L'Architecture d'Aujourd'hui (France)/ Feb, 91/ "Portrait: Troughton McAslan"
Blueprint (UK)/ Jun, 90/ Cover Story: "Poets of Pragmatism"
Progressive Architecture (USA)/ Apr, 90/ "Recent Work of Troughton McAslan"

Redhill Station
Architect's Journal (UK)/ 13 Mar, 91/ "On the Right Tracks"
Building (UK)/ 6 Oct, 89/ "On the Upward Curve"

Riverside Apartments
Architect's Journal (UK)/ 16 Jul, 86/ Cover Story: "In the Nautical Tradition"
L'Arca (Italy)/ Jul, 87/ "A Ship on the Riverside"

Rosebery Avenue
Architectural Review (UK)/ May, 89/ Current Project

Rosebery Avenue/Hardwick Street
Architecture Today (UK)/ May, 92/ Cover Story: "The Taming of Technolory"

Shepherd's Bush Studio
Architecture Interieure Cree (France)/ Apr, 86/ "Shepherd's Bush, Londres"

St Peters Street, No. 3
Architect's Journal (UK)/ 10 Aug, 88/ "Success of Limitations"
Abitare (Italy)/ Dec, 90/ "Industrial Appeal in a Victorian Warehouse"

Waverley Station
The Scotsman (UK)/ 11 Nov, 91/ "A Waverley project worth debating"
Architect's journal (UK)/ 22&29 Aug, 90/ "Alternative Show

JAMIE TROUGHTON (left)

Jamie Troughton was born in Scotland in 1950 and obtained an MA in Architecture from the University of Cambridge in 1975. He trained with Norman Foster until 1978, joining Richard Rogers and Partners during that year to become a team leader on the Lloyds Redevelopment.

He established Troughton McAslan in 1983 with John McAslan.

Within the practice, Jamie Troughton specialises in business strategy, corporate policy, and management.

ジャミー・トロートン(左)

1950年スコットランド生まれ．1975年ケンブリッジ大学建築修士．1978年までノーマン・フォスターのところで働き，その後リチャード・ロジャース・アンド・パートナーズに移り，ロイズビル計画のチームリーダーとなる．1983年ジョン・マッカーズランとトロートン・マッカーズランを設立．事務所では主に経営戦略や組織の骨格となるポリシーを打ち出し，総合管理を担う．

JOHN McASLAN (right)

John McAslan was born in Scotland in 1954 and educated at Edinburgh University, obtaining an MA in Architecture in 1977, and a Diploma in 1978. He worked in the USA with RTKL in Baltimore and Cambridge Seven in Boston before joining Richard Rogers and Partners in 1980.

He established Troughton McAslan in 1983 with Jamie Troughton.

John McAslan specialises in design within the practice and regularly lectures to architects and students on the practice's work, both in the UK and abroad. He is actively involved in a number of architectural conservation groups and is a Trustee of the Whitechapel Art Gallery in London.

ジョン・マッカーズラン(右)

1954年スコットランド生まれ．1977年エジンバラ大学建築修士，78年ディプロマ取得．米国ボルチモアのRTKL，ボストンのケンブリッジ・セブンで働いた後，1979年にリチャード・ロジャース・アンド・パートナーズに所属．1983年ジャミー・トロートンとトロートン・マッカーズラン設立．マッカーズランは設計活動において主にデザインを担当，仕事の実践について英国内外で建築家や学生たちに広く講義活動に従事．多くの建築保護団体に積極的に参加し，ロンドンのホワイトチャペル・アートギャラリーの評議員も務める．

THOMAS FISHER

Thomas Fisher has been the Executive Editor of Progressive Architecture since 1987. Prior to joining the magazine in 1982, he worked in architectural offices in Hartford, Connecticut, and Cleveland, Ohio, and served as the Historical Architect for the state of Connecticut. He has an undergraduate degree in architecture from Cornell University and a graduate degree in interdisciplinary studies from Case Western Reserve University. He is a frequent juror and lecturer at architectural schools around the United States.

トーマス・フィッシャー

1987年以来プログレッシブ・アーキテクチャ誌の編集主幹．1982年に同誌に参加する以前は，コネチカット州やオハイオ州の設計事務所で設計活動に従事し，また，コネチカット州の歴史建築家として活躍．コーネル大学建築学科卒業，ケース・ウエスタン・リザーブ大学学際研究の大学院終了．全米の多くの建築学校で教鞭をとる．

KENNETH POWELL

Kenneth Powell is an architectural and property writer based in London. After a varied academic career, he worked for the conservation pressure group SAVE Britain's Heritage. Combining a commitment to new architecture with a continuing interest in conservation, he serves on the committees of the Victorian Society and Thirties Society. He is now Architecture Correspondent for the Daily Telegraph newspaper and writes for journals. His books include two studies of the work of Norman Foster and a forthcoming account of the Lloyd's Building.

ケネス・パウエル

ロンドンを中心に活躍する建築評論家．アカデミックな経歴の後，英国の保護圧力団体であるSAVE英国遺産のために働く．常に保存への関心を持って新しい建築を考えるという姿勢で，ビクトリアン・ソサエティやサーティーズ・ソサエティの委員会に参加．デイリー・テレグラフ紙の建築コラムニストであり，いくつかの新聞・雑誌に寄稿している．「ノーマン・フォスター」などの著書があり，最新刊は「ロイズ本社ビル」．

ROWAN MOORE

Rowan Moore is an architect based in London. Trained at Cambridge University, he is now a partner in the firm of Zombory-Moldovan Moore Ng, and has written for other publications including The Independent newspaper, Vogue and Progressive Architecture. He edits a new magazine on architecture, Foundation.

ローワン・ムーア

ロンドンを中心に活躍する建築家．ケンブリッジ大学卒業．ゾンボリー・ボルドバン・ムーア設計事務所の創立当初からのパートナー．ブループリントのコラムニストであり，その他にもインディペンデント紙，ボーグ誌，プログレッシブ・アーキテクチュア誌などに寄稿している．目下，財団による新しい建築雑誌を編集中．

PAST OFFICE MEMBERS
Stephen Archer
Bob Atwal
Mohammed Azhar
Peter Beard
Janet Brown
Martin Campbell
Jason Cornish
Sharon Davis
Bobby Desai
Madeleine Deschamps
Stuart Elgie
Colin Glover
Joanna Green
Thomas Grotzeck
Jonathan Hill
Annabel Hodgson
Jeremy King
Birgit Klauck
James Lambert
Colin MacKenzie
Jennifer Mallard
Christopher Mascall
Malcolm McGregor
Roger Meadows
David Medas
Nick Midgley
David Mikhail
Gary Mountford
Jonathan Parr
Chris Perry
Stephen Pimbley
Suzie Pote
Matthew Priestman
Grant Robertson
Jamie Shorten
Judy Slater
Colin Smith
Stephanie Smith
Paul Summerlin
Yann Taylor
Paul Voysey
Tracie Walter
Andrew Weston
Jane Witz

PRESENT OFFICE MEMBERS
Alison Bick
Hugh Broughton
Adam Brown
Christophe Egret
Nick Eldridge
Yasser El-Gabry
Martin Harris
Ken Hutt
Michelle Kelly
Kit Lewis
Kevin Lloyd
John McAslan
Gregory McLean
Aidan Potter
Piers Smerin
Murray Smith
Maureen Tadman
Jamie Troughton
Mark Wilson

Credits

CLIENTS

Allied Breweries Ltd
Apple Computer (UK) Ltd
Barrie Tankel Partnership plc
British Foreign and Commonwealth Office
British Railways Board
Comune di Monteriggioni
C T Bowring and Company Ltd
De La Warr Pavilion Trust
Derwent Valley Holdings plc
Design House Ltd
Fletcher King
Great Portland Estates
Imperial Land Ltd
Jaison Property Development Company Ltd
Jubilee Line Extension
Kobe Steel Corporation
Leeds Initiative and Leeds City Council
Local London Group Ltd
London Docklands Development Corporation
London Merchant Securities Group of Companies
London Regional Transport Ltd
London Underground Ltd
MEPC Development Ltd
Olympia & York Canary Wharf Ltd
Portmans Ltd
Pilcher Hershman
Ross Jaye Ltd
Rother District Council
Royal Institute of British Architects
Soldiers, Sailors and Airmens' Families Association (SSAFA)
St Catherine's College, University of Oxford
Shilton plc
Stanhope Properties plc
Terryash Properties Ltd

CONTRACTORS

AJR Renovations Ltd
Bovis Construction Ltd
Brick Studio Ltd
Denver Building Services Ltd
William Green Builders Ltd
Heath Construction (St Albans) Ltd
Hilton Building Services
J Jarvis and Sons plc
John Lelliott Construction Group
Lovell Construction Ltd
Mowlem Management Ltd
Nico Construction Ltd
John Nugent Construction plc
Princeton plc
Quality Glass (Stoke-on-Trent) Ltd
A Roberts (Building) Ltd
Schal International Ltd
Takenaka Corporation, Japan
Trollope and Colls
Wiltshier (London) Ltd

CONSULTANTS AND COLLABORATORS

Adamson Associates (UK) Ltd
Alan Baxter & Associates
Anstey Horne & Company
Atelier One and Atelier Ten
Barker and Barton
Barrie Tankel Partnership plc
Beavis Walker
Boyden & Company
Bradstock Group plc
Bucknall Austin Project Management
Cameron Taylor Partnership
Cundall Johnston Partnership
Davis Langdon & Everest
Richard Davis
DEGW Ltd
Louisa Denman & Associates
Esterson Lackersteen
W G Edwards and Partners
Fibbens Fox Associates
Flack & Kurtz
Max Fordham Associates
Mary Fox Linton
Charles Funke Associates
Edmund Hambly Ltd
E C Harris and Partners
Howard Associates
Helmut Jacoby
Jampel Davison and Bell
Kandor Modelmakers Ltd
Kenchington Ford plc
Landesign Group
Lighting Design Partnership
Keith March
John Minshaw Designs Ltd
Montagu Evans
Frank Newby
J H Nicholsons and Company
Ove Arup & Partners
Pell Frischman Group
PHD Associates
Joe Pool Associates
Kenneth Powell
K R Plowright and Company Ltd
J Roger Preston and Partners
Public Art Development Trust
Nigel Rose & Partners
Rowe and Maw
F J Samuely & Partners
John Savage Associates
Steensen Varming and Mulcahy Partnership
Takenaka Corporation, Japan
Tirant Associates
Unit 22 Modelbuilders
Walfords
Whitby & Bird
Ian White Associates
YRME Partnership

PHOTOGRAPHY

Robin Barton
Richard Bryant
Martin Charles
Peter Cook
Richard Davies
Brian Harris
John Donat
Hiroyuki Hirai
Alastair Hunter
John Miller
Eamonn O'Mahoney

BUILDING ILLUSION

ビルディング イリュージョン　カルロス・ディニーズに描かれた建築

カルロス・ディニーズの仕事は，レンダラー，イラストレーターなどといった分類には当てはまらないほど広い領域を持つ，アメリカの建築画家である．彼によって「描かれた建築」は，時には現実以上にそのプロジェクトを生き生きと感じさせる．

1960年代，ミノル・ヤマサキのワールドトレードセンターのプレゼンテーションに参加．その後，有名な建築家や事務所と組んで次々と大きなプロジェクトを成功に導いてきた．

この本では，「描かれた建築」をテーマにカルロス・ディニーズのイリュージョンを集大成する．

好評発売中

責任編集者	カルロス・ディニーズ
総　　頁	216頁(カラー204頁)
文　　章	日本語，英語
定　　価	9,800円
装　　幀	ハードカバー，ジャケット付
サ イ ズ	A4変形版

株式会社プロセスアーキテクチュア　〒151 東京都渋谷区笹塚1-47-2-418 Phone03(3468)0131 Fax03(3468)0133

近藤典生，もうひとつの世界

エコロジカル・パークの思想とその方法

著者は育種学，遺伝学を専門とする研究者で，研究対象としての生きた動植物を確保する一方策として，動植物公園づくりに関わり始めた．動植物の生態を知りつくした著者によるこれらの公園では，動物も植物も，自然の中にあるがままの日常を営んでいる．

本書では，作品と共に，地球儀温室計画案の壮大な構想を合わせて紹介する．公園づくりの考え方から環境問題，資源問題を論じ，その哲学に迫るとともに，動物達の魅力あふれる表情を伝える写真集となっている．

●対談／「自然思考の公園づくり」近藤典生＋進士五十八
「動植物の生態と公園づくりの手法」近藤典生＋朝倉繁春

●作品／伊豆シャボテン公園，地球儀温室，長崎鼻パーキングガーデン，鹿児島市平川動物公園，ボリビア共和国日本庭園，長崎バイオパーク，ひめはるの里のクリスタルグリーンハウス，名護自然動植物公園，地球儀温室計画案

定価￥2,900(税込)

都市環境のデザイン……空間創造の実践……

編・著　高橋志保彦

都市デザインは，単なる１つの分野でなく，様々な分野の関係で成り立つ「つなぎの文化」といえる(編・著　あとがきより)．本書はアーバンデザインの専門家，その他の関係機関など，その道の第一人者の叡智を結集してつくった都市を，様々な切り口からケーススタディを通して検証したものである．全国から16例を選出し，「アーバンオアシス」「みち空間」「都市のアメニティ」の３章に分け，そのプロセスを浮き彫りにする．

●主な事例・作品／1987年・新宿新都心，梅田センタービル・外部空間，大宮駅西口再開発構想，大阪ビジネスパーク，住友生命仙台中央ビル，イセザキモール，仙台東一番町商店街，アーケードシティ・高松，平塚市中心街・街づくり，ミュージアムステーション・阪急三番街，多摩センター，公園都市・呉市，全県公園化構想　山梨県・甲府，長崎・中島川界隈──JR長崎駅，他

定価￥3,900(税込)

SEKINE／Message from Environment Art Studio

編集　林 芳史

近代的な造形を超えて，総合的に環境を包含する環境美術の開拓を目指してきたパイオニア，関根伸夫の力強い空間演出を，その代表作のみを選りすぐって浮き彫りにする．常に人間の生の始原的感動に視線を注ぐ関根伸夫の世界に迫る．高級美術印刷による美的作品集である．

●文／関根伸夫，林 芳史

●作品／東京都庁舎，江南女子短期大学，市町村アカデミー，筑波北部工業団地近隣公園，塩釜市総合体育館，奥久慈憩の森，世田谷美術館壁泉，グランドヒル市ヶ谷，新潟駅南口広場，箱根彫刻の森美術館彫刻，他

定価￥3,000(税込)

現代日本のランドスケープ

自然と共生，都市空間の中でのうるおいの創造等，さまざまな環境の中での建築外構，公園，広場，庭園など，建築家及びランドスケープデザインの第一線で活躍する作家の代表作品をオールカラー写真と資料を加えて編集したものである．

1988年11月発行の「現代日本のランドスケープ」に収録されなかった作品やその後の新作品を加えた最近10年間の38作品，さらに「花博EXPO'90」も併せて紹介する．

●作品／八ヶ岳高原音楽堂，山梨県立芸術の森公園，天保山ハーバービレッジ，三井倉庫箱崎ビル，滋賀県立陶芸の森公園，味野公園，府中市郷土の森，修善寺「虹の郷」，国営みちのくの杜湖畔公園，高塚公園，総和町ネーブルパーク，勾当台公園，豊島区立西池袋公園，滋賀県文化ゾーン「夕照の庭」，大仙公園・日本庭園，高松邸の庭，京都スパイラルガーデン(京北の庭)，ベルコリーヌ南大沢，熱帯ドリームセンター，浦安シンボルロード，日比谷モール，国際花と緑の博覧会，他

定価￥9,800(税込)

JAPAN LANDSCAPE
人・都市・自然のコミュニケーションマガジン 季刊ジャパン・ランドスケープ

季刊ジャパンランドスケープ

好評発売中

No.1～11，No.14は品切れです。
No.12「スポーツの景」，No.13「橋の景」(共に，定価2,580円)は在庫が少なくなっています。お早めにお申し込み下さい。

季刊「ジャパンランドスケープ」は全国有名書店でもお求めになれますが，品切れになるおそれがありますので定期購読をおすすめいたします。なお，お申し込み時に発行されている号は定期購読対象外となりますのでご了承下さい。

●定期購読
1年(4冊) 10,300円
2年(8冊) 18,540円
3年(12冊) 24,720円

発行●㈱プロセスアーキテクチュア
〒151 東京都渋谷区笹塚1-47-2-418
電話03-3468-0131㈹ FAX03-3468-0133
編集●㈱マルモ・プランニング
〒150 東京都渋谷区道玄坂1-16-6二葉ビル
電話03-3496-7046

No.15●特集 海の景
●CROSS OVER TALK／「海辺の文化と景観論」樋口忠彦＋宮城俊作
●序論／「メディアとしての海洋空間」近藤健雄
●Seaside Landscapeの潮流／海辺の都市開発，海辺のリゾート，海辺の環境保全
●トピックス／激動のシーサイドランドスケープを探る
●CREATIVE FORUM／豊饒の海へ
●人と作品／伊東豊雄
●LANDSCAPE NEW WAVE／国営みちのく杜の湖畔公園，芸術の森公園，水戸芸術館，他

No.16●特集 時空(とき)の景
●CROSS OVER TALK／「風景の記憶と自然」岩田慶治vs石井鬼十
●対談／「建築・現象・ランドスケープ」安藤忠雄vs佐々木葉二
●トピックス／時のかたち――環境芸術における時空造型の試み，時を駆け，時を超えるランドスケープ
●CREATIVE FORUM／からくり時景
●人と作品／石井幹子
●LANDSCAPE NEW WAVE／ベルコリーヌ南大沢，中村市トンボ自然公園，他

No.17●特集 テーマパークの景
●対談／「テーマパークとランドスケープデザイン」
●PEOPLE SCAPE／「ディズニーランドにおけるランドスケープ計画」
●テーマパークからアミューズメントタウンへ／東京ディズニーランド，ユニバーサル・スタジオ・フロリダ，東京セサミプレイス，長崎バイオパーク，他
●トピックス／テーマパーク最新トレンド情報
●CREATIVE FORUM／楽園漫遊
●人と作品／井上卓也
●LANDSCAPE NEW WAVE／夕照の庭，他

No.18●特集 森の景
●序論／「人と森のランドスケープ」熊谷洋一
●人と森のニューライフ／森にあそぶ，森をつくる，森と生きる
●トピックス／森との新しい出合いのために
●CREATIVE FORUM／森の詩
●PEOPLE SCAPE／細川護熙
●人と作品／関根伸夫
●LANDSCAPE NEW WAVE／箱根・神仙郷，熱海・瑞雲郷／三井倉庫崎ビル／都民の森／勾当台公園

No.19●特集 色彩の景
●PEOPLE SCAPE／「環境に播かれる種――大地と人の絆を育む造形家」ダニ・カラヴァン
●環境の中の色彩を考える／風土と色彩，街と色彩，エレメントと色彩
●CREATIVE FORUM／艶
●トピックス／港町・函館の色彩紀行，藤沢市の都市景観づくり，他
●LANDSCAPE NEW WAVE／西宮市大谷記念美術館庭園，カナダ大使館庭園，他
●LANDSCAPE WORKS／上野　泰

No.20●特集 駅の景
●座談会／「駅のランドスケープ」
●序文／「ステーションフロントの時代」樋渡達也
●PEOPLE SCAPE／佐藤　昌
●駅の計画論・手法論／川越駅，浜松駅，土気駅，丸亀駅，緑園都市駅，他
●CREATIVE FORUM／プラットホーム
●LANDSCAPE NEW WAVE／目白庭園，国営ひたち海浜公園，シーバンス，スノーアートとやま，フォレストヒルズガーデン，他
●LANDSCAPE WORKS／山本紀久

JAPAN LANDSCAPE
人・都市・自然のコミュニケーションマガジン 季刊ジャパン・ランドスケープ

定価2,580円
好評発売中

No.21 ●特集● エコ・シティの景

ドイツに見られるエコロジカルニューウェーブ

日本のケーススタディ
野川は甦ったか――生きた川を取り戻すために
トンボの好む水環境を再生
西京桂坂――花鳥風月のある街

■PEOPLE SCAPE
グロッセ・リュック

■LANDSCAPE WORKS
進化生物学者のエコロジーパーク
――近藤典生博士の理念と方法

■LANDSCAPE NEWWAVE
創造の丘ナシオン
柏の葉公園中央ストリート
晴海客船ターミナル
しながわ水族館

■特別企画
ペイザジストと呼ばれる人々
――フランスの造園教育とその社会的役割

■OVERSEAS REPORT
ポルトガルの石畳に魅せられて／アメリカンプランニングのパラダイム，他

■連載
都市風景塾／Keyword Playground／テクニカルノート／新製品紹介／Book Review

JAPAN LANDSCAPE
人・都市・自然のコミュニケーションマガジン 季刊ジャパン・ランドスケープ

好評発売中　定価2,580円

No.22 ●特集● 石の景

現代に生きる石の精神

現代作家にみる石心、石使い
神の宿る石を置く外空間作家 ――深谷光軌
伝統を礎に現代空間に挑む造園家 ――荒木芳邦
石を生けるデザイナー ――伊藤邦衛

■特別インタビュー
現代石材事情―石材メーカーの動向を探る
永田助親／柘植英雄／高田誠之助／大澤秀行

■LANDSCAPE NEW WAVE
カントリーパーク（熊本県農業公園）／アートレイクゴルフ倶楽部／清原中央公園・清原南公園／リトル・ノルウェー公園

■PEOPLE SCAPE
スティーブン・スミス

■Overseas Report
ランドスケープアーキテクチュアについての5つの思考
エコ・シティ――自然環境と人工環境の回復・保全のためのコンセプト

■連載
Creators Voice／都市風景塾／Keyword Forum／テクニカルノート／JLひろば／キャンパス・ナウ

PROCESS : Architecture 96 海洋建築の構図

PROCESS : Architecture　Material appears in English and Japanese　96
Composition of Oceanic Architecture
海洋建築の構図

水際から海域において見られる建築と海，河川とのかかわりから生み出されてくる建築的空間を海洋建築と総称し，計画的側面，デザイン的側面，技術的側面に焦点をあてる．
ここでは集まった事例を施設の機能や構造形式によって分類するのではなく，水の利用形態と建築空間との対応関係から，「水を引く」「海に架ける」「海に浮く」「海を抱く」「海に潜る」の５つのキーワードで分類し，計画中のものも含めてその概要を紹介する．

●論文／「海洋空間を創造する海洋建築」畔柳昭雄
●作品／マリナシティ，カナダプレイス，長崎オランダ村，ブライトンピア，ピア39，バリアリーフ・フローティング・ホテル，浮かぶ劇場「世界劇場」，大阪海遊館，シアトル水族館，シドニー水族館，海中展望塔「足摺海底館」，他

責任編集者	畔柳昭雄，渡辺富雄
発行日	1991年６月
総頁	160頁（カラー144頁）
文章	日本語，英語
定価	2,990円（本体2,903円）

PROCESS : Architecture 97 デザインされた都市：ボストン

PROCESS : Architecture　Material appears in English and Japanese　97
Boston by Design　A City in Development: 1960 to 1990
デザインされた都市：ボストン

世界の海の玄関といわれるボストン．ウォーターフロントのみクローズアップされがちであるが，３世紀以上の歴史を持つボストンの魅力は建物，広場，街並みにあふれている．歴史と伝統を保存しながらの開発を模索する姿に，環境と開発のバランスのとれた都市のルーツを探ることができる．本書ではこうしたボストンの形成や現状，未来を分析し，都市計画から建築ガイドに至るまで，航空写真をふんだんに使って紹介する．

●論文／「ボストン都市散策」神田　駿
「ボストンは存在する」ジェーン・ホルツ・ケイ
「ボストンの生きてきた道」小林正美
●プロジェクト／サウスウェストコリドー，チャールズタウン・ネイビーヤード，セントラルアーテリー地下埋設計画，他

責任編集者	神田　駿，小林正美
発行日	1991年８月
総頁	152頁（カラー127頁）
文章	日本語，英語
定価	2,990円（本体2,903円）

PROCESS : Architecture 98 自然エネルギーと建築

「環境志向型」建築は，太陽や風などのクリーンな自然エネルギーを活用することによって，非再生型エネルギーへの依存を減らし，かつ環境へ与える影響を和らげることができる．ＰＬＥＡ国際委員会は，世界各地の「環境志向型」建築の実践例の収集を計画し，この作業は日本建築学会パッシブデザイン研究グループによって進められてきた．本号はその成果を気候別に分類し，まとめたものである．

●論文／「地球的かつ地域固有の建築」ジェフリー・クック
「建築と技術：1990年代の環境を意識したデザイン」シモス・ヤナス
●作品／ネゲフ高地教育センター，大島の家，ガピオタス村熱帯病院，ソーラーハウスビレッジNo.3，世田谷区立宮坂地区会館，ニューカナーン自然センター園芸実験棟，苫小牧市立中央図書館，ウルム神経外科研究所，他

責任編集者	小玉祐一郎，ジェフリー・クック，シモス・ヤナス
発行日	1991年９月
総頁	160頁（カラー144頁）
文章	日本語，英語
定価	2,990円（本体2,903円）

PROCESS : Architecture 99 東京を開く：尾島俊雄の構想

PROCESS : Architecture　Material appears in English and Japanese　99
Imageable TOKYO: Projects by Toshio Ojima
東京を開く
尾島俊雄の構想

首都東京の都市環境を主眼に，都市のアメニティ，21世紀へ向けての再開発，ひいては首都大改造の具体的構想をイメージしてきた．絵に描いた餅といわれ続けてきたものだが今日のように豊かな時代に我々はすぐに食べられる餅をこれ以上つくる必要はない．尾島のイメージを中心に研究室が25年間繰り返し調査，研究してきた成果としての具体的構想を紹介する．

●構想／首都ランドマーク構想，銀座再開発構想，東京駅前地区再開発構想，新宿駅周辺再開発構想，池袋アーバンコンプレックス構想，下町マンハッタン構想，東京湾開放構想，首都圏臨界高層都市，アンダーグラウンドスペースネットワーク構想，ペントハウス構想，インダストリアル構想，エコロジカルハウス構想，レジデンシャルハウス構想，インテリジェントシティ構想，サテライトオフィス構想，アメリカンシティ構想

責任編集者	尾島俊雄，尾島俊雄研究室
発行日	1991年11月
総頁	156頁（カラー142頁）
文章	日本語，英語
定価	2,990円（本体2,903円）

PROCESS :Architecture 100 レンゾ・ピアノ・ビルディング・ワークショップ

1991年5月23日，関西国際空港旅客ターミナルビルの建設が始まった，ピアノはこの日を「夢がかたちに変わる最初の時」と表現している．建設業の家に生まれたピアノの幼年期の経験は，建築家になってからも彼に影響を与え続けた．

この100号特別号では，彼の仕事を4つの時期に分け，その発展のプロセスを探る．

●序文／「モノローグ」レンゾ・ピアノ
●作品／ポンピドーセンター，IRCAM音楽音響総合研究所，シュルンベルグジェ社改築，パラッディオのバシリカ修復計画，メニルコレクション美術館，IBM移動巡回パビリオン，コロンブス大陸発見500年記念国際博覧会，聖ニコラス・フットボール競技場，ベルシー・ショッピングセンター，関西国際空港旅客ターミナルビル，他

責任編集者　レンゾ・ピアノ・ビルディングワークショップ
発行日　1992年1月
総頁　256頁
文章　日本語，英語
定価　4,600円（本体4,466円）

PROCESS :Architecture 101 ジャーディ・パートナーシップ

アメリカの建築家ジョン・ジャーディは13年前に事務所を創設，以来独自の建築言語「Mixed-use」「Host place」「Placemaking」などを使って，空間をディスプレイする街の脚本家である．代表作にはファッションアイランドの増改築画，1984年ロサンゼルスオリンピックのサインやゲートなど装飾計画を演出．また，幕張タウンセンターなど日本でのプロジェクトも進行中である．

●作品／1984年ロサンゼルスオリンピック，ユニバーサルシティ，ファッションアイランド，幕張タウンセンター，ホートンプラザ，リバーフロント博多

責任編集者　ジャーディ・パートナーシップ
発行日　1992年2月
総頁　160頁（カラー136頁）
文章　日本語，英語
定価　2,990円（本体2,903円）

PROCESS :Architecture 102 シカゴ：超高層建築の時代

ミース・ファン・デル・ローエによるレイクショアドライブの出現以来，シカゴのスカイラインは激変する．サリバンやバーナム&ルートが活躍したシカゴ派の全盛期から半世紀後，シカゴは再び高層建築が競い合う建築の実験都市と化する．この時代をリードしたのはミースとその弟子たち．ミースの哲学が力強くシカゴの建築界をつらぬいていた．しかしそのシカゴにもポストモダンの波は押し寄せる．本書では，レイクショアドライブから，40年間の代表的ビル50例をあげて，設計思想の変遷をあとづける．

●作品／レイクショアドライブ・アパート，インランドスチール，シカゴ・シヴィックセンター，マリナシティ，シアーズ・タワー，ジョーン・ハンコック・センター，イリノイ州政府センター，333ウエスト・ワッカー・ドライブ

責任編集者　高山正実
発行日　1992年3月
総頁　152頁（カラー120頁）
文章　日本語，英語
定価　2,990円（本体2,903円）

PROCESS :Architecture 103 SWAグループ ランドスケープとプランニング

カリフォルニアを基点として全米に5つの事務所を持つSWAグループは，その組織網を生かして地域に則したプランニングやランドスケープデザインを展開している．専属の写真家，地質学者，大学で教鞭をとるプリンシパルなどが，多角的な独自の組織基盤を支えている．本誌では，大規模なコミュニティからディテールのデザインまで，グループによる作品の魅力をあますところなく紹介する．

●主な記事／「SWAの沿革」メラニー・サイモ，「座談会」アラン・テムコ＋SWA，「専門活動」写真，地質情報調査(GIS)，SWAプロフェッショナルプログラム
●作品／アーバインランチ，サザンカリフォルニアコミュニティ，アリゾナセンター，ウィリアムズスクエア，カーチスセンター・ファウンテンコート，アーバイダリゾートコミュニティ，那須ハイランドパーク，他

責任編集者　カルビン・プラット
発行日　1992年5月
総頁　152頁（カラー132頁）
文章　日本語，英語
定価　2,990円（本体2,903円）

PROCESS :Architecture 104

好評発売中　定価2,990円

City Score : Up To Date

語りかける都市：そのテーマとメディア

本誌55号「街並みのスコア」(現在品切れ)に続く池沢寛氏の都市散策シリーズ．都市には人を魅きつけるものがある．本号ではこの魅力をいろいろな切り口でながめ，さまざまな言語で私たちに語りかける都市の表情を追う．

主要テーマ
風土とヴォキャブラリー，リゾートの環境，シティパーク，タウンスケープにおける街路樹，楽しさをもたらすもの，都市のなかのアトリウム，環境保存と開発調和と対比，他